PRAISE FOR *REGGIE JACKSON*

"A well-rounded treatment of one of baseball's most celebrated and controversial figures. . . . Perry reaffirms the notion that when it comes to sports superstardom, monstrous talent combined with enigmatic character truly yields the stuff of legend. Few Hall of Famers have done it with the path-breaking mix of panache, bombast, and raw achievement that defined Jackson's career. . . . A provocative portrait sure to win as many fans . . . as its red-hot subject." —*Kirkus Reviews*

"Any discussion of baseball in the '70s must begin with Reggie Jackson—the first and perhaps the last of his kind—and now any discussion of Reggie must begin with Dayn Perry's insightful, immensely enjoyable biography." —Rob Neyer, senior writer, ESPN.com

"Perry teases out the combustible, contradictory, provocative aspects of Jackson's personality—not to mention his talent for demolishing a baseball—that still make him such an irresistible personality to this day." —*Booklist*

"Dayn Perry gives us the full Reggie: Mr. October and Mr. Swagger, racial avatar but not a racial militant. This is a book about more than baseball and will appeal to more than fans."

—Larry Tye, author of *Satchel: The Life and Times of an American Legend*

"Perry does a nice job of surveying Jackson's career."

—Associated Press

"Reggie Jackson was a towering figure during his controversial Hall of Fame career. He was prideful, jealous, emotional, and talented. His ego—both alluring and revolting—as Dayn Perry cleverly described it, could make a fan forget what a force he was. Perry, a damn fine writer, brings an insightful, fresh analysis to the career of Mr. October."

—Peter Golenbock

ANDREW COLLINGS

ABOUT THE AUTHOR

Dayn Perry wrote for ESPN.com and Baseball Prospectus before becoming a baseball columnist with FOXSports.com. He is the author of *Winners: How Good Baseball Teams Become Great Ones*, and he lives with his family in Chicago, Illinois.

www.DaynPerry.com

REGGIE JACKSON

ALSO BY DAYN PERRY

Winners: How Good Baseball Teams Become Great Ones
(and It's Not the Way You Think)

REGGIE JACKSON

The Life and
Thunderous Career
of Baseball's
Mr. October

Dayn Perry

itbooks

AN IMPRINT OF HARPERCOLLINS PUBLISHERS

*it***books**

A hardcover edition of this book was published in 2010 by William Morrow, an imprint of HarperCollins Publishers.

HarperCollins books may be purchased for educational, business, or sales promotional use. For information please write: Special Markets Department, HarperCollins Publishers, 10 East 53rd Street, New York, NY 10022.

FIRST IT BOOKS PAPERBACK EDITION PUBLISHED 2011.

Designed by Lisa Stokes

The Library of Congress has catalogued the hardcover edition as follows:

Perry, Dayn, 1972–
    Reggie Jackson : the life and thunderous career of baseball's Mr. October / Dayn Perry.
    p. cm.
    ISBN 978-0-06-156238-9
    1. Jackson, Reggie. 2. Baseball players—United States—Biography. 3. New York Yankees (Baseball team). I. Title.
  GV865.J32P47 2010
  796.357092—dc22
  [B]

2009047988

ISBN 978-0-06-156237-2 (pbk.)

11 12 13 14 15   OV/RRD   10 9 8 7 6 5 4 3 2 1

For Mary, my wife, my love, my luckiest break

CONTENTS

REGGIE JACKSON

PROLOGUE

October 18, 1977,
World Series, Game Six

EVERYONE WANTED TO forget something.

New Yorkers wanted to forget the Son of Sam murders, the empty city coffers, the blackouts, the looting in Crown Heights and Bushwick, and the 30,000 fires set in the South Bronx over the last few years. George Steinbrenner wanted to forget that he was a convicted felon and that Yankees fans still thought of him as "some fucking guy from Cleveland." Thurman Munson wanted to forget about his contract and the failures of the previous October. Billy Martin wanted to forget that his job was in danger, that he drank too much, that another marriage was falling apart, and that he hated his best player. Reggie wanted to forget about the promises and enemies he'd made. But to forget, it would take one more win.

That one win over the Dodgers would give the Yankees their first championship since 1962. It had been their longest drought since before the days of Babe Ruth and Lou Gehrig. The team wanted it. The city—beleaguered by a hot, deadly summer—needed it.

In the first game of the 1977 World Series, the Yankees had edged the Dodgers in twelve innings. Game two was over once it began, as the Dodgers scored five runs in the first three innings and won 6–1. As the Series shifted to Los Angeles, Reggie was batting .136.

In game three, he scored twice and drove in a run in a 5–3 Yankees win. In game four, he homered in the sixth inning to give the Yankees a critical insurance run. They won 4–2. The Dodgers struck back in game five, beating the Yankees 10–4. In his final at bat of the night, Reggie hit another home run. The Yankees went back to New York with victory one win away.

THE UNIFORM FELT especially good stretched over Reggie's body. His muscles seemed more lithe and fluid than usual, his equipment lighter, his movements more deliberate. It was as though his body moved on its own, made its own decisions. He'd felt something like this a few times before, and then good things had always happened. But never had it been quite like this. By force of superstition, he wore two new pairs of socks and placed two towels in his locker. He hung a square gold medallion around his neck—one with Jackie Robinson's name engraved on it. Then he attached to his belt a button—one with Jackie Robinson's face on it.

In the retelling, myth would have it that Joe DiMaggio, the Yankees eminence on hand to throw out the first pitch, approached Reggie in the clubhouse and told him that this surely would be his night. But that never happened. The portents didn't come until batting practice, when Reggie launched perhaps twenty balls out of the park. By the end of his display, the fans in the right-field seats cheered as though game six had already started. Reggie felt good—impossibly good. "This Series is in the hands of the Lord," he said before taking the field. He did not believe his own words.

In the top of the first, Mike Torrez retired the first two Dodger hitters on easy groundouts, but then Bucky Dent ranged to his right and fumbled away a Reggie Smith bouncer. Torrez's second pitch to Ron Cey bounced off Thurman Munson's glove, and Smith hustled to second. Cey walked. Torrez pitched Steve Garvey low and outside but missed with his first two offerings. His next sinker nicked the strike zone's outer half. The Yankees pitchers had worked outside for much of the Series, and too often Dodgers hitters tried to pull those outside pitches. This time, though, Garvey shortened his swing and thumped it low down the right-field line and into the corner. Reggie lumbered over, hesitated, and didn't corral the ball until Garvey rounded second base. Garvey wound up on third, and the Dodgers had a 2–0 lead. In the bull pen—now covered with a tarp to prevent fans from throwing coins and rocks into it—Dick Tidrow warmed up. But Torrez, still throwing his sinker outside to right-handers, struck out Dusty Baker to end the inning. Back in the dugout, Billy Martin pulled Reggie aside. "Don't worry about it," he said through clenched teeth.

Burt Hooton, the right-hander who had tamed New York in game two, worked quickly in the home half. The Yankees swung freely and went in order. In the top of the second, Torrez needed just five pitches to retire the side. On the final out, Hooton lifted a bloop to right, but Reggie, playing shallow, made an easy play. He jogged to the dugout and flipped the ball toward the mound.

As Hooton warmed up, Reggie stood at the on-deck circle and watched. Then he adjusted the batting glove on his right hand, took four smooth practice swings, and approached the plate. He picked up a handful of dirt with his left hand and stepped in. He mashed the helmet down so low on his head that you wondered whether he could even see. Then he clawed the dirt with his cleats and kicked up dust behind him, like a bull ready to charge. He leaned in, rippled with physical gifts—six feet tall, 203 pounds, 17-inch biceps, and a broad chest that tapered into a 32-inch waist and thickset legs. He chopped his bat across the plate and stared into Hooton's eyes. Stay back, he reminded himself. Lay off the inside stuff. Keep your front side closed. Go hard the other way.

Hooton threw a fastball high. Reggie, against all instincts, held off. Ball one. The next pitch cut inside on his hands. Reggie took it, as he'd taught himself to do. He thought for an instant that it had bitten the plate, but home-plate umpire John McSherry called ball two. Then Reggie looked for a fastball. Instead, Hooton threw a knuckle-curve in the dirt for ball three. He nibbled, probably out of fear. Next came a fastball away—too far away.

Reggie still had the feeling he'd had in batting practice—the energy that crackled from his shoulders down to his fingers—but Hooton had given him no way to channel it. He sprinted to first and flipped his bat toward the dugout.

Hooton went to 2–1 against Chris Chambliss and then threw a fastball at the knees but over the heart of the plate. Chambliss hit it hard. As the ball carried, Reggie ran from first to second and then slowed to a jog and held up two fingers. The ball landed twenty feet beyond the wall in right center. Reggie and Chambliss touched home and tied the game, 2–2.

Hooton, behind in the count to Chambliss, had challenged him. He'd thrown a fastball and not the knuckle-curve with which he'd teased Reggie. They're afraid of me tonight, Reggie thought as he celebrated at home plate with Chambliss and Graig Nettles.

Elias Sosa warmed up in the Dodger bull pen. Hooton, however, recouped and set down Nettles and Lou Piniella on routine plays. Hooton then struck out Bucky Dent with a perfect knuckle-curve—the best pitch he'd thrown all night.

In the third, Torrez worked ground-ball outs from Davey Lopes and Bill Russell. But then Torrez left the ball up to Reggie Smith, who hit a solo home run over the 385 sign in right center. The Dodgers led again, 3–2.

The Yankees fell in order in the bottom of the third. In the fourth, Dusty Baker drove a 3–1 sinker to deep right center, but Reggie tracked it and made an easy, two-handed catch on the warning track. In most ballparks, Baker's drive would've been a home run. Dick Tidrow warmed up for the third time. Rick Monday then punched one over Dent's head for a single. Next came a shot from Steve Yeager down the third-base line. Monday coasted into third, but the ball ricocheted off the sidewall straight to Piniella in right field. Piniella then wheeled and threw out Yeager as he slid into second base. Martin jogged from the dugout, and he and Munson talked with the laboring Torrez. Torrez then struck out Hooton.

Munson strode to the plate to start the bottom of the fourth. In the on-deck circle, Reggie dropped to his left knee. He studied Hooton. Hooton started Munson with a breaking ball up in the zone for ball one. He threw high again with his next pitch, a fastball, and Munson tore a sharp single to left. After such crispness in the third, Hooton was hanging his pitches. As Reggie stepped in, he sensed a rare opportunity—and a necessary one, given Torrez's struggles. Munson edged away from first. Hooton delivered.

The Dodger scouting report said to work Reggie inside. He didn't fear the ball, but his muscled arms and chest made it difficult to turn quickly on an inner-third fastball. Early in his career, he stood at the edge of the batter's box, but doing so left him naked to the slider away. Instead, he learned to resist the inside pitch. He always aimed to hit the ball to the left of the second baseman. Doing so gave him an extra instant to adjust. That same Dodger scouting report also said, "He rises to the occasion."

Hooton spotted his fastball lower this time, but as it approached the plate it drifted over the outer half. Reggie's swing was thick, strong, reassuring . . .

GAME SIX HAD ended but the night had just begun, and Reggie held court in front of teammates and newsmen. He fished out the Jackie Robinson medallion he'd worn around his neck. He showed it to them. "What do you think this man would think of me tonight?" he asked.

When Reggie posed that question, Robinson had been dead for almost five years. But if the man who broke baseball's color line had been there, he probably would have said, "I think you changed things."

What Robinson had begun, Reggie advanced. Robinson had shown young blacks that they could participate and compete, but Reggie showed them that they could do so without compromise. They, like Reggie, could break from the necessarily passive models of the past.

He roomed with white players, fought with white teammates, feuded with white managers, broke the dress code, made salary demands, admired his home runs for too long, held forth in the press, jousted with team owners, and dated white women at a time when miscegenation was outlawed in many states and shocking in those where it wasn't. Certainly, a few other black ballplayers—Dick Allen and Jim Rice, for instance—shared his swagger and insolence, but they never captured the national imagination like Reggie did. And, most important, they lacked Reggie's championship veneer. Reggie proved, beyond all doubt, that black individualism didn't impede team success.

He remains, though, a tangle of ironies. Reggie freed black ballplayers to express their individuality without himself ever being a vital member of the black community. It wasn't that he failed to share the community's aims or was in any way hostile toward black progress. Instead, he was a man of mixed heritage who had been raised among whites, continued throughout his career to live among whites, and rarely consorted with blacks in any meaningful sense. Reggie decried racism from time to time, but he did so only when there was no personal cost.

His 563 home runs and impossible gift for the moment made Reggie a baseball legend, but his reluctant and conflicted pioneering made him a cultural icon. He is, at once, more than the breadth of his statistics and more than the changes he wrought. Reggie himself coined a phrase for it. "Sometimes," he once said in his familiar pensive way, "I underestimate the magnitude of me."

After so many years, Reggie's life—Reggie's "magnitude of me"—begs for fresh testimony.

ONE

"Aspirations"

ONE MORNING IN 1950, the young Reggie Jackson went for a ride in his father's delivery truck. Usually on those rides around Wyncote, Pennsylvania, Reggie's father, between drop-offs, would teach him Spanish words or tell him stories about baseball games and battles, all in far-off places. But on this ride Martinez Jackson was too quiet. Even at age four, Reggie could tell the difference between a comfortable silence and a dangerous one. Finally, his father pulled the truck into their driveway. He wiggled the gearshift into park but didn't get out of the car. Martinez leaned across the steering wheel and turned his head toward the window. He sobbed for a moment and took a deep breath. "Your mom and I are splitting up," he said. "She's leaving today."

Reggie didn't know what "splitting up" meant, but he understood "leaving." Why? He wanted to know. Where? He wanted to ask. But Martinez climbed out of the truck and shuffled toward the house before he could ask those questions.

His mother, Clara, was upstairs. Reggie wondered what she was doing behind the closed bedroom door. His father sat down at the modest dining table and flipped through the newspaper. Reggie understood that the man wasn't reading, just trying to avoid certain thoughts.

Martinez was a wiry, handsome sort who smiled archly and from certain angles looked like Cab Calloway. His looks, the occasional roll of money in his pocket, and his hustler ways all made him popular with the women in town. In Martinez's mind, having a wife and six kids at home meant he was entitled to have a good time every now and then. He did. Yet though he succeeded at arranging dalliances, he failed to hide them from Clara. Martinez gambled, ran numbers on occasion, and bootlegged illegal corn liquor. Clara could forgive those sins, but she couldn't—wouldn't—abide his infidelities.

Reggie went to the room he shared with his two brothers, plopped down on his bed, and uneasily drifted off. Two hours later, his father roused him from sleep. "You need to come outside," Martinez said.

The boy yawned, then ambled to the front lawn. He had already forgotten the conversation in the truck. Clara, dressed in Sunday clothes, stood on the grass with her scant belongings packed in a small suitcase. Martinez, head down, toed the ground like a chastened boy. Only then did Reggie remember that his mother was "leaving." Martinez nudged the six children into an orderly queue.

Clara stared at the children. Reggie, Beverly, James, and Tina were hers. Joe and Dolores were Martinez's from his first marriage. Clara yanked James, Dolores, and Tina from the line, and Reggie watched her lead the three children to the car. She backed out of the driveway and pulled away.

She settled 150 miles away in Baltimore. Soon Beverly left to join her, and James returned to Wyncote. Reggie, though, had little contact with Clara over the years, and eventually he told people he didn't have a mother.

———————

NESTLED BEYOND THE northern border of Philadelphia, Wyncote was originally a town of displaced Anglicans and Quakers, but after the First World War, German Jews moved there in droves. By World War II, Jews made up the majority of Wyncote's population, and their presence increased over the years.

Martinez came to Wyncote from New Jersey in the late 1930s. He worked as a tailor and soon married Clara. Eventually, though, his gambling schemes caught up with him, and, to avoid imprisonment, he enlisted in the Army Air Corps. Two months later, the Japanese attacked Pearl Harbor. In the war, Martinez flew a P-51 Mustang during the invasion of North Africa, and he worked his way up to lieutenant before being honorably discharged with a hip injury.

Upon his return, Martinez pooled his soldier's pay with the family's modest savings and bought a two-story wood-frame house on Greenwood Avenue. The family lived on the two main floors, and Martinez used the attic for his dry cleaning business.

During Reggie's time, Wyncote was a racially enlightened place, at least by the standards of the day. In that sense, Reggie's upbringing was rare among professional baseball players. Unlike most black players of his generation and the preceding ones, Reggie was neither born in the South nor raised in an urban black community. In Wyncote, Reggie never had to deal with Jim Crow or the bruising poverty of the urban ghetto or the sharecropping economy. Instead, Reggie helped Martinez with the family business, performed chores around the house, kept up with his schoolwork, and played sports when he had the time.

In Wyncote, Reggie was almost always the only black kid on his sports teams and in his circles of friends. (Wyncote had a small black community, Hilltop Lane, but Reggie rarely ventured there.) At the time, he thought little of it. A motormouth, a troublemaker at times, and, despite his then-diminutive size, a physically powerful kid who delighted in defending himself, Reggie paid little price for being his unleavened self. The progressive-minded Jewish commu-

nity in Wyncote demanded little of Reggie in the way of social con-
formity. And his father took pains not to distinguish among the races
around him. Martinez didn't identify himself as black, and the town
of Wyncote didn't make him feel especially black. Martinez, whose
mother was a light-skinned Hispanic, even *looked* white and passed
himself off as such when he needed to. Reggie learned from his father
that it was normal, even desirable, to assimilate into white society.

Those racially unburdened years allowed him to develop a social
ease with whites in general and Jews in particular. His friends were
Jewish, his girlfriends were Jewish, his teachers and coaches were
Jewish, and his father's customers were Jewish. Martinez even peppered his conversations with Yiddish phrases. ("He's got kup," he
would often say of Reggie, invoking the Yiddish for "good sense.")
Reggie learned to trust white people.

Years later, when asked what he'd taken from such unlikely environs—a neighborhood white in color and collar—Reggie thought for
a moment and said, "Aspirations."

Reggie's aspirations led him to sports. He told his family, his
friends, his coaches, strangers, anyone who would listen that he would
one day be a sports star. At first it seemed like an unlikely goal. He
simply didn't *look* like an athlete. He was gap-toothed and diminutive.
He had calm features, and he smiled a lot.

But he immediately forged a reputation as a gifted athlete.
Whenever a ball got stuck in a tree on the Wyncote Elementary
School playground, the principal would call Reggie out of class to
dislodge it with another ball. In the entire school, even among the
male staff members, only Reggie had the arm and accuracy to do the
job—most often on the first try. He relished the attention that sports
brought him.

Yet, according to Reggie, some of that shine wore off when, at
age thirteen, he played for the nearby Greater Glenside Youth Club.
Glenside squared off against a team from Fort Lauderdale, Florida,
in the annual "Dixie Series." Reggie, in his 1984 autobiography, said

the team from Florida wouldn't take the field against a black player. Reggie's coach capitulated and benched him. Martinez confronted the coach, who stammered something about roster limits and new rules. "You'll face this kind of thing from time to time," Reggie's father told him.

Or at least that's the story Reggie told for years. In reality, though, Reggie played regularly throughout the series and did so without incident.

It's human nature to magnify or even feign hardships endured, and Reggie was as prone to doing so as any of us. Later in his life, he envied the blacks he met who had survived more than he had. He wanted, as part of his own story, the edifying properties of struggle. So he massaged his personal history.

Despite the revisions to come, Reggie in high school was every bit the teenager in the halcyon America of the early 1960s. He dreamed about cars and girls. He wore his Cheltenham Township High School letterman's jacket, madras shirts, and cuffed blue jeans. He listened to Elvis and Buddy Holly and the Kingston Trio. He worked on the 1955 Chevy that his father had bought him. He hung out with his white friends at the ice cream stand or Kenyon's, the local hamburger joint, and he occasionally sneaked a beer at Schmidt's or Ballantine's.

At Cheltenham High, Reggie enjoyed the spoils of being an athlete. He had girls, respect in the hallways, teachers who made sure his grades were in order, the adoration of the community, and chants of "Reg-gie! Reg-gie!"—the chants he'd hear for the rest of his life— that tolled through the gyms and fields. He played baseball, football, and basketball and ran track, and at each sport he excelled. Above all, he wanted to be a professional football player. In 1963, though, Reggie saw those dreams threatened.

In Reggie's junior year, the big rivalry game against Abington Township was scheduled for the Saturday before Thanksgiving. But on Friday, an assassin's bullets struck down President John F. Kennedy as he traveled through Dallas. With a pall cast over Wyncote and the rest of the nation, the game was pushed back to Thanksgiving Day.

In the early moments of the game, Reggie, the team's star tail-back, cut back against the grain and wrenched his knee. After his coach attended to him, he was carried off the field on a stretcher and taken to the local emergency room. Most parents were at the game to see their sons, in the words of the poet James Wright, "gallop terribly against each other's bodies," but Martinez was nowhere to be found. Reggie's assistant principal, Ed Guarneri, tried to reach Martinez by telephone to tell him that his son needed him, but he couldn't track him down. Guaneri signed the release papers and sat at Reggie's bedside. Guaneri held his hand and told him, yes, he would play football again. The doctors who treated Reggie were less certain.

Reggie did recover, and he did return to the football field sooner than anyone thought he would. That same season, however, he came in too low trying to make a late-season tackle against Marple-Newton and snapped his neck. He finished the game.

Only after the pain set in hours later did he go to the hospital and receive the grim news: he'd fractured five cervical vertebrae. Reggie spent the next six weeks in traction and then another month in a partial neck cast. Doctors again underestimated his recuperative powers and told him he might not walk again, let alone play football. Reggie defied their expectations in the hugest of ways.

After he healed, Reggie also carried on as Cheltenham's best hit-ter on the baseball team. At practice one day, Reggie, determined to hone his skills against lefties, took extra batting practice. He asked one of the team's left-handers, Gene Waldman, to pitch to him. "Throw high and inside," Reggie told him. "Real tight, move me back."

It was almost seven o'clock. Reggie lost the first pitch in the gloaming, and it struck him flush on the face. He fell to the ground, and blood poured from his mouth. His coach again rushed him to the emergency room, where doctors told Reggie that his jaw was broken in five places. They wired his mouth shut and solemnly told him he wouldn't be able to play for the rest of the season. He missed just three practices and one game.

His senior year proved to be no easier. Midway through the school year, Reggie arrived home one day to find a line of police cars outside. He burst through the front door, but two officers restrained him. Reggie saw his father cuffed and then led away on bootlegging charges. The family couldn't afford bail, and the judge sentenced Martinez to six months in jail.

His older brother, Joe, had joined the Air Force, his other brother, James, worked constantly to maintain the modest family business, and Clara was still in Baltimore with his sisters. The booming cheers in the gymnasiums and stadiums sustained him, but his days always ended in the unbearable quiet at 149 Greenwood Avenue. He hated the ticking of the clocks and the creaking of the floorboards. He hated the one and only trip he made to see his father at the prison in Norristown. He hated seeing his father in the drab gray jumpsuit and telling him, "We're all right," when they both knew it was a lie. So he channeled the angst the only way he knew how.

As a guard on the basketball team, he averaged better than 18 points per game. As a running back on the football team, he averaged 8.0 yards per carry and led the district in touchdowns. On the baseball diamond he batted .550 and, when not playing first base, threw numerous no-hitters and once struck out twenty batters in a game. People noticed. Alabama and Georgia were both willing to integrate their football programs for him, but the idea daunted the eighteen-year-old who had only fearful notions of the American South. Oklahoma would also break the color line for him, but it told Reggie that he must stop dating white girls.

As for his baseball skills, the Giants had first noticed Reggie when he was eleven years old, and a venerable Giants scout named Hans Lobert followed Reggie closely during his senior year. Lobert tried desperately to sign him, and Reggie knew it would mean he might one day play alongside his baseball idol, Willie Mays. The Dodgers and Twins also made overtures, and the hometown Phillies gave him a tryout. ("This boy does everything well with exception of hitting," one of their scouts wrote. "Not impressed with his bat.")

Martinez, however, wanted his son to go to college. A model father he never was and never would be, but he did emphasize to Reggie the importance of an education. He believed that football offered the surest way for Reggie to earn his degree. College baseball at the time was something of a backwater sport and even more of an afterthought in colder climates, where the baseball seasons were necessarily shorter. Martinez appreciated that baseball presented opportunities for blacks, but he wanted Reggie to be the first in his family to go to college. So Martinez, counseling his son from behind bars, begged him to get an education. "So you don't end up like me," he cautioned.

Reggie loved football, but he couldn't give up baseball. Dartmouth and George Washington offered him baseball scholarships, but at that point no school would let him play baseball *and* football. Reggie's high school football coach, John Kracsun, made some calls on his behalf. One was to Frank Kush, an old coaching friend from Kracsun's days in the western Pennsylvania coalfields who had gone on to Arizona State. Kracsun told Kush that Reggie was a gifted running back who also wanted to play baseball. "We can work something out," said Kush.

"One other thing," said Kracsun. "He's a black kid."

"Can he play?" asked Kush.

"He can play."

Many football coaches in the mid-1960s would not countenance a black player. Most major colleges in the South had yet to integrate their athletic programs, and even in other parts of the country race remained a complication. Kush, however, cared about nothing except a player's ability and his willingness to work. After Kracsun's phone call and a subsequent scouting trip in the Northeast, Kush decided Reggie had both. He told Reggie that he'd be granted a full football scholarship—tuition, room, board, and $15 per week in spending money—and that he'd also be allowed to play baseball for one of the best programs in the country. That and the notion of going to school on the other side of the country swayed Reggie. He took the free recruiting trips that came his way, but he'd made up his mind.

It was a bold step for a young man who'd never ventured far beyond Wyncote's borders. And at the time, he had neither a mother nor a father to tell him it would all be okay. But Reggie held fast to the motto that ran under his senior portrait in the Cheltenham yearbook: "Sovereign Independence."

As he walked through Sears, Roebuck and picked out the clothes he could afford—two pairs of shoes, three of everything else—he could scarcely wait to leave his hometown behind. His father was still in prison when Reggie received his high school diploma, and he was still in prison when Reggie, encumbered by a pair of suitcases and a gym bag, climbed into his friend's '56 Pontiac and left for Tempe, Arizona.

TWO

"He Looks Whiter All the Time"

TEMPE WAS INDEED a far meridian, some 2,400 miles from Wyncote and on the other side of the country. To Reggie, it felt like the other side of the world. The land was arid and treeless, and the air was hot but, unlike his hometown, not turgid with Atlantic humidity. If you drove even ten minutes outside of Tempe or Phoenix, you saw nothing but the distant, rockbound horizon.

Like so many other young men who thrive in high school athletics, Reggie's entry into a big-time college program sobered him. Now *everyone* on the team was a hometown hero on an unswerving course for glory. Those accustomed to being the biggest, strongest, and fastest found themselves, for the first time, surrounded by athletes as good as or better than they were.

The reality around Reggie—the big, strong, intense *men* who were now his teammates and competitors—tempered his expectations. No longer did playing two sports appeal to him. To keep his scholarship, let alone thrive, he would devote himself entirely to football.

As his freshman season progressed, Reggie began to sour on his circumstances. Kush laughed and mocked his players when they were hit hard in practice. He ridiculed them when they got tired. He called them "pussies" and "mama's boys" and told them they weren't tough enough for football. He'd line up his halfbacks—of whom Reggie was one—against the entire defensive line and call the same running play over and over again. If he further doubted his players' mettle, then he'd force them, in the 100-degree heat, to run sprints up "Kush's Mountain," a steeply pitched hill near the ASU practice field.

As his sophomore campaign—his first with the varsity—loomed, Reggie looked forward to measuring himself against the best football players in the country. But things didn't unfold as he'd hoped. Kush, impressed with Reggie's tackling skills, moved him to defensive back. Reggie, though, savored the "glamour" position of running back, and the switch to a less conspicuous role displeased him.

Just when Reggie most needed something to take his mind off the frustrations and terrors of playing for Frank Kush, a young lady named Juanita "Jennie" Campos came along. Reggie had seen her around campus before. She was a petite Latina with a warm, inviting smile and dark, thick, curly hair. She'd caught Reggie staring at her a couple of times, and finally he summoned the courage to ask her to lunch in the cafeteria. She agreed.

She didn't know who Reggie was, and she seemed blissfully unaware of anything having to do with sports on campus. The more they talked, though, the more he liked that he could engage Jennie on other grounds. They both spoke Spanish, and they'd both grown up in single-parent homes (Jennie's father had been killed in action when he crashed his B-29 bomber into the mountains of North Korea). He told her how much he'd been hurt when his mother had abandoned him, and she told him how much she missed her dead father. They had their first date at a dormitory dance in the spring.

Jennie was intelligent—smarter than Reggie—and he liked that about her. "I wanted to see westerns, and Jennie liked foreign films," Reggie said later. "She read serious books; I read the sports pages." With Jennie, he felt less need to nurse his ego. He also felt like a man when she told him that he was the first boyfriend she'd ever had who made her feel safe and protected. But trouble soon followed.

An assistant football coach went to one of Jennie's uncles, a wealthy benefactor of the athletic department, and asked him to break up the couple. Reggie was black, and, according to the racial ordering of the day, Jennie, the Hispanic girl, was white. "It won't be good for Reggie's career or for the school," the coach told Jennie's uncle. Jennie's uncle relayed the concerns to her. "People really care about this?" Reggie asked. But he and Jennie were strong enough to ignore the warnings, and their romance blossomed.

Reggie also adjusted on the field. Doubts about his ability to compete with the other athletes at ASU started to fade, and he earned more attention and plaudits. As he readied himself for the upcoming season, a return to baseball preoccupied him. He imagined himself mashing home runs out of Packard Stadium and riling up the dirt around home plate with his swings. He even thought fondly of the racial makeup of the baseball team. It had the kinds of faces—white faces—he was accustomed to seeing back in Wyncote, and, in his most honest moments, he knew he missed that. When Reggie had first moved into Sahuaro Hall, the athletic dormitory on the ASU campus, he'd found himself, for the first time in his life, living and working among other blacks.

At first he strained for acceptance. Reggie imitated some of the mannerisms he saw and dialects he heard, and he even told a few lies to burnish his past with more "blackness." But whenever Reggie costumed himself in that blackness, it felt false and affected. Eventually, he stopped trying.

Instead, he befriended two white baseball players, Joe Paulsen and Jeff Pentland. Reggie told them he wanted to play again. He boasted of the hitter he'd been back in high school and said that making the team would be easy for him. Finally, Paulsen and Pentland challenged Reggie to prove it.

One afternoon, after a typically draining Kush practice, he made his way to the nearby baseball field, where Coach Bobby Winkles lorded over a varsity workout. Reggie, still decked out in his football uniform save for his helmet, asked Winkles if he could take a few swings the next day. "I think I can play, sir," he said. Winkles said he'd give him a look.

That next day, with Winkles and the rest of the team looking on, Reggie, dressed in football pants and spikes, dug in. He hadn't swung a bat in almost a year, and he faced a varsity hurler for the mighty Sun Devils.

The sequence went something like this: swing and a miss, homer to right, homer to right, swing and a miss, swing and a miss, 440-foot homer to center, take, take, homer to center. "Okay," he gushed to Coach Winkles, "do I make the team?"

Winkles paused for a moment, and then, tempering his enthusiasm as much as he could, told Reggie he thought they'd have a place for him in practices. At the time, NCAA rules barred freshman players from varsity competition, but Winkles could see that Reggie would make a difference one day.

That season Reggie watched, learned, and savored the time away from Kush. Winkles forbade his players to argue with umpires, and he demanded that they run out every ball, sprint on and off the field between innings, and answer "Yes, sir" and "No, sir." Winkles was tough, but he wasn't as backbreaking as Kush. To Reggie, he was a sweet relief.

Reggie's early practices were notable for violent strikeouts and misplays in the outfield. Off the field, however, Reggie dominated the physical fitness tests that were mandatory for all ASU athletes. The parts were still greater than the sum, but Reggie's dormant baseball skills began to return.

———

FOLLOWING REGGIE'S FRESHMAN baseball season, Winkles told him to hone his skills over the summer. Since Reggie would spend the summer in Baltimore with his mother, Winkles arranged for him to play with an Orioles-affiliated amateur team based in the city, one sponsored by Leone's Tavern in South Baltimore.

Reggie ironed out the details over the telephone. His being an articulate young man who had grown up around whites and didn't have an accent meant that his new handlers didn't realize something about him—that he was black. In Reggie's own words, he "talked like a white boy." When he reported, Walter Youse, the Orioles scout with whom he'd spoken, could muster only "*You're* Reggie Jackson?"

The team to which he'd been assigned had never before had a black player. Nevertheless, it gave Reggie a tryout. They put him through the usual battery of drills on an overgrown field at Swann Park in South Baltimore. On that field, flanked by crumbling row houses, chugging refineries, and the littered banks of the Patapsco River, Reggie dazzled them.

In the 60-yard dash, Reggie clocked close to a world-class time. In the outfield he outthrew the best arm on the team. When he ran to first base, he came close to Mickey Mantle's legendary scout time, and with the bat he put on his typical power display. "He looks whiter all the time," Youse said.

During the summer season, which lasted from June to August and consisted of eight games a week, Reggie set all manner of team records for Leone's. He did so despite missing a tournament in rural Virginia that barred black players. The Orioles approached him about a contract, but NCAA rules prohibited him from signing a contract in one sport (baseball) while maintaining eligibility in another (football). Rather than forfeit his college scholarship, he passed on a $50,000 signing bonus.

Reggie returned to ASU in the fall, and his baseball career took off. He showed up with a letter from Kush saying he had permission to skip spring practice if he made the varsity baseball team. He did that and more.

Reggie replaced the legendary Rick Monday in center (Monday that year became the top overall pick in baseball's first-ever amateur draft). Reggie had played first base and pitched in high school, and manning the most vital outfield position scared him. "I don't care if you can't catch a cold, I don't care if you drop balls, I don't care if you strike out every day," Coach Winkles told him. "You're going to be out there."

Winkles's dogged trust sustained him. As a sophomore, Reggie set the team record for homers in a season; batted .327; paced the team in hits, total bases, runs, RBIs, and stolen bases; and was named first-team All-American. Against archrival Arizona, he became just the second collegian ever to hit a ball completely out of Phoenix Municipal Stadium. The sellout crowd treated Reggie to an ovation he'd never before experienced. It drove home what he had already come to believe about baseball: that the opportunities for adulation and glory were far greater. Though baseball offered failure without the shield of a face mask or a mass of bodies, that same exposure also allowed one to be adored in uncommon ways.

The Sun Devils went 41–11 on the year, but they failed to repeat as national champions. Still, ASU was a high-profile program, and Reggie was its best player. Danny Murtaugh, who managed the Pirates to a pair of World Series titles, scouted him on behalf of Pittsburgh, and Tom Greenwade, the scout who had signed Mickey Mantle, followed Reggie for the Yankees. The Orioles and Giants also followed him closely. In his final game as an amateur, Reggie showed the many scouts in attendance his potential: he homered, doubled, laid down a bunt single, made an acrobatic running catch in center, and gunned down a runner at home plate.

"Maybe you're aware of this, and maybe you're not," Winkles told him in his office one day, "but you're certain to be drafted high in the first round."

Reggie knew that. He'd talked to the scouts. The money appealed to him. But so did getting his degree, continuing to play for Winkles, and, on the football team, returning to the running back position—something Kush had promised him. Reggie also feared leaving Jennie behind.

"You're going to get offered a lot of money," Winkles insisted.

The day before the draft, the *Chicago Tribune* reported that the New York Mets, the holder of the top pick in 1966, were expected to draft Reggie. What happened next is unclear.

The Mets passed on Reggie in favor of a high school catcher from Lancaster, California, named Steve Chilcott. According to Reggie, Winkles told him that the Mets wouldn't draft him because he had a white girlfriend.

There was a long and hopeless history of persecution on those grounds. The boxer Jack Johnson had been imprisoned in Leavenworth for the "crime" of transporting a white woman (who would later become his wife) across state lines. Joe Louis had endeavored to keep secret his affairs with Lana Turner and Sonja Henie, lest his career be ruined. Vic Power had toiled as one of the best prospects in the Yankees' minor-league system for years, but the Yankees had traded him because he dated white women. College basketball legends Elgin Baylor and Walt Hazzard had both been harassed because they went out with white coeds, and the University of Washington had kicked the fullback Claude Robert off the team because a prominent alumnus saw him at a nightclub with a white woman.

Reggie habitually courted light-skinned women, but for him it was not an exercise in sexual activism; it merely reflected his origins. Reggie sought out white friends, and later in life he would choose white business associates and advisers. His father even *looked* white. Reggie could not grasp that his preferences in women rankled a team from New York. Then again, George Weiss ran the Mets in 1966.

Weiss, the architect of the great Yankees teams of the 1950s, was president of the Mets by the time Reggie entered the draft. Weiss was a bigot of long standing who'd passed on Willie Mays because he was black. "I will never allow a black man to wear a Yankee uniform," he once proclaimed. "Box holders from Westchester don't want that sort of crowd. They would be offended to have to sit with niggers."

By 1966, Weiss had begun to tolerate black players on the roster, but not any who breached his notions of good behavior. So perhaps the Mets, at Weiss's command, would not draft Reggie as long as he indulged in miscegenation.

Winkles, however, denies he told Reggie such a thing. "I know nothing about that," Winkles says today. "I was never informed why he wasn't drafted by the Mets." Joe McDonald, a functionary in the Mets' front office at the time, also denied Reggie's allegations. "There was absolutely nothing to Jackson's charge," he told the writer Maury Allen in 1981. "We simply drafted the first player we thought could help us."

Indeed, the Mets had good reason to believe in Chilcott. Casey Stengel scouted him for the Mets and watched him record eleven hits in twelve at bats. The report Stengel turned in glowed as brightly as the young catcher's performance. Perhaps Reggie, who has a history as a racial fabulist, could endure not being the number one pick only if he could blame it on conspiratorial elements. Whether bigoted or merely incompetent, the Mets passed on Reggie.

When Joe McDonald approached the podium at the Plaza Hotel in New York City and called Chilcott's name, the Mets made one of the hugest mistakes in baseball history. And the Kansas City Athletics knew it. Charles Oscar Finley, the owner of the Athletics and holder of the second pick, smiled a knowing smile.

Finley hustled his way to the microphone as though this opportunity—one he couldn't quite believe—might vaporize before him. "I take Reggie Jackson!" he bellowed. "Reggie Jackson!" he repeated even more loudly, just to ensure that everyone knew this boy now belonged to him.

THREE

"Yes, Sir"

CHARLIE O. FINLEY would on occasion joke that his middle initial stood for "owner." The owner of the Kansas City Athletics was just that—a man who owned things. Finley didn't "employ" you or "sign" you; he owned you.

Whatever words were used to describe Finley—irascible, brilliant, miserly in the extreme, petulant, defiant, sentimental, bullheaded—they would be accurate in one instant and impossibly wrong in the next. He lived to defy whatever simple taxonomy you applied to him.

Among the normally staid fraternity of baseball owners, Finley was a tilting-at-windmills maverick given to argument and caprice. He was an outsider and an irritant to the status quo. But he was also a tireless worker and, at times, a man of uncommon vision. There was simply nothing simple about Charlie Finley.

He grew up poor in Alabama and foundered for years as a rank-and-file worker at the U.S. Steel mill in Birmingham. He watched two generations of Finley men while away their years in the Hueytown and Shadyside neighborhoods of Birmingham, their lives punctuated only by the blare of the mill whistle. Unsatisfied, he defied odds and circumstance.

As a boy, Finley bought rejected eggs from a local market at 5 cents per dozen, and then he went door-to-door in Birmingham and sold them for 15 cents per dozen. During the days of Prohibition, he picked grapes from neighbors' yards under cover of night and sold the wine he made from them. While his friends played in abandoned lots or fished at a nearby pond, young Finley mowed lawns in his neighborhood and sold *The Saturday Evening Post*.

He tasted baseball for the first time in 1931, when the Birmingham Barons minor-league team hired him as a batboy. He made 50 cents per game, plus tips from the players and a used baseball. More important, though, was that the game had hooked him. Inspired by what he saw on the field, he took those used baseballs, taped them up, and formed a sandlot team of his own.

By 1933, hard times had forced the Finley clan north to Gary, Indiana, and the countless foundries, plants, and mills of the greater Chicago area. It was a dark, sooty, and blighted place where the airborne dust and grime seemed to blot out the sun, even in the height of summer. Finley worked hard to lose his Alabama accent, which he believed made him sound ignorant. In high school, he finagled a transfer to Horace Mann, where the rich kids went. Finley was hellbent on marrying above his station, and Horace Mann was the place to do that. So with cold calculation he charmed Shirley McCartney, the daughter of Gary's wealthiest plumbing contractor. It was easy for the tall, lean, and somewhat dashing Finley, who was quick with a compliment and a well-timed one-liner.

After graduation he worked the night shift at U.S. Steel's Gary plant for 47½ cents an hour. In keeping with his incessantly repeated motto ("sweat plus sacrifice equals success"), Finley worked his way up to a supervisory position. He and Shirley married in 1946.

Finley spent his scarce free time as a slick-fielding first baseman for the Ensweiler Printers of the Gary Twilight League, one of several semipro leagues in the region. On occasion, he'd also make the trip to the grandstands of Comiskey Park to take in a White Sox game. All of it made Finley want to be a part of the sports world, but he couldn't fathom how that would come to pass.

He sold insurance on a full-time basis and distinguished himself as one of the Travelers Company's top salesmen. However, his indefatigable pace finally caught up to him. In November 1946, Finley was climbing a flight of stairs to meet a potential client when he collapsed and coughed up blood. After being admitted to a Gary hospital, Finley learned that he'd developed a grave case of tuberculosis. Doctors gave him a fifty-fifty chance of survival and confined him to the Parramore Sanatorium in nearby Crown Point.

Finley's work and material possessions defined him. He'd drive clients past the largest, most palatial estate in Gary and lie to them that it was his home. He'd overextend himself to buy lushly appointed Cadillacs and Oldsmobiles. As he convalesced, his carefully built life slipped from his grasp. In a bit of irony that would haunt Finley for years to come, the record-setting peddler of medical insurance had failed to sell himself a policy. His wife, Shirley, was forced to take a $30-per-week job as a proofreader at the *Gary Post-Tribune*.

The suddenly powerless Finley lashed out. He snapped at his nurses, called the doctors incompetent quacks, demanded a private room (which he wouldn't get), and, more than once during Shirley's visits, slapped his wife across the face.

Frustrated, ailing, and desperate, Finley put his restive mind to work. All around him were bustling, highly paid medical professionals. He thought about them—their needs, their vulnerabilities, their peculiar fears.

As he lay there, sweating, laboring to breathe, and at one point down to 96 pounds, he concocted an idea to sell doctors group disability policies that would protect them and their families from sudden loss of income. He canvassed some of the doctors at Parramore. Their responses encouraged him.

Once he had healed enough to return home, he shopped his idea to insurance companies. Several dozen nos later, he found a taker and formed Charles O. Finley & Company, Inc., in Chicago. After a few years, he logged more than $40 million in annual premiums (including a leviathan of a sale to the American Medical Association). At long last, Finley was a rich man. His mind returned to baseball.

In 1954, he put up $3 million in a bid to purchase the Philadelphia Athletics from Connie Mack, but his lack of personal connections did him in. In 1956, he led a syndicate that offered $5 million for the Detroit Tigers, but once again he was spurned. Then Finley tried to buy into Bill Veeck's group that was to purchase the White Sox, but that too failed. Then he aimed for an expansion franchise in Los Angeles, but he lost out to Gene Autry. Finally, in 1960, following the timely death of Athletics owner Arnold Johnson, Finley got his chance. After a trip to probate court and some late-hour maneuvering, Finley purchased 52 percent of the Kansas City Athletics. By 1961, he'd scraped together an additional $4 million to buy the remaining shares from local minority owners. The A's hadn't managed a winning season in almost a decade, but they were his. "I wanted to get into baseball in the worst way," Finley later said, "and that's what I did."

In lieu of attracting fans with quality baseball, which wouldn't be possible until Finley could rebuild, Finley turned to creative and occasionally absurd promotions. In the seasons to come, he put a petting zoo beyond the outfield fence and installed a mechanical rabbit to deliver the ball to the home-plate umpire. He laced the foul poles with pink fluorescent lights and ordered his players to ride into the stadium on mules on Opening Day. He hired a team astrologer and an eleven-year-old team vice president (the young Stanley Burrell, later the rapper MC Hammer) and signed a succession of track stars to function as pinch runners extraordinaire. At one point, he lobbied the league to install a telephone at home plate so his manager could argue balls and strikes from the dugout. The gimmicks rarely worked, but all the while he was rebuilding the team from the bottom up.

At first blush, Finley seemed to be the kind of ruthlessly self-made man that Reggie, in his thirst for success and material uplift, had come to admire. During those early days, though, Reggie caught only strobe-lit glimpses of Finley—what Finley allowed him to see. He saw the paternal instincts, the lightning-quick mind, the trappings of success, the smooth carriage, and the promises of things to come. He didn't see the pettiness, the selfish cruelty, the impossible stinginess, and the hints of bigotry.

As negotiations loomed, Reggie felt out of his depth. He called his father back in Wyncote and asked him for help. Martinez's neglect still stung Reggie, but he had nowhere else to turn. He paid his father's way to Chicago, and they checked into the Congress Hotel on Michigan Avenue. From there they walked a few blocks in silence to Finley's offices at 310 South Michigan. Finley cut a tall and lanky figure. He smiled widely and welcomed them with a booming voice and powerful handshake. From his white loafers to his dark, thicket-like eyebrows, Finley exuded confidence and control. He leaned back in his chair, propped his feet up on his desk, and after a torturous pause offered Reggie $50,000 to sign. "No thank you, Mr. Finley," Reggie said.

"We want $100,000," Martinez said. It was what Finley had given Rick Monday the previous year.

"I can't pay you that kind of money," Finley said.

If the offer was $50,000, Reggie told him, he'd return to Arizona State and continue his education. Finley studied Reggie and his father for several seconds. "Seventy-five thousand," he said. "You go back to the hotel and think about it, and we'll get together at my house for breakfast tomorrow."

Reggie and his father talked through much of the night. His father urged him to sign and take the money, while Reggie wanted to return to ASU and the world that had become so comfortable for the twenty-year-old. He phoned Coach Winkles and asked his advice. "Take the money," Winkles told him.

The next morning, Finley flew Reggie and Martinez to his home in Indiana on his private plane. He served them expensive steaks, cantaloupe à la mode, and fresh corn harvested from his own fields. As they ate, he regaled them with tales of how the A's would become champions with Reggie in the lineup and how Reggie would one day become a wealthy superstar. All around him were the spoils of a successful life—the rolling farmland; the indoor basketball court; and the legions of dogs, cats, horses, and grandchildren. Reggie would have it all for himself one day, Finley promised him.

"Mr. Finley," Reggie said, "if you give me the money you offered yesterday, plus two thousand dollars a semester for my college tuition and a new Pontiac, I'll sign." Finley indulged in another of his long pauses before he said, "There isn't anything more to talk about. We do have a deal. Reggie, you're going to win me a World Series some day."

WHEN HE ARRIVED in Lewiston, Idaho, his first stop in the A's minor-league system, the absence of black faces reminded him of home. He was one of just two blacks in town, the other an old-timer called "Chicken Willie" who drove the team bus. The second thing that reminded Reggie of Wyncote was the unrelenting quiet—a quiet that he found at times calming and at times disconcerting. Lewiston seemed like an oddly familiar place.

Reggie got off to a hot start: in twelve games, he hit .292 and slugged a robust .563. Exactly half of his hits went for extra bases, and each of his two homers broke a window in a house across the street from Bengal Field. Reggie made just $500 a month, but he measured himself against the $85,000 bonus package.

In those two weeks, he traveled by bus around the Northwest and got a taste of the nomadic life of a minor leaguer. Back in Lewiston,

Reggie spent quiet nights at the Lewis and Clark Motel. Sometimes, he'd have dinner at Bojack's, but mostly he watched television in his room or made long-distance calls to Jennie back in Arizona.

On one of those otherwise quiet nights, Reggie took a fastball squarely on the head and spilled to the ground. Although he never blacked out, the team dispatched him to the local emergency room as a precautionary measure. Reggie dozed off on the ride to St. Joseph Hospital, but the next day doctors discharged him after X-rays showed no lasting damage.

In his autobiography, Reggie claimed that he'd been denied a private room on the basis of race. Three years after that, in an interview with *Sports Illustrated*, he claimed that he'd been denied admission to the hospital altogether. St. Joseph's records, however, show that it admitted Reggie. At the very least, he lied to *SI*.

Soon after Reggie's release, Finley promoted him to Modesto of the California League. Once there, Reggie glimpsed the dynasty to come. In 1962, Finley had signed—for just $500—a Cuban infield prospect and son of a lariat maker named Dagoberto "Bert" Campaneris. Then, in 1964, he inked a right-hander out of Hertford, North Carolina, named Jim Hunter. Hunter had been a coveted prep hurler, but his brother had accidentally shot him while duck hunting. The mishap had left thirty shotgun pellets in Hunter's foot and his baseball career in doubt. Most teams ceased pursuing Hunter, but Finley took a chance and signed him for $75,000. After he did, Finley told Jim Hunter that he was now Catfish Hunter. The story—concocted by Finley—was that as a boy Hunter had gone missing and that his parents had found him asleep on the bank of stream, one catfish in hand and one on his fishing line. "Whatever you say, Mr. Finley," Hunter said.

In 1965, Finley brought Rollie Fingers, Joe Rudi, Rick Monday, Sal Bando, and Gene Tenace into the fold. In 1966 he signed Reggie, and in 1967 he signed Vida Blue. By the time Reggie arrived in Modesto, Fingers, Rudi, catcher Dave Duncan, and eleven other future major leaguers waited for him.

Modesto would be a stiffer challenge for Reggie. It was a rung higher on the organizational ladder, and, unlike the bandbox in Lewiston, Modesto's park was more in line with the dimensions of major-league stadiums. He spent the remainder of the 1966 season in Modesto, and in fifty-six games he batted .299, slugged .611, hit roughly one home run every ten at bats, and tallied more RBIs than games played. In full-season minor-league ball, each league crowned a first-half champion and a second-half champion. Without Reggie, the Modesto A's claimed the first-half crown by two games; with Reggie, they won the second half by sixteen games, mostly because of a powerhouse offense. Duncan hit forty-six homers, and Reggie chipped in twenty-one in less than half a season.

Reggie and several of his teammates lived at the Carvel Hotel for $6 a day. The collegial atmosphere reminded him of his time at ASU, except that this time he lived, happily, among white players. He called Jennie often and wrote her long letters on Carvel stationery.

Reggie also had a discretionary income for the first time, and he rewarded himself. He bought alligator-skin cowboy boots, alpaca sweaters, Ban-Lon shirts, leather belts, and high-end sunglasses. In the clubhouse and with the spare semblance of media that followed the team, he was impossibly cocksure. As he began to absorb his own promise and the promise of those around him, he knew they had forged something special.

THE FOLLOWING SPRING, Reggie for the first time set foot in the American South. His ideas of it came straight from Martinez. When Reggie was a boy, Martinez would regale him with tales of his days playing in the Negro Leagues against and alongside such luminaries as Satchel Paige, Cool Papa Bell, Judy Johnson, and Josh Gibson. Reggie, when asked about his father, would repeat those stories. However, Martinez, though he did play baseball on some lesser circuits, didn't make it to what's commonly thought of as the Negro

Leagues. The closest he came was when he drove the Newark Eagles' bus for $7 a day. As the Eagles' bus driver, he got a firsthand look at the segregated South. There he kept an eye out for local vigilantes, slept in flophouses, and ate meals on the bus when the team couldn't find a "colored" diner to serve them.

Reggie thought of those stories—stories that had left him in fearful marvel—when he reported to Camp Campbell, North Carolina, to fulfill a brief ROTC detail. However, his neck injury from high school flared up once again. The camp doctor diagnosed Reggie with an arthritic spine and then discharged him after just a month of training.

He drove the Pontiac that Finley had given him from the Camp Campbell medical barracks to Waycross, Georgia, where minor-league spring training awaited. Because of his time in the hospital, Reggie was already ten days late for camp. He tried to make it to camp on one tank of gas, but he was finally forced to stop just outside Waycross a little after 10 P.M. Not long after Reggie pulled into the darkened filling station and pumped gas into his car, a pickup truck approached. From within, a voice hissed at him, "Hey, nigger."

Reggie froze and then slowly turned toward the truck. "Hey, nigger," the voice said again, and someone else in the truck laughed. "You get off our streets, and you stay off our streets."

Reggie looked away. He held his breath until the truck motored off into the dark. Trembling, he climbed back into his Pontiac and drove the final few miles to Waycross, taking special care not to exceed the speed limit.

After a few days of treading carefully—eating and rooming with the few other blacks in camp, not wandering into town after dark—Reggie learned Finley's plans for him. Finley beamed over the young team he'd built, and he wanted to show off the residue of his genius in his hometown.

Finley would dispatch Reggie and several other top prospects to Double-A Birmingham, the A's Southern League outpost. After

Reggie's recent experiences, spending perhaps a season in the heart of the Deep South harrowed him. He went to his manager, John McNamara, and asked him whether he could beg off, perhaps be sent somewhere else, even somewhere lower within the organization. "There are other places I can go," Reggie said. "Send me to Vancouver, send me anyplace. But if Birmingham is going to be anything like here, don't send me to Birmingham."

"Can't do that, Reggie," McNamara said.

When Finley had a plan in mind, reason could not touch him. "Bombingham," in the years immediately following the Civil Rights Act of 1964, was a perilous place for a young black man, particularly one like Reggie, a naif to the social byplay of the region. But Finley allowed nothing to soil his vision. The boss himself called Reggie to tell him. The team had won the California League championship in Modesto, and Finley wanted it to win the Southern League championship in his hometown.

Reggie asked for $1,000 a month. Finley guffawed at the idea of doubling his salary and countered with an offer of $600. Reggie told him he wouldn't go. He would finish spring training and then go back to Arizona until Finley decided to pay him something commensurate with the struggles ahead.

Finally, on the last day of spring training, Finley raised his offer to $800 a month. Reggie had been imagining himself back in Arizona with Jennie. He would take a class or two and watch the season tick away thanks to Finley's stubbornness. By the time Finley caved—as Reggie believed he would—the season would be waning. That meant Reggie's time in the Deep South would be kept to a minimum. But Finley stepped up.

IN 1967, BIRMINGHAM, Alabama, was still a city on the grinder's wheel, a place where a civil society one day *might* exist. Reggie thought he knew what waited for him there on the front lines of the civil rights struggle. He did not. Birmingham was the land of church burnings, Bull Connor and his police dogs, and simmering hatred. More than Reggie knew at the time, he was walking into history.

When he arrived, he drove past the Trailways terminal, where, six years earlier, the Ku Klux Klan had attacked the Freedom Riders. Soon after Reggie reported to the team, a cab hustled him and two black teammates to the west side of town. The A's put them up at the Gaston, a "Negro" motel that four years earlier had been bombed in an attempt on Dr. Martin Luther King, Jr.'s life.

Reggie's prior years had been mostly free of prejudice, so he was woefully unprepared for it. In Wyncote he'd experienced little overt racism, at ASU he'd been a star athlete, and at Lewiston and Modesto he'd been one of the few blacks in town and thus not part of a more sweeping "threat" to whites. Birmingham, however, was clotted with blacks demanding humanity and whites unwilling to give it to them.

Once the games began, fans called him "nigger" and "boy." Reggie took a cab to the park, played his best, took a cab back to the Gaston, and ate dinner in his room. When he drove himself around town, he took care to always go five miles under the speed limit. Outside the clubhouse, he strained not to draw attention to himself.

Eventually, three of his white teammates, Joe Rudi, Rollie Fingers, and Dave Duncan, sensed Reggie's difficulties and asked him if he wanted to move in with them. Reggie, who was tired of going to his room alone, making lonesome phone calls to Jennie at all hours of the night, and feeling like a stranger in the only part of town that would accept him, said yes.

For a few days, all was as normal as it could be. Reggie enjoyed the company. He went to and from Rickwood Field with his teammates rather than driving alone, and he talked and drank beers with them afterward.

One night Rudi said to him, "Dave and Rollie and I are thinking about moving."

They'd been in the apartment for just a few days, it was close to the park, and nothing was wrong with the place. Reggie pressed him for a reason. Finally, Rudi told him, "They've threatened to throw me out if you continue to stay with me."

"They can't do that," Reggie said.

"Well, they can, Reggie," Rudi said. "But I told them that if you go, then we all go."

Reggie's self-sufficiency, honed over his young years, had made him proud, and he didn't want anyone to suffer on his behalf. "I'm not gonna let you guys do that," he said to Rudi.

Reggie couldn't slink back to the Gaston, so he chose the Bankhead, another black hotel not far away. The room came with a black-and-white television and a phone, and Reggie added to it a small radio. Immediately he missed seeing his teammates off the field, but he knew that seeking them out would only cause trouble for them.

Not long after he arrived at the Bankhead, he met the white owner's daughter, an attractive and coquettish girl named Sally. Reggie, of course, loved white women, and during that lonely time in his life he craved physical intimacy. They'd speak casually when she saw Reggie around the motel, and they'd have quick conversations when her father wasn't around. Reggie knew he could have her. Sally barraged Reggie with invitations to dinner and movies and walks in the park and anything else she should think of. But he'd been in Birmingham long enough to know the stakes. If a black man dating a young white woman would get you scorned in Arizona, it would get you killed in Alabama. He fended off her advances time and again.

After several nights, he decided he couldn't stand another meal alone in his room. So he went to the nearby Red Lion Inn, where he could at least hear the sound of other voices as he ate.

The maître d' ignored him, so Reggie made his way to a quiet table in the corner and seated himself. The white waiter came to him and said nothing as Reggie ordered a steak, some fries, and a Coke. In a few minutes the waiter returned, held the plate of food over the table, and dropped it. A blood-raw steak toppled off the plate and created a clamor that drew every eye in the place. "Nigger," the waiter hissed, "don't you ever come back here."

Reggie sized the man up for a second, but only a second. His heart thumped. He couldn't swallow. "Yes sir," he whispered.

He bolted from the Red Lion and ran the full six blocks back to his motel, crying much of the way. He felt like a coward. If a white kid had spoken like that to him back in Wyncote, Reggie would've beaten him savagely. Here, though, it was different. There was more to lose, and that cowed Reggie. The lies he'd told in an effort to share the miseries of other black athletes back at ASU were no longer necessary.

From that point onward, Reggie rarely left his room. He ate takeout alone, watched TV, listened to the radio, wrote letters to his family, and talked to Jennie on the phone.

REGGIE'S PERFORMANCE ON the field belied his struggles off it, and Finley ordered him promoted to Kansas City in June. Reggie welcomed the respite of a new city.

Finley had longed to show off his slugger ever since pen had been put to contract—in fact, two A's scouts had had to talk Finley out of starting Reggie's professional career in Birmingham. But after Reggie cut a swath through Double-A, Finley had seen enough.

At the time, the A's were a vaguely respectable 25–28, but they trailed seven teams in the American League standings. Finley decided they needed something. He called up Reggie from Birmingham, and on June 9 Reggie made his major-league debut. Normally, he had an indomitable confidence, but this, he knew, was the pinnacle. Soon, he would test his mettle against the best baseball players in the world. His confidence abandoned him, so he feigned it instead.

After he found his locker and unpacked his bags, he announced to his new teammates that he had superstar ability, that he would play regularly, and that he would be the leader. Reggie didn't believe his own words. Everyone else didn't believe his nerve.

In the first half of a double-header against the Cleveland Indians, Reggie came to the plate three times against starter Steve Hargan. He flied out to center, struck out, and grounded out to third in a 2–0 A's win. In the second game, Reggie notched his first major-league hit, an arcing triple to center off reliever Orlando Pena.

Over the next three weeks, Reggie played regularly, but on July 2, he was batting just .189 with no home runs. With the A's in ninth place, Finley optioned him back to Birmingham.

He rejoined his Birmingham teammates on the road in Evansville, Indiana, and in his first game back he ripped a game-winning triple. It was just what he needed. He continued hitting, but the South brought back a host of unwelcome emotions. He begged Jennie to come visit him, and she promptly flew to Birmingham.

One evening, Reggie and Jennie went over to Rudi's apartment, and they enjoyed a barbecue with Rudi and his wife and Duncan and Fingers and their dates. As they left, the landlord stood waiting for them in the parking lot. "I don't want no niggers in here anymore!" she shouted at Rudi. Reggie's grip on Jennie's arm tightened, but he said nothing. In Birmingham, you said nothing.

As they drove silently back to his motel, he thought back to when he and Jennie had first dated. He remembered that Jennie had said he made her feel secure and tended to. After that night, she could no longer say that. Reggie felt shame at his cowardice and shame that Jennie had witnessed it.

Later, after he'd been spirited away from Birmingham, he'd loathe himself for the meekness that had issued from him. The "Yes, sir's" and "No, sir's" and the silently bowed head whenever he heard the word "nigger" spat at him—Reggie's desire for self-preservation trumped the rudiments of black activism he had within him. Hatred was right in his face most of the day, but never once did he defend himself or demand to be treated as a man. He hated that side of himself, but most often he affirmed his blackness only when it was safe to do so.

THE TEAM WON the championship that Finley had envisioned, and a Birmingham country club wanted to throw it a party. Privately, a representative from the club asked the manager, John McNamara, if Reggie could be persuaded not to attend. McNamara, who had refused to let the team eat at any diner that wouldn't serve Reggie, smiled broadly. "You know, that is an excellent idea. Really excellent," McNamara said. "But you ought to know that if Reggie isn't there, it's going to be awfully lonely for you people throwing the party because I'm not going to be there either, and neither is one member of this baseball team."

Despite the prejudice he faced on a daily basis, Reggie, between the white lines, was as fearsome and fearless as ever. He ended the season with a .293 batting average and a slugging percentage of .562, and he became the first player ever to bang a home run off one of the light towers at Rickwood Field. He tallied sixty extra-base hits in just 114 games played—all deeply impressive for a twenty-one-year-old who played in the high minors and toiled under difficult circumstances. For his troubles, sixteen white sportswriters from eight different cities unanimously voted Reggie Southern League MVP for the 1967 season. Mostly, though, Birmingham had peeled his eyes open to white prejudice, and to the limits of his own courage.

He wanted out.

FOUR

"I'm Not Working in One of Those Birmingham Steel Mills"

NOT LONG AFTER Birmingham's victory over Albuquerque in the Dixie Series, Reggie was back in the majors. He continued to struggle. On the season, he hit just .178, but on September 17, 1967, in Anaheim, Reggie touched Angels left-hander Jim Weaver for the first home run of his major-league career—a fastball low and away that he turned on and blasted 400 feet to right field.

Over the off-season, Reggie went back to Tempe and attended classes at ASU on a full-time basis. Like most athletes, Reggie first majored in physical education—the least rigorous of academic disciplines—but by this point he was working toward a biology degree, one he would never finish.

He had his own apartment close to campus, and he spent his evenings there with Jennie. In the afternoons after class, he'd work on his outfield play. Reggie wanted to be thought of as something more than a one-dimensional player. His idol, Willie Mays, was a masterly hitter, runner, defender, and thrower, and Reggie wanted to achieve a similar depth of skill. So he worked hard to balance his brute strength with grace and precision.

Meanwhile, his relationship with Jennie deepened. A number of his close friends were already married—his teammates Rudi and Duncan, for instance. And so was Gary Walker, a young white man from Arizona who by then worked as Reggie's agent. Reggie envied the calm it gave them, and the pangs of homesickness added to the feeling. Reggie and Jennie began to talk about marriage.

There was no grand proposal, no cinematic moment that told them they were meant to be together. Rather, it seemed to both of them that it was the natural thing to do. Reggie had thought of marriage ever since Jennie had visited him in Birmingham. That she knew what he had gone through in the South and had seen firsthand the limits of his will made him feel laid bare and vulnerable, but it also drew him closer to her.

All the while, Finley was uprooting the Athletics. After years of scheming and perfidy, Finley and the A's headed to Oakland, California. The move prompted Missouri senator Stuart Symington, frustrated by Finley and the loss of the A's, to call Oakland "the luckiest city since Hiroshima." The news, though, pleased Reggie. He had fond memories of Modesto, and he welcomed any move that would take the team farther away from the South.

Reggie reported to Bradenton, Florida, for his first major-league spring training. Spring training facilities had been integrated for just a few years, and for Reggie that distinguished the experience from Birmingham. What bothered him, though, was the contemptible drudgery of, as the name suggested, training.

He took to his remedial defensive work in Arizona, but when he arrived in Bradenton the A's tampered with his mechanics at the plate. In Reggie's mind, they were assaulting his skills. When A's manager Bob Kennedy would ask him to hit the other way, he'd ignore him. When the celebrity roving coach Joe DiMaggio, in the course of their daily, hour-long training sessions, would tell him to shorten his swing, he'd ignore him. Reggie never openly refused to follow orders, but he would quietly do things the way he'd always done them. As a young hitter, he didn't want to go with the pitch, hit to the gaps, take it the other way, or give himself up to advance the runner. He wanted home runs. "That's where the money is," he said.

Nonetheless, he impressed the A's. Finley had decided going in that his prized prospect would break camp with the team, and Reggie's flashes of power in spring training reinforced the owner's confidence. When the team went north to Oakland, Reggie was with it.

THE YEAR 1968 was a sad and roiling time for America and the sports world. Sports had always served a dual purpose: to provide common people with a source of leisure and to distract them from the more vital events of the day. Slaves and soldiers in the Civil War had played a rudimentary form of baseball to help them forget the horrors about them. Babe Ruth had helped ferry the nation through the Great Depression. Franklin D. Roosevelt had written his famous "Green Light Letter" to Baseball Commissioner Kenesaw Mountain Landis to implore him to keep the games going during World War II. In the days following the assassination of President Kennedy, NFL Commissioner Pete Rozelle had opted to play a full schedule of games. That's what sports were supposed to be—something to bind society in its routines and assumptions. And that's what it was for so many years: a foil to war, economic collapse, and other social miseries.

But in 1968—Reggie's rookie season—that all changed. Sports and global events became intertwined in a way never seen before. Former NFL lineman Rosey Grier and former decathlete Rafer Johnson subdued Robert F. Kennedy's assassin in Los Angeles. Muhammad Ali, declaring that "no Vietcong ever called me nigger," was convicted for refusing induction into the military. Arthur Ashe won the U.S. Open in tennis and used his newfound platform to speak out against racism and injustice. Tommie Smith and John Carlos jarred the world with their Black Power salute at the Mexico City Olympics. The libertine and occasionally gender-bending Joe Namath defied expectations and social norms and guided the upstart New York Jets to a victory in Super Bowl III. The soft-spoken Lew Alcindor converted to Islam—a faith viewed as being dangerously subversive at the time. Even a handful of nonpolitical happenings—Forward Pass won the Kentucky Derby because the first-place horse failed a drug test, and the golfer Bob Goalby won the Masters because one of his competitors signed an incorrect scorecard—seemed to reflect the confounding nature of the times. Sports were no longer an escape; they were, for the first time, less a consoling fiction than a hard reminder.

In Reggie there percolated, thanks to all of this, a sense of self-investment. He was headed for Oakland, where he would toil amid the Black Panther movement, the beatniks of Haight-Ashbury, and the athlete-activists at San Jose State, where a near boycott of the Mexico City games had taken root. So with conviction, Reggie told the assembled writers on the final day of spring training, "I'll be rooming with Dobson from now on."

Dobson was Chuck Dobson, a twenty-four-year-old right-hander and one of the best pitchers on the A's at the time. He was also white. In the sprawl of baseball history, a black player and a white player had never roomed together. To hear Reggie and Dobson tell it, they weren't trying to overturn the mores of the sport; instead, Dobson needed a roommate to get him out of bed on time, and Reggie said he could. "I don't want to be known for rooming with a white guy," Reggie said, "and I don't think Chuck wants to be known for rooming with a Negro guy." As ever, Reggie preferred to live with whites. On another level, though, he saw an opportunity to agitate and make small amends for his behavior in Birmingham.

The long-standing and vigorously encouraged habit of white and black players' rooming with their own grew out of baseball's bizarre notions of interracial sex. Most baseball players slept around on the road, and females would be in their rooms. If a white player and a black player roomed together, then a white woman would share quarters, however indirectly, with a black man. So teams, unable to cope with the prospect, shunted whites toward whites and blacks toward blacks.

It would've been safer, and perhaps less keenly felt throughout baseball, had it been a pair of veterans who toppled the old ways. Rookies were supposed to lead a serflike existence in Major League Baseball, lugging bags, being the butt of jokes, and trying not to be noticed. It shouldn't have been a rookie, and it certainly shouldn't have been a black rookie like Reggie.

Reggie's boldness jarred Finley. In one of his first meetings with Oakland Coliseum officials, Finley had wondered aloud whether black ushers should work white sections of the ballpark. An official had explained to him that there were no white and black sections in the stadium. Finley received the same answer when he asked whether black fans would be allowed to buy tickets behind the Oakland dugout. More shocking still was when his prized black rookie went even further in assailing tradition.

However, Reggie's nerve was soon forgotten. Finley had arranged for his team to go on a three-city barnstorming tour in which it would play exhibition games against the Cincinnati Reds. The tour would take the team to Shreveport, Louisiana, and Indianapolis, but it would play the first game in Birmingham. Reggie dreaded the prospect; his only relief was that the team would spend but one night in the city that had terrorized him.

On April 4, mere days before they were to open the season in Baltimore, the team's bus rolled into Birmingham and went first to the motel that would house the white players. As Reggie waited to be driven across town, he spotted the morning headlines: Dr. Martin Luther King, Jr., had been assassinated at a Memphis motel. The news shocked and saddened Reggie. His toils in Birmingham had given him an abiding respect for King. He referred to the pioneering King as "my president," and he marveled at the man's courage, so much greater than his own. The tragedy dampened his faith and revived his loathing of the South. For a country already fractured by racial unrest, it was a grave blow.

The A's numbly played the games in Birmingham and Shreveport, but shortly after they arrived in Indianapolis, Reggie and the rest learned that rioting had broken out in more than a hundred cities. For a few desperate days America seemed on the brink of collapse. Baseball Commissioner William Eckert canceled the A's exhibition against the Reds and pushed back Opening Day almost a week, just long enough for the collective shock and anger to turn to grief.

The A's traveled to Baltimore for the opener against the Orioles, but because of unrest in the city, the team lodged in suburban Towson. Reggie, however, stayed at his mother's house in Baltimore, near the heart of the riots—riots that would eventually demand federal intervention. Even as he grieved for King and feared for his family's safety, he focused on the season to come.

Opening Day finally came on April 10. The riots tamped down attendance to fewer than 25,000—remarkably low for Opening Day in Baltimore—and from the field Reggie could see the neighborhood fires burning. As they warmed up, the contrast struck him: on the inside were the pop of leather gloves, the snap of maple bats, the bellowing of vendors, the glare of the afternoon sun. Outside the walls of Memorial Stadium the sirens, flames, breaking of glass, and windblown ash punctured whatever calm there was.

That day, the A's fell to the Orioles, 3–1. Reggie, who batted second and manned right field, provided the lone Oakland run when he homered to left center off right-hander Tom Phoebus.

Next it was on to Washington, D.C., another city rife with violence, for a pair of games against the Senators. Oakland won the first game, but Reggie proved his rawness when a Ken McMullen fly ball bounced off his head. Reggie then made his first trip to New York for two games in Yankee Stadium.

In the second game, the rookie launched a towering blast into the right-field bleachers, some 450 feet away. Yankees publicity man Bob Fishel announced to the crowd that Reggie was one of the few players ever to hit the ball to those distant reaches. The struggles and timidity of the previous season seemed worlds away, and the King assassination shrank from his memory.

In Oakland, Reggie and the A's played in front of more than 50,000 fans for the home opener. The A's were new to the city, they brimmed with young talent, and only one team had managed a better record in spring training. However, Dave McNally and the Orioles shut down the A's. The next night attendance plummeted to just 5,304. Despite the paltry support, Reggie felt like a big leaguer at last. He won the game in the thirteenth when he tagged up and hustled home on a short pop-up to the outfield. He ended the month of April with a .309 batting average.

He slumped in May, and manager Bob Kennedy dropped him from second to eighth in the batting order. When that didn't help, Kennedy worked him higher in the order. Reggie resumed hitting. He hit home runs, he struck out, in anger he snapped bats like saplings, he threw out runners on the bases, and he misplayed fly balls. Even in failure, he entertained.

During those early weeks, Reggie spoke with Jennie often and told her that he finally felt stability and a sense of belonging. They made plans to marry over the All-Star break. On June 29, Reggie and the A's returned to Yankee Stadium. As he would so often in the Bronx, he launched a critical, game-winning home run. But then the A's went on to lose seven straight and fall out of first place for good. As the first half ended, Reggie had thirteen home runs to his credit, but he was overlooked for All-Star honors. He and Jennie proceeded with their wedding plans.

They married on July 8 at the Our Lady of the Blessed Sacrament Catholic Church in Jennie's hometown of Miami, Arizona. Among the two hundred guests were Reggie's father and a few of his football teammates from Arizona State, who served as groomsmen. At the reception, Reggie grabbed the microphone and bellowed, "Thanks for coming to *my* wedding." Later he asked his friends to autograph a plate so that he could "keep it as a memento of *my* wedding." Reggie's self-centered display upset Jennie. "I'm afraid these young people will have trouble," the priest confided to Jennie's mother.

After the wedding, the couple moved into Reggie's apartment in the Lake Merritt section of Oakland. Reggie and Jennie spent every moment together that they could. They made love, talked deep into the night, and appointed their new home with the furnishings they could afford. They missed each other when the A's were on road trips, and for the first several months of the marriage their love and the newness of domestic life upheld them.

Reggie liked her on his arm, and he liked her at home waiting for him. But their new life together challenged Jennie. She was more intelligent and self-aware than Reggie, so she struggled to be a good baseball wife. The wives of ballplayers dressed a certain way, behaved in a certain manner, restrained their opinions, and were quick with smiles and charm. The rivalries and petty grievances of the clubhouse inevitably made it to the cocktail parties. Jennie cared for none of it. She had nothing in common with the other wives, who were either crass and stupid or aloof and given to finishing school affectations. When kids would ask her for an autograph merely because they'd seen her with Reggie, it seemed to her that the world's priorities were hopelessly amiss.

Jennie enjoyed quiet dinners with Sandy Bando and Sharon Rudi, but when a larger group of wives was thrown together, the social congestion and the secondhand jealousies—whose husband had the better season, whose husband was underpaid or overpaid—disheartened her. As Reggie withdrew from her and became more absorbed in the game he played, Jennie felt she couldn't share those feelings with him.

As the season went on, the organization was at once awed by Reggie's power and put off by his strikeouts. DiMaggio, at Finley's bidding, worked regularly with Reggie to shorten his swing and persuaded the young slugger to switch to a heavier bat. Reggie listened to him and nodded attentively at his advice, but once the game began he swung as violently as ever. Early in the second half it became clear that Reggie would challenge the single-season strikeout record of 175.

On July 13, a pitch from Cleveland's Mike Paul struck Reggie on the wrist. He had to wear a bandage and miss the next two games. A week and a half later he slid into third base and sprained his thumb. The team trainer bandaged him again and told him that he'd miss at least the next pair of games. Reggie then cut himself while removing the bandage.

The news didn't sit well with Finley, who wanted his popular young slugger to play the entirety of the current home stand. Finley had the trainer call the dugout and order Kennedy to fill out a new lineup card, this one with Reggie on it. The pained and angered Reggie went 0 for 3 with a strikeout. "Finley will pay for this come contract time," he said after the game against Minnesota. "I'm not working in one of those Birmingham steel mills."

Reggie ended the 1968 season with 29 of Oakland's 94 homers, and he paced the club in slugging percentage, total bases, RBIs, and extra-base hits. But he also led the league in strikeouts with 171 and in outfield errors with 14. Other than Catfish Hunter's perfect game against the Twins on May 8, Reggie's numbers and undeniable promise were the stories for Oakland that year. Stan Bahnsen of the Yankees just edged him out for American League Rookie of the Year honors. The 1968 season was "The Year of the Pitcher," in which a bloated strike zone led to the lowest league ERA since before Babe Ruth wore the Yankees pinstripes. Yet Reggie—despite his age, rookie status, league conditions, and run-suppressing home park—thrived. The team finished in sixth place and notched the A's first winning season since 1949. That wasn't enough to save Bob Kennedy's job, though.

Following that rookie season, Finley called Reggie and ordered him to hone his skills in winter ball, but Reggie, still angry over being forced to play while injured and still committed to his education, said he was going back to Arizona State. "School?" Finley yelled. "I want you in winter ball."

"I'll be at school," Reggie told him and hung up the phone.

As spring training approached, Reggie and Finley worked out a contract for the 1969 season. Finley opened negotiations by offering him a $16,000 contract. Reggie and Gary Walker thought twenty-nine home runs were worth more, so they countered with an offer of $20,000. Finley went up to $18,000 but budged no further. As camp opened, the two sides were still haggling. That Finley was so bull-headed over a sum of $2,000—nothing to a man of his resources—stunned Reggie. He held out for the first two weeks of spring training, and Finley at last offered $20,000.

After just a few days in camp, Reggie felt quicker and stronger than he ever had. He talked about building on his successes of 1968 and putting up the kind of numbers that would make him a star. One day, with the start of the regular season in the offing, he took out a piece of paper in front of the writers and wrote the number "40" on it. He saved it.

FIVE

"If I Played in New York,
They'd Name a Candy Bar After Me"

OAKLAND'S NEW MANAGER was Hank Bauer, and he was as tough as his name. Bauer had grown up the son of a bartender in East Saint Louis and was so poor as a boy that he wore clothes made of feed sacks. He was a talented, multisport athlete in high school, and a minor-league contract with the White Sox saved him from a life of repairing blast furnaces. Bauer went on to win seven World Series as a Yankees outfielder, notch a hit in a record seventeen straight Series games, take shrapnel in his leg at Okinawa, and win another World Series as manager of the 1966 Baltimore Orioles. Toward the end of his playing career, he spent two seasons in Kansas City and then went on to manage for Finley for part of 1961 and all of 1962. Finley fired Bauer after a 72–90 season, but his toughness and leadership had made an impression. When Finley grew weary of Kennedy, he called Bauer. Bauer's Marine Corps crew cut, sturdy jaw, and heroic personal history made him an intimidating figure, and he savored rules and regimentation. The A's learned this early, as Bauer insisted in spring training that his players wear coats and ties after sundown. Reggie, having toiled under the likes of Frank Kush and Bobby Winkles, was comfortable with hard-nosed types. Reggie and Bauer would have no problems. American League pitchers, however, would have plenty of problems with Reggie in 1969.

The game was different that season. The previous year, run scoring had cratered, and fans, the owners believed, grew bored with pitching duel upon pitching duel. Prior to the 1969 season, the owners voted to lower the mound, shrink the strike zone, and use a ball with an all-rubber core—all to inject more offense into the game.

Reggie batted just .204 for the month of April, and Bauer, frustrated by Reggie's strikeouts, benched him against left-handers. However, by the end of the month he heated up. On April 20, he blasted a home run almost to the top of the center-field scoreboard in Kansas City. In the first game of the double-header, Rick Monday had hit one in almost the same spot. A writer suggested that Monday's clout probably would've gone farther than Reggie's had it not hit the scoreboard. Nonsense, said Reggie. If *his* homer hadn't hit the scoreboard, he said, it "would've gone 700 feet." To prove it was a serious estimate, he took out the home-run ball and scribbled on it, "April 20, 1969, 700 feet."

Four days later, in a series finale at Minnesota, Reggie belted a first-inning, opposite-field home run off Dave Boswell. He came up again in the third inning and again hit a home run off Boswell, this time deep to right field. By the time Reggie batted again, in the fifth inning, reliever Dick Woodson had taken over. Woodson, on the orders of Twins manager Billy Martin, threw his first pitch behind Reggie's head—a feat for a right-handed pitcher throwing to a left-handed hitter. Woodson's next pitch buzzed Reggie's ear and sailed to the backstop.

Reggie picked himself up and, batting helmet in hand, sprinted toward Woodson on the mound. Woodson cast aside his glove and raised his fists. Reggie then executed a form tackle that would've made

Frank Kush proud. The dugouts and bull pens emptied. Dave Duncan barged into the scrum, but Martin pulled him out and choked him with both hands. Hank Bauer pried Martin away. Reggie, meanwhile, held Woodson in a bear hug at the bottom of the pile. After umpires unpacked all the bodies, they ejected Reggie. Bauer dragged Reggie off the field as he screamed at the Twins' dugout.

Later in the inning, Rick Monday broke for home on a fielder's choice, and Woodson covered. Monday was out at the plate, but he came in spikes high and left Woodson with a five-inch cut on his leg. The A's held on to win, 6–4.

After the game, Martin denied calling for the brushback. "If I order a guy to throw at a batter, it won't be behind him or over his head," he said. "It will be at his Adam's apple."

Reggie, meantime, would not apologize. "What can you do?" he said. "If I don't go out, then I'm less than a man."

Less than twelve years earlier, Cleveland outfielder Larry Doby had been the first black player to be involved in an on-field fight. By Reggie's time, black players were often part of the peacemaking contingent that descended upon every baseball fight, but they were rarely central to the action. Rarer still was for a black player to do what Reggie had just done: instigate a fight with a white player.

He also frustrated onlookers by admiring his handiwork. Since his days at Arizona State, Reggie had lingered a bit too long in the box after he'd struck the ball hard, fair, and far. He motored around the bases, but he didn't bow his head like a penitent's. After an initial pregnant pause, he'd begin with a strutlike walk as the ball soared and then pick up into a proud, easy lope about halfway down the first-base line. As he approached the bag, he'd drop his inside shoulder and take a wide turn at first base. A few steps before home plate, he'd slow to a walk once again. It was methodical, but it had flair. And pitchers hated it.

In some ways, though, baseball needed someone to lift it from the torpor of the 1960s. Reggie flashed what the columnist William C.

Rhoden has called "black style." That style expressed black distinctiveness and agency and at the same time rejected the way white paymasters insisted the game be played. Consciously or no, Jackie Robinson had brought black style to the base paths, and Willie Mays had brought it to the outfield. With his trots and swagger, Reggie brought it to the plate.

Those trots became more frequent by the end of May, at which point he'd tallied fifteen home runs. He went on to bat .365 in June and launch fourteen more homers. On June 11, he homered twice in Washington with President Richard Nixon in attendance. Nixon sent him a telegram of congratulations. In a weekend series at Fenway Park that began on June 13, Reggie dominated again. His home run in the opener on Friday night merely hinted at what was to come. On Saturday, he blasted a Ray Jarvis pitch to deep center in the third. In the fifth, he hit one to the same distant spot off reliever Lee Stange. In the seventh, he thumped a bases-loaded single off Bill Landis, and in the next inning, with the bases loaded once again, he cleared them with a bloop single off Gary Roggenburk. He ended the day with ten RBIs, one shy of Tony Lazzeri's American League record.

When Reggie arrived in the clubhouse after the game, the rest of the A's gave him a standing ovation. In the finale on Sunday, Reggie was 3 for 4 at the plate with another homer and four more RBIs. During his final plate appearance of the series, Boston catcher Russ Nixon demanded that the umpires examine Reggie's bat. Then Bill Landis pegged him with a fastball and forced in a run. As the A's trainer checked Reggie's arm, Sal Bando, the next batter, took his place in the box. "Thanks for leaving somebody on the bases for a change," he said to Reggie. Reggie jogged to first base, and Bando hit a grand slam.

The sweep in Boston pushed the A's into first place, and Reggie led the league in home runs. On July 2, he hit three homers against the Seattle Pilots, which put him ten games ahead of Roger Maris's 1961 record pace. Finley was at the game, and afterward he told

Reggie that he'd never before seen a player hit three home runs in a single game. "Then you ought to come out more often," Reggie deadpanned.

The next week, Reggie made his first of nine *Sports Illustrated* covers, and back at the Coliseum in Oakland, the fans in right field called themselves "Reggie's Regiment." Finley had official Reggie's Regiment membership cards printed and given out to the fans. Reggie kept hitting.

Opposing teams employed the "shift" against him—stationing three infielders on the right side in an attempt to cut down more of his line drives—but nothing daunted him. Bauer asked him to lay down drag bunts on occasion to keep the defenses honest, but Reggie resisted. "They shifted on Ted Williams, and he defied it," Reggie said. "He hit between the fielders—or over them. They shift on Willie McCovey, too. But I feel like them. If I hit the ball on the nose, the fielders will not catch it, even if they are stacked on top of each other."

Unlike most skilled batters, Reggie didn't swing based on location or whether a pitch was in his "wheelhouse." Rather, he had a mind for sequences and patterns. He swung based on what type of pitch he thought would come next—"calculated anticipation," he called it. If he guessed incorrectly, he'd swing and miss with a cut so fierce that you were roused by what might have been. If he guessed correctly, most often a signature home run followed.

Sometimes in the early innings Reggie would miss a pitch badly and even stupidly so as to make the pitcher think he couldn't handle that particular offering. Reggie hoped that he'd see the same pitch at a more critical moment later in the game, at which point he'd let the guy on the mound know that he'd walked into a trap.

In 1969, a lot of pitchers walked into that trap. When the All-Star break arrived on July 20, Reggie had thirty-seven home runs, which put him ahead of both Maris's and Ruth's record tempos. But he paid a price for his displays. Opposing pitchers plunked Reggie seven times in the first half, so he wore a protective bandage on his right wrist. Reggie said it was all "part of the game" and asked only that his own pitchers take steps to protect him. Finley, however, was less diplomatic. After Seattle beaned Reggie twice, Finley called the supervisor of AL umpires and bemoaned the "criminal attack on Reggie."

"As owner of this club, I'll be damned if I'm going to put up with this shit!" bellowed Finley. "Jackson has to be protected!"

Finley felt he needed to spare Reggie from more than just vengeful pitchers. In the two weeks before the break, Reggie granted more than a hundred interviews, the subject of which was his pursuit of the mythical lady he called "Ruth Maris." Finley hated anything that took attention away from him, and Reggie's openness with the writers did just that. Ostensibly to spare Reggie from the media crush, Finley ordered him not to give interviews after batting practice. Reggie ignored Finley's mandate. And all eyes remained on him at the All-Star Game in Washington, D.C.

The 1969 season marked baseball's designated centennial, and the site of the All-Star Game, RFK Stadium, had been renamed as such earlier that year in honor of the murdered Democratic presidential candidate. It was an important occasion for baseball and for a slowly healing nation. A number of great players were All-Stars that year— Hank Aaron, Willie McCovey, Johnny Bench, Bob Gibson, Frank Robinson, Ernie Banks, Harmon Killebrew, Carl Yastrzemski—but the media flocked to Reggie.

There were two All-Star story lines. One was Reggie's home-run pace, and the other was the New York Mets' surprising rise to consequence. The Mets had been diabolically bad since their inception in 1962, but in 1969 under second-year manager Gil Hodges, they barged to a 53–39 record at the break.

The All-Star Game is a time for leisurely appreciation of the sport—a time to fawn over luminaries and admire their craft. It is not, most would tell you, an occasion for rabble-rousing. Yet Reggie, when asked about the Mets' season, couldn't resist. "The only thing I know about the Mets," he said, "is that they wouldn't draft me because I had a white girlfriend." The bouquet of microphones and tape recorders in front of his face grew larger. "That's what I heard," he went on. "I can't say if it is true or not, but I would've played in New York."

Back in New York the story resonated. Some were angry at Reggie for sullying the occasion, while others pondered what it would be like to have a player of his gifts and personality in their midst. Most, though, wondered why the Mets would object to Reggie's dating a white woman. Gotham's appetite had been whetted.

The game itself was forgettable for Reggie: he went 0 for 2 at the plate but cleanly fielded the two balls hit to him in center in a 9–3 AL loss. His mind, and almost everyone else's, was on his pursuit of Maris's record. As the season wore on, the pressure on him would only increase. This he knew. The media would study him with the closeness of a diamond appraiser, and his private moments would be more rare than he could imagine.

During Maris's pursuit of Ruth eight years previously, he had famously wilted and at times lost his hair from the stress of his chase. Maris at the time had been twenty-six and in his fifth major-league season. Reggie was twenty-three years old and in just his second full campaign. He would have to overcome not only the increased media presence but also his own callowness.

Yet the All-Star break didn't cool him off. Reggie returned home to Oakland and hit three homers in the first five games of the second half. On July 29, Reggie hit his fortieth home run of the season. After the game, with the writers clustered about him, he produced the piece of paper on which he'd written the number 40—his prediction of how many homers he'd hit in 1969—and tore it up in front of them. With more than two months to play, he needed twenty homers to tie Ruth.

After the A's began a road trip early in August, the interview requests in each city reached impossible levels. One writer followed him into the cage during batting practice. Fans interrupted his meals, called his hotel room at all hours, and even showed up at his door. Reggie used an assumed name at check-in. Finley called him constantly and offered words of encouragement that merely added to the pressure. At the plate, he swung harder than ever at balls he couldn't possibly square up on. His habits at the plate worsened.

Reggie failed to homer in sixty-five straight at bats. Commissioner Bowie Kuhn ordered an official inquiry to determine whether the baseballs in use were "juiced" or in some other way not up to specifications. His investigations turned up nothing untoward, but Reggie felt that Kuhn was trying to cast doubt upon his accomplishments. His confidence frayed a little more.

Reggie had managed forty-five home runs before the end of August, but Maris at that same point had had fifty-one. On September 9, Reggie woke up to find almost his entire body covered by a strange and agonizing rash, the result of stress. He was admitted to the hospital and missed the next ten games.

Late in the season, the A's dropped fourteen of eighteen and fell out of the race for good. Finley caught up with the team at the Grand Hotel in Anaheim, split a bottle of whiskey with Hank Bauer, and fired him. The new manager would be John McNamara, the man who had helped Reggie survive Birmingham. McNamara was young, a player's manager, and an antidote to Bauer's hard style. He wouldn't try to temper Reggie's game. For the first time in weeks, Reggie's spirits lifted.

The enthusiasm was short-lived. Reggie hit just two homers over the final thirty games of the season to finish with forty-seven. Not only did he fall far short of Maris's mark, but Harmon Killebrew and Frank Howard also passed Reggie's total in the waning days. Nonetheless, it was a season of distinction. Those forty-seven homers were the most ever in a season by a player age twenty-three or younger, he led the league in runs scored and slugging percentage, and he ranked second in walks, doubles, and total bases. And he had done it all despite playing his home games in one of the toughest hitters' parks in baseball. On the season, the A's surged to eighty-eight wins and second place on the strength of Reggie's bestowals. He finished fifth in the AL MVP voting.

Oakland was on baseball's rural route (as Reggie said that year, "If I played in New York, they'd name a candy bar after me"), but Reggie's chase had enraptured the nation. Besides the history involved, fans and media responded to Reggie as a personality. Baseball players were generally wary of the writers and were reserved with their comments to a fault. It had always been that way, but the sports media had evolved. A generation prior, writers had understood that stories harmful to the players and decision makers they covered were not to be written. Eventually, though, the cultural mood of America had changed, and media consumers were no longer interested in rank mythmaking. So sportswriters had changed the way they wrote about the games and, by extension, how they related to the players.

The most famous practitioner of the new approach was Dick Young, the venerable and confrontational scribe whose columns for the New York *Daily News* and, later, the *New York Post* helped put writers on a different, more precarious footing with athletes. Young's stock in trade was candor and pointed criticism. Eventually, several teams banned him from the clubhouse, and Jackie Robinson dismissed him as a bigot—but not before his provocative style caught on.

By the mid-1960s, Young, along with *Newsday*'s Stan Isaacs and Stan Hochman and Larry Merchant of the *Philadelphia Daily News*, led a self-styled clan of young sportswriters known as the "Chipmunks." In Young's own words, a Chipmunk would "tell people they're full of shit and then go out and face them the next day."

No longer would writers confine their coverage to on-the-field happenings. Now the reading public demanded to know what players were like in the clubhouse, on the road, and in their private lives away from baseball. Tough questions, intrusive reporting, and columns larded with value judgments—it was the way the Chipmunks did things.

As a rejoinder to the writers who no longer served their interests, ballplayers withdrew and even grew hostile. When they dealt with the media, they resorted to the safety of the insipid, and the writers, frustrated by the players' newfound reserve, dug deeper. Then Reggie came along.

Reggie heeded only a deep need to pontificate on his favorite subject—himself. The result was often fiendishly good copy for the writers. "I am like a storm when I hit," he said, as his eyes ripened, of his prowess in 1969. "First there's sleet—slow, sharp sleet out of dark skies. Then comes a mass of clouds and a howling wind. And thunder, very noisy, very frightening thunder. The wind now grows in intensity. Leaves are blowing everywhere off trees of every description. Limbs and boughs are snapping off and falling. There is a great noise. There is a heavy, heavy downpour all around. But just you wait. That's only the way it is now. Only once in a while, like rain. Someday, though, my hitting will be just like this. Every day, as sure as that sun is up there, my hitting will be all there. All around. Everywhere you look."

On another occasion: "It was as if all the power of the earth and the sky and the sands and the waters were in these hands."

He spoke—baroquely, incessantly, heedless of how the message was received—like no other ballplayer the writers had ever encountered. He even liked most of the writers, a decided rarity among athletes. A man of Reggie's immodesty cherished a captive audience, and the writers gave him that. Reggie's knack for the pull quote, sense of what the scribblers wanted to hear, and ability to shape a narrative with his words and actions prompted the great Leonard Koppett to call Reggie "the best sportswriter among ballplayers."

Televised baseball also yearned for a player like Reggie, whose blinding speed, powerful arm in the outfield, all-or-nothing exhibitions at the plate, and perfectly tapered musculature all made him seem tailored to the visual medium. And Reggie understood that medium. During *Game of the Week* telecasts, for instance, Reggie, when leading off an inning, would wait until the network was back from commercial break before he stepped into the box.

He was also becoming baseball's most towering black superstar—a player who combined excellence, style, and personality but who also, unlike Willie Mays, had the good fortune to play when the television set was a near ubiquity in American homes. The only question for Reggie and his many fans was: What's next?

SIX

"Fuck You"

THE HOME RUNS had mounted in 1969, but so had Reggie's troubles with Jennie. She had long felt out of place in the world of baseball, and Reggie's rising star only made things worse. But she tried. She feigned interest in his consuming passion—hitting—and she behaved as deferentially as her nature would allow. She could not, however, abide disrespect.

Jennie had been looking forward to unwinding with Reggie at the end of the long season and trying to recapture the closeness they once enjoyed. However, when Reggie returned to Arizona, he spent some of his time with Sal Bando and the rest of it working on the land development business he'd started with his agent, Gary Walker. His success that season had also given him a higher opinion of himself. "He really started to strut," Jennie told the writer Bill Libby years later. "He really thought he was something. . . . He came and went as he wanted. There was no talking to him, there was no living with him."

Worse, though, were his betrayals. During the season, she discovered scribbled phone numbers in his pockets and tucked under the wipers of his car, intercepted letters from out-of-town mistresses, and heard him talk on the phone late at night in hushed tones. Jennie knew that some baseball wives tolerated such behavior in exchange for a life of ease—"I don't care what he does as long as I get a new fur coat," one wife once told her—but she wanted no part of such a demeaning arrangement.

When she confronted Reggie, he said, "It's none of your business." When she asked him to promise he'd stop having affairs, he refused. He withdrew from her and spent his downtime listening to music on headphones or running menial errands.

Inside, he churned. Reggie had long resented that his own father's affairs had battered his family, but now that he had money and status he found himself unable to resist the same temptations. He underwent psychotherapy.

He and Jennie separated briefly over the off-season, but Reggie couldn't concentrate on his training or even complete a thought. He called her, and they reconciled. But they did so without the illusion of permanence.

OVER THE OBJECTIONS of Gary Walker, who wanted more, Reggie asked for $60,000 for the 1970 season. Finley offered $35,000. Talks stalled. Finley wrote letters to Reggie and called him at all hours of the night. He hoped that his young slugger, in the fugue of near sleep, would accept his latest lowball offer. He had functionaries call Reggie, feign his best interests, and beg him to sign. When those efforts failed, Finley suggested to the media that Reggie didn't hustle enough and had shown little fortitude during his September collapse. He reminded the public that Reggie was still a very young man who'd been paid a handsome sum to sign out of college. Reggie, in Finley's words, was "ungrateful."

That Reggie, the black player, owed gratitude to Finley, the white owner, was a common enough sentiment. Finley knew this, and he shamed Reggie on those grounds. Finley's tactics and the hints of racism therein dismayed and angered Reggie. "If Finley doesn't want to pay me what I'm worth to play in Oakland," he said, "let him trade me to New York, where they'll pay me more."

By the time spring training began, Finley upped his offer to $40,000. Reggie was unmoved. He was in his adopted hometown of Tempe, and his teammates, mere miles away, were preparing for the regular season. Their nearness agonized him. He worked out regularly, but such haphazard training didn't get you ready to play baseball at the highest level. Besides, he was devoting too much of his time to studying for the Arizona real estate exam.

The holdout continued. Reggie showed up in spring training to seek the advice of some veteran players. He talked to older black players such as Ernie Banks and his childhood idol, Willie Mays. Banks and Mays were part of a more yielding generation of black players, and they counseled him from that perspective. They told Reggie not to worry about whether Finley treated him fairly. The important thing, Banks and Mays both said, was to get into camp on time so he could have another great season. The money would come later.

Reggie, though, wanted to be told he had done the right thing, made a high-minded stand that advanced the cause of players. He wanted reassurance; he got correction.

Reggie's stance began to soften, but his anger at the process grew. At the same time, Curt Flood was holding out to protest his trade from Saint Louis to racially hostile Philadelphia. Flood's mission of conscience would make it all the way to the Supreme Court, and his and Reggie's holdouts marked the first time black players had dared to take such a step. For Reggie, it marked a clear break with the old guard of black players—the very ones who had told him to give up. Yet Finley remained confident that his young star would sign. "Reggie is a good boy," he said.

Finally, having missed most of spring training, Reggie agreed to a contract that would pay him $45,000 plus a monthly stipend to cover his apartment rent in Oakland. For Finley, the negotiations had been an exercise in pettiness and acrimony. For Reggie, they had been an education: Finley, he had learned, was a businessman, not a father. "That was the last time I was ever naive about player-owner relations," Reggie told the writer Maury Allen.

Once Reggie finally did report to camp, just ten days before the regular season began, he remained aggrieved. Writers asked him how it felt to play for McNamara once again, and they asked whether the young, rising A's could win the pennant. But Reggie wanted to talk about how he would get back at Finley, how he would get his money. The owner might have been more practiced at the feints and lies of business, but Reggie was learning.

According to Reggie's reading of the contract, Finley had to cover the costs of his apartment rent, regardless of what the rent amounted to. So Reggie chose a furnished luxury apartment just across Lake Merritt from Finley's Oakland rental. When Finley received the bill, he was furious. He called Gary Walker and demanded to renegotiate the clause. However, when Reggie threatened to walk out and go back to Arizona, Finley relented. But he fumed.

Reggie took small comforts in his daily life in Oakland. Most mornings, he'd enjoy pork chops and rice at Lois the Pie Queen's near the Berkeley line, and on off days he'd go to the Del Rio brothers' garage in San Leandro and tinker with cars. On rare occasions, he'd caucus with fellow black athletes such as Kareem Abdul-Jabbar, Archie Clark, and Lucius Allen to discuss the hardships of being a black star. Those distractions didn't fully ease his mind, though.

Finley was unsympathetic. He wanted Reggie punished for playing contractual games. Even if it hurt the team, Finley wanted to diminish and humble the young slugger, so that he'd never challenge his owner again.

THE A'S SPENT the first few weeks of the season in Oakland and other northern climes, and the cold air made it even more difficult for Reggie. At the end of April, Reggie was hitting just .137 with three home runs. On May 19, the A's traveled to Milwaukee with Reggie's batting average at .191 and the team in third place.

Finley summoned McNamara and his coaches to his Chicago offices. The owner emerged with a decision. "We've decided not to use Jackson against left-handers," he told the writers after arriving in Milwaukee. "And if he doesn't start hitting right-handers, there's only one thing left. He might have to go down to Triple-A."

The writers who covered the A's had already learned to play Reggie and Finley against each other. When one said something particularly withering about the other, they'd scurry off to the offended party for reaction quotes. Never did it work better than when Finley threatened to defrock Reggie and return him to the minor leagues. "Don't be telling me that shit, going back to the minors," Reggie said after Finley's words were read back to him. "I'll tell you one thing, I wouldn't go."

"That big asshole," he went on. "If he would've signed me, I would've been ready. If he'd been fair, paid me the money, if he would've cared about this team, he should've had me in on time."

After the series against the Brewers, Finley held his annual team barbecue at his farm in Indiana. Reggie was the only player not to show up.

Soon Reggie was on the bench. McNamara, the manager whom Reggie had come to trust so deeply after Birmingham, followed Finley's orders in silence. McNamara managed his first full season in the majors with little job security. He simply couldn't align himself with Reggie. But Reggie couldn't—or wouldn't—understand McNamara's straits. The betrayals outraged him.

After one of Reggie's increasingly common off nights, Herb Michelson, a part-time reporter who covered the A's home games for the *Sacramento Bee*, roamed into the clubhouse at precisely the wrong time. "You talk too much!" Reggie shouted at him without provocation.

Michelson, taken aback, responded that Reggie also talked too much. Reggie moved in closer and cut Michelson a chilling glare. He then raised a bat over his head and held it over Michelson's head. For several arresting seconds, Reggie seemed about to bludgeon him. Finally, he lowered the bat and walked away.

At the plate Reggie pressed, and the struggles continued. He didn't lift his average above .200 for good until June 12, and for the first time in his career he heard boos from the hometown fans in Oakland. On more than one occasion, he pondered retirement. His foul moods kept his teammates at a distance, and he couldn't confide in Jennie, from whom he had drifted even further. One night after a game, he drank with Catfish Hunter and admitted he wished he were white. Then, Reggie reasoned, Finley would treat him fairly.

The struggles continued. "Be yourself, Reggie," Gene Tenace told him. "You'll come out of it. The guys still like you."

"You mean it?" Reggie asked. "The guys like me?"

His brashness, his vocal nature, and his occasional combativeness concealed a driving desire to be liked by his peers. When he didn't perform, when he didn't hit, he couldn't imagine what there was to like about him. The hitter was inseparable from the man, and in 1970 the man wasn't hitting.

McNamara finally called Reggie into his office for a meeting. McNamara asked him to accept an assignment to Triple-A Des Moines. Considering the depths of Reggie's slump, what McNamara proposed—at Finley's bidding, of course—made sense. But Reggie would not indulge them. "I'm a major-league ballplayer," he snapped at McNamara. "I'm no minor leaguer. I don't like to travel roads I've been on."

McNamara asked Reggie to sleep on it and give it further thought. Reggie said he would not. Finley called him late one night—just as he had in the course of contract negotiations—and kept Reggie on the phone for a full four hours, imploring him to accept a demotion. But he wouldn't.

Angered by Reggie's disobedience, Finley once again ordered McNamara to play him erratically. By that point, Reggie and McNamara weren't speaking, so the writers told Reggie that Finley had benched him for the final three games of the first half. He had hoped that the time away during the All-Star break would allow wounds to heal on all sides. All he wanted was to be in the lineup and left alone. But Finley had no designs on change.

Once again, Reggie thought about quitting. He told Jennie they would go back to Arizona together. They'd start a family and repair their damaged union. Things would get better away from Finley and away from a boy's game that had become a man's toil. "I'm sticking with you," she said. "I know you're right. I know I'm right."

Perhaps if he'd been able to be with Jennie at that time, he would've done it. However, Jennie was stricken with a case of hepatitis, and the doctors forbade Reggie to see her. He was left alone with his thoughts. And the more he thought about it, the less a life away from baseball appealed to him. Even with his business interests, money would become an immediate and unceasing worry, and time away from Jennie, which he needed, would become a rarity. Was the marriage even salvageable? Could he live without the women in other cities and the money and lifestyle that baseball afforded him? "I hate it when I hurt my wife," he said at the time. "I want it to work, but it may not. I may not be ready to make a marriage work."

Finally Reggie grew desperate enough to call Finley and ask to be returned to the lineup. Reggie promised that he wouldn't attack him in the press and would do as he was told. Satisfied that Reggie had kissed has ring, Finley lifted his orders. But he continued to terrorize his young star.

Reggie learned that Finley had called Jennie during one of the A's road trips and pressed her for information on her husband's state of mind. Finley had done so under the guise of concern, but Jennie believed he was seeking something to use against Reggie. Finley would go to any lengths to gain a negotiating advantage. That much Reggie knew. This time, though, the sense of intrusion was too much.

Reggie was back in the lineup to start the second half, but, paranoid and eager to prove himself, he couldn't relax at the plate. In the field, he was distracted and unfocused. In early August, Finley ordered him benched once again.

In a game against Cleveland on the eleventh, Reggie entered the game as a pinch runner, but McNamara lifted him for a pinch hitter before he could come to the plate. Frustrated, he gathered his things and retired to the clubhouse before the game had ended. "Did you see that shit?" Finley bellowed in front of the writers. "Pinch-hit for that Jackson, and he puts on his warm-up jacket and goes into the clubhouse. Call that team spirit? What kind of team spirit is that?"

"If I were a ballplayer," Finley continued, "I'd certainly try to see all nine innings of a game. If there is anyone who needs to learn what the game is about, it's Jackson."

Finley holed up with McNamara in the manager's office and demanded that Reggie be fined. McNamara explained that since the A's had no specific rule barring a removed player from leaving the dugout, they couldn't punish Reggie. Finley was miffed. After he emerged from the meeting he informed his players, while glowering at Reggie, that thenceforth there would be exactly such a rule. "Thank God our fans show more interest than some of our players," Finley said. Tommy Davis had left the dugout that same day when Reggie had pinch-run for him, but not a word was said about that.

———

THE GAME ON September 5 against the Royals was Fan Appreciation Day in Oakland, and it was one of those promotions that Finley undertook with a terrible sense of mission. When he worked on one of his marketing gambits, Finley fretted, schemed, micromanaged, and abused his functionaries beyond even his usual extremes. So when fewer than 10,000 fans showed up to the Coliseum for the game against the Royals, his mood soured.

Reggie, meanwhile, was batting just .223, he'd had only one home run in the last six weeks, and this would be the fifth straight game that he hadn't started. Yet it wasn't just the fallen numbers that bothered Reggie. He'd thought that he and Finley had achieved some kind of détente over the All-Star break, but Finley continued to assail him. Before the game, he was cross and restrained with the reporters—something deeply out of character for him. One teammate told those reporters not to read too much into Reggie's change in attitude. "You know how fucked up he is this season," he said.

On the strength of Chuck Dobson's crisp pitching, the A's led until the seventh inning, when Rich Severson doubled home the tying run. In the eighth, Felipe Alou singled to put Oakland back in front. Sal Bando followed with another single, and Dick Green walked. With two outs, bases loaded, and the A's on top 4–3, manager John McNamara told Reggie to grab a bat. He detested pinch hitting. It upset his rhythms and removed him from the essential flow of the game. On this day, though, he had nothing else.

Kansas City brought in lefty Tom Burgmeier to neutralize. High up in the owner's box, Finley leaned in. Burgmeier nodded at the catcher's sign, slumped out of the stretch position, and heaved a fastball at the inner third of the plate. In a swing that seemed like something plundered from better days, Reggie uncoiled on the pitch. The ball landed deep in the center-field bleachers, and the A's led 8–3. He had hit the first grand slam of his career.

Reggie's trot around the bases, at odds with his boiling mood, was slow and measured—the pace of a man who savored a forgotten taste. The 9,824 fans in attendance leaped out of their seats and cheered. As fireworks snapped overhead, six fans slipped over the fence, bounded onto the field, and slid into third base. Reggie approached home plate amid the chaos and glared skyward, toward Finley. Finley stood and applauded with a zeal to match that of the fans. A wide smile broke across his face, and the old man raised his hands in triumph. Later he would say that his treatment of Reggie had all been an orchestration, that he had "goaded him into doing what he was capable of."

How dare he, thought Reggie. What had just happened defied everything Finley had believed and perpetrated. He could not share in it. After Reggie touched home plate, he stopped, flung his batting helmet offstage, and raised his middle finger at the old man. He mouthed, "Fuck you."

Lest it look like some fleeting impulse—or lest fans think they didn't see what they thought they saw—he sustained the gesture and glared up at the suddenly angered Finley. Reggie wanted to get across one message: *I hate you for what you've done to me.*

After the game but before the writers had been admitted to the clubhouse, Reggie nailed above his locker a *Baltimore Sun* article that laid out the scenarios that would bring the disgruntled star to the Orioles. "I just hit a home run with the bases loaded," Reggie said after the writers arrived. "It's just a nice time for a guy to do something like that when he's getting shafted."

The fallout came a few days later in Minneapolis. The A's were in town for a series against the division-leading Twins, and Finley decided that now, rather than back in Oakland with too much hometown media in earshot, was the time to confront Reggie. Finley, Reggie, McNamara, Sal Bando, and the coaching staff met in the manager's suite at the Ambassador West. Finley produced an article in which Reggie, after a reporter asked him what words he had mouthed at the owner, said, "You can't print it."

"What do you think of this?" asked Finley.

"I'm proud of it," said Reggie.

"It's a disgrace to baseball. Why did you do it?"

"Because I hate the way you treat me," Reggie shot back, "the way you treat people."

McNamara owed Reggie after he'd failed to stand up to Finley earlier in the year, he'd developed a mutual respect with hitting coach Charley Lau, and Bando, the team captain, knew firsthand of Finley's dark ways. He *deserved* for these men to take his side. But Reggie looked to them and got silence and bowed heads.

Finley pulled from his briefcase a public apology, which he told Reggie to sign. "No way," said Reggie.

"Okay," said Finley. "We'll all just stay right here until Jackson signs the paper."

Finley told him that if he didn't sign it, he'd fine him $5,000 and suspend him without pay for the rest of the season. Reggie cried. Finally he said he'd sign the statement. He never did sign it, but Finley proceeded as though he had.

Reggie finally gave up. He would no longer fight Finley, he would no longer trust anyone within the organization, and he'd stop trying to figure things out on the field. Finley's statement read, "Last Saturday, I made gestures and comments I wish I never made. I would like to apologize to the fans, my teammates, John McNamara, and Mr. Finley."

In the series that followed, Reggie went 0 for 9 with five strikeouts at the plate and in the field dropped an easy and crucial fly ball. The Twins swept, and once again the pennant would elude Oakland. The lone highlight of the season was the no-hitter twenty-year-old Vida Blue spun on September 21. The next night, however, Minnesota clinched a second consecutive AL West title.

Reggie ended the endless season with numbers that inspired no one, least of all himself: a .237 batting average, a league-leading strikeout total of 135, and the most errors of any outfielder. But he had taken his walks, which had led to a respectable on-base percentage of .359, and his twenty-three home runs and solid slugging percentage of .458 were also commendable. Yet his successes were lost on Finley and, worst of all, on himself.

NOT LONG AFTER the regular season ended, Finley fired McNamara. Because the A's had failed to win the division, Finley had already decided to change managers, although he didn't know how it would play with the fan base. But when catcher Dave Duncan made some all-too-candid comments about Finley's way with managers, the owner believed he had the cover he needed. "There's only one man who manages this club," Duncan said just after the season ended. "Charlie Finley. And we'll never win as long as he manages."

Finley preferred for this not to become public knowledge. He'd forced Hank Bauer to lie about his level of involvement, and he was displeased when Duncan threw back the curtain. He made McNamara pay for it. "We had only two problems on our ball club of players spouting off, my good friend, Reggie Jackson, and Duncan," Finley told the press shortly after he dismissed McNamara. "No manager can allow one of his players to criticize unfairly, knowing the facts himself, without getting pinched."

Then the rub: "John McNamara didn't lose his job," Finley declared. "His players took it from him."

Reggie believed McNamara had betrayed him twice, so his firing didn't devastate him. However, that Finley would off-load blame for the firing onto the players was, to his "good friend" Reggie, beyond the pale.

At the same press conference, Finley also announced he'd fired hitting coach Charley Lau. "One day," Finley explained, "I found out that Duncan was sleeping with Charley Lau."

After a long pause, Finley went on to explain that by "sleeping with" he meant they were sharing a room to cut expenses. However, through his puzzling choice of words, Finley let the innuendo of sex hang in the air. He didn't want his coaches consorting with the players, but he phrased his explanation to anger Duncan.

Finley wasn't done. Also out was the popular broadcaster Harry Caray. Caray was no cheerleader in the booth. Frank and critical in his game calls, Caray appealed to working-class Oaklanders, who appreciated effort and efficiency. Finley, though, wanted a salesman, not a critic. The breaking point came when Caray refused to indulge Finley on what was, to the owner, a vital matter: changing his famous "Holy cow!" call to "Holy mule!"—a reference to Charlie O., Finley's beloved mascot.

The new manager was Dick Williams, the man who'd guided the 1967 Red Sox to impossible successes. Early on, Williams attempted to appeal to Reggie's sense of neglect. "I expect Reggie Jackson to play every day," he told Ron Bergman of the *Oakland Tribune*. "I have no thoughts of benching him against left-handers."

It was precisely what Reggie wanted to hear, but he feared it wasn't up to Williams. He also didn't trust him yet. "I've heard a lot of bad things about him from other players, unfavorable comments," said Reggie. "I've heard that when things get tough, he wouldn't stick up for you."

In his first conversation with Williams, Reggie asked to be traded—he knew it wouldn't happen, but he wanted Williams to know the extent of his dissatisfaction. Williams told him that he hoped it wouldn't come to that. In the days to come, rumors circulated that Reggie would be dealt to Pittsburgh in exchange for Willie Stargell or to Baltimore for Paul Blair and Tom Phoebus. When nothing materialized, Reggie sulked.

As THE WINTER began, Reggie's thoughts consumed him. He still had baseball, but he knew that Finley had the power to take it all away from him. He and Gary Walker flew to Chicago to attempt a workable peace.

They met Finley at his insurance office on Michigan Avenue. Reggie, for half an hour, ticked off his grievances. He then asked Finley to trade him. Finley stared at him and exhaled deeply. "I listened to everything you had to say. Now I'm going to talk for thirty seconds," the owner said. "Number one, I love you. Number two, I'm not going to trade you. Number three, let's go to lunch."

It wasn't a catharsis for Reggie, but he felt better. Finley had turned on the fatherly wiles, and Reggie responded to them, just as Finley knew he would. It was an imperfect peace, but it was peace.

Brought low by the 1970 season, Reggie badly needed a change of environment. Finley urged him to play winter ball in the Caribbean, and this time Reggie, abashed by his struggles, agreed to go.

His manager on the Santurce Crabbers, one of Puerto Rico's storied Winter League clubs, was the legendary Frank Robinson. Then in his midthirties, Robinson was still an effective hitter for the Baltimore Orioles and just four years removed from his Triple Crown performance of 1966. As a leader, he communicated with sharp words and sharper glares.

Reggie spent his first several days in Puerto Rico at the Hotel San Juan, but Robinson soon invited him to stay in his apartment and save money. At once honored and intimidated to share close quarters with a man like Frank Robinson, one of the great black stars of the post–Jackie Robinson era, Reggie accepted. For the next two months, he spent almost every waking moment with Robinson.

Reggie struck out fourteen times in the first week of play. "You're having a slump," Robinson told him. "Everybody has slumps. Keep your damn head up. If you're going to be a leader in this game, you've got to lead all the time." Reggie nodded. "If you want to talk after every at bat," his manager said, "then we'll talk after every at bat."

They did. Back in the dugout, after each of Reggie's trips to the plate, he'd ask Robinson what he'd done right and what he'd done wrong. Robinson told him. Reggie didn't take instruction well, and it took some time for him to open up to Robinson's relentless counsel-ing. But slowly they rebuilt his swing.

On Robinson's advice, Reggie crouched more deeply at the plate. Doing so gave him a better angle at the ball and a better rate of con-tact. By happy accident, Reggie also discovered he needed corrective eyewear. While he shopped for sunglasses in Old San Juan, the store-keeper persuaded him to have an eye exam. The doctor found Reggie to have severe astigmatism and prescribed him a pair of glasses. That left Reggie with 20/10 corrected vision. He homered in five of his next six games and lifted his batting average by seventy points the rest of the way.

Robinson's steadfastness continued to impress Reggie. The base-ball season was long and riddled with ups and downs, both physical and psychological. He couldn't read too much into any single fail-ure or triumph. He needed to remain centered without losing those innermost fires. When Reggie would throw his helmet in frustration, break his bat over his knee, or, on one occasion, whip his bat into the stands of Hiram Bithorn Stadium, Robinson would look on in disap-proval. "Be a man," he'd say. "Be a pro."

Reggie hit twenty homers—the second highest total in Santurce team history—and he left promising to emulate Robinson's quiet, steady strength on the field. He needed some of that to survive this game, Reggie told himself. He needed some of that to survive Finley.

FOR 1971, FINLEY reduced Reggie's salary to $40,000. In Puerto Rico, Robinson had counseled him to think of his owner's position and interests whenever possible. It made the struggles seem less per-sonal. Reggie accepted Finley's offer in uncharacteristic silence and showed up to spring training in exceptional shape.

Through the first ten games of spring training, Reggie totaled ten home runs and seventeen RBIs. His new stance allowed him to uncoil powerfully upon the ball, his new glasses allowed him to pick up the ball earlier out of the pitcher's hand, and his new attitude helped him focus more keenly on each element of his game. Ted Williams, who entered his third season as manager of the Washington Senators, enthused that Reggie was "the most natural hitter I've ever seen."

The A's dropped the first three games of the regular season, but soon they won and won often. In one April stretch, Reggie notched game-winning hits in three straight games. During one of those games, a 6–1 win in Minnesota, the veteran Tommy Davis, another black player with a "difficult" reputation, noticed a flaw in his swing. Davis told Reggie that his back leg was out of sync when he strode toward the pitcher and then demonstrated how he could correct it. Reggie followed his advice and then powered two home runs, each well more than 400 feet in distance.

The end of April, however, found him struggling. He batted just .220 for the month, but he didn't let that dim the rest of his game. In May he hit, and by the end of the month he had recorded nine outfield assists, including five runners cut down at home plate.

For most of 1971, though, the story was not Reggie but Vida Blue. The fire-throwing lefty had been a gifted high school quarterback at DeSoto High School in Mansfield, Louisiana, and had signed a letter of intent to play football at the University of Houston. Blue's family, though, was living in poverty, and when Finley drafted him in the second round and offered him $25,000 to sign, he leapt at the chance.

Tall and sinewy with deep sable skin and a placid face, Blue was reserved by nature. Just two things moved him to intensity: pitching and Charlie Finley. Early in Blue's career, Finley leaned on him to change his first name to "True," as he'd similarly done with "Catfish" Hunter and "Blue Moon" Odom. Blue, however, saw himself as a ballplayer and not one of Finley's clownish promotions. "How about if you change your name to True Finley?" he asked the owner.

The A's first called up Blue in 1969, but at age nineteen he struggled, and the team dispatched him back to Iowa. He returned to the majors in July 1970 and thrived. In 1971, though, he dwelled on another plane entirely. On road series, the writers would pool about Blue's locker and for the most part leave Reggie alone. While the attention frustrated Blue, the lack of attention frustrated Reggie. He was hitting again, and after the toils of 1970 he felt he deserved the press, at least more than the unproven Blue did. Attention had always been nourishment for Reggie. Back in Wyncote, one of his football teammates had once shown up for practice with a new pair of size 16 shoes. The other players crowded around and marveled over them. The jealous Reggie snatched one of the shoes, ran to the bathroom, and filled it with water.

On June 1, the A's won in Yankee Stadium thanks to a complete-game victory by Blue (one that *raised* his ERA to 1.36) and a two-run homer by Reggie. The writers, though, wanted to talk only to Blue. "Don't talk to him, Vida," Reggie said and nodded toward a writer who was trying to pry a boilerplate quote from the shy left-hander. "They're all the same."

Blue ignored him. Reggie continued. "You don't need the press," he told him. "Just wait until you ask for a raise next year. You'll see that they'll take the side of management. You'll see."

Blue gave him a hard stare and went on talking to the reporter. Then an unsuspecting clubhouse attendant approached Reggie and asked him what kind of drink he wanted. "Get me the kind niggers drink!" Reggie shouted. "I'm a nigger, you know I'm a nigger, and we all drink the same thing."

THE ALL-STAR GAME in Detroit made history. Blue would start for the AL, and Dock Ellis of the Pirates would start for the NL. For the first time in baseball history, two black starting pitchers opposed each other in the Midsummer Classic. Blue had seventeen wins at the break, an unheard-of midseason total in the modern era. The focus was understandably on him. By the end of the game, though, it was Reggie's show.

Blue gave up home runs to Johnny Bench and Hank Aaron in the early innings. In the third, AL manager Earl Weaver called on Reggie, who was battling a customary leg strain, to pinch-hit for his teammate. With Luis Aparicio on first, Reggie unloaded on a Dock Ellis high slider. With a sound like a rifle report, the ball soared beyond the right-center fence, beyond the outfield bleachers and the upper deck, over the roof of Tiger Stadium, and off an electrical transformer that soared almost a hundred feet above the park. As the ball completed its impossible arc, the cheers turned into stunned gasps. Later, scientists at Wayne State University concluded that Reggie's home run, had it not bored into the transformer, would have traveled an unimaginable 650 feet.

In the same inning, Frank Robinson, the man who had helped Reggie rediscover his skills in Puerto Rico, also homered and gave Blue a lead the AL wouldn't relinquish. Blue earned the win, but afterward the writers flocked to Reggie, the game's MVP, to ask him about his historic blast. He was in his habitat once more—making the big hit and rhapsodizing about it before a captive audience of writers. "I didn't travel two thousand miles to strike out," he said.

Not long after the All-Star break, Finley purchased Mudcat Grant off waivers. Grant had been a reliable reliever for Oakland in the past, but in September of the previous year Finley had shipped him off to the Pirates for a nominal return. The A's needed another arm in the bull pen, and Grant could also counter Reggie.

Grant was a black player cut from a simpler cloth. Unlike Reggie, Grant smiled a lot, was unfailingly polite to Finley, and in the past had been quietly submissive at contract time. In other words, he wasn't a mouthy, combative, attention-seeking black man like Reggie. Finley hoped that Grant's presence in the clubhouse would influence Reggie, and he hoped that Grant would change the team's growing reputation. That reputation, in his mind, was as a team that enabled black players like Reggie to "misbehave." That couldn't be good for business, he reasoned. To Reggie, though, Grant was just another player, and he ignored Finley's roundabout efforts to change him. He worried about winning.

On September 15, the A's beat the White Sox in Comiskey Park and clinched the division title. In celebration, Finley transported all his players to his farm in nearby La Porte, Indiana, for a feast. This time Reggie attended.

IN THE AMERICAN League Championship Series, the A's would face the Baltimore Orioles. Blue would start the play-off opener, but he was in trouble before he ever took the mound. All season, he had been ill at ease with all the attention thrust upon him, and his mood worsened as the games became more important. As he prepared for his game one start, he learned of a *Parade* magazine story that claimed that Blue's girlfriend was white. Reggie knew the power of such insinuations.

One of Blue's girlfriends was white, but a lot of his other girlfriends weren't. Young, famous, and handsome, he behaved accordingly. The *Parade* piece bewildered and angered the young ace. As a consequence, he brushed off all the media leading up to the Baltimore series. Mentally, Blue wasn't fit.

Physically, Chuck Dobson wasn't fit. His elbow failed, and he wasn't able to go against Baltimore. His absence forced Diego Segui into the play-off rotation, and that made Blue's game one start all the more vital. With Blue fretting, the rains arrived, postponing the opener. That meant no off day and less rest between starts for Blue. Before game one, it also meant more time to think.

When they finally played, Blue cruised initially, but the Orioles reached him for one run in the fourth and four runs in the seventh. Reggie batted third and played right in his first postseason game. He went 0 for 3 in the 5–4 loss. In game two, Reggie managed a hit, a double in the first off Mike Cuellar, but Cuellar gave up only one run and pitched a complete-game, 5–1 victory.

Because of the rainout, the A's, down 2–0, made the cross-country flight back to Oakland and played game three the next day. Segui and Rollie Fingers failed to stop the Orioles attack, but Reggie did his best to prolong the series with two opposite-field home runs off Jim Palmer. Yet the A's lost 5–3 and were swept out of the play-offs. After Palmer struck out the side in the ninth, Reggie collapsed onto the dugout steps in anguish. There he sobbed—genuinely according to some, theatrically according to others—for almost half an hour.

SEVEN

"The Worst Feeling I've Ever Had . . . Was the Day We Won the World Series"

FOR THE A'S, the winter brought turmoil, not rest. A robber shot Blue Moon Odom in the neck, and Blue's salary fight with Finley grabbed the headlines. Blue had won the Cy Young Award and the MVP in 1971, and he assumed, just as Reggie had after his 1969 campaign, that a hefty payday was in the offing. Finley, though, was miserly beyond his estimation. "Well, I know you won twenty-four games," Finley told Blue early in negotiations. "I know you led the league in earned run average. I know you had three hundred strike-outs. I know you made the All-Star team. I know you were the young-est ever to win the Cy Young Award and the MVP. I know all that. And if I was you, I would ask for the same thing. And you deserve it. But I ain't gonna give it to you."

This was Oakland. You weren't paid according to merit or achievement or market forces; you were paid merely enough to keep you from quitting. Such were the depredations of a rigged system.

Blue's long holdout wasn't the only story leading up to the 1972 season. For the first time in the modern era, the players voted to strike. Reggie, as one of the most vocal player reps, helped unite the players behind union head Marvin Miller. It was, of course, an argument over money. Specifically, the players wanted the compounded interest earned off their pensions cycled back into the pension system. The owners, meanwhile, wanted those monies for themselves.

Finley broke ranks. He disclosed that the owners, prior to negotiations, hadn't even known about the surplus in the pension fund, and he also opened the Coliseum to his players in defiance of league orders. He rallied a bloc of like-minded owners and forced an end to the strike. By the time the work stoppage ended, the A's had lost seven games from their schedule. They finally opened the season on April 15. On that day, they bested the Twins 4–3 in eleven innings. Reggie went 0 for 3 on the day, but in the final frame he bunted the eventual winning run to third.

Not until early May did Blue and Finley come to terms on a contract. As was the case with Reggie in the winter of 1969, Finley had gotten the better of Blue in the strict terms of dollars and cents, but what Reggie and Curt Flood started that off-season—the end of black assent in contract negotiations—Blue had continued.

WHEN SPRING TRAINING opened in 1972, Reggie showed up with a flowing mustache. At that time, no players wore facial hair, mostly because a number of teams banned them from doing so. (It's believed that no player had worn a mustache in the regular season since Wally Schang of the 1914 Philadelphia A's.) Reggie's teammates needled him, and his coaches shook their heads in disapproval. Undaunted, Reggie announced in the clubhouse that not only would he keep the mustache, but he might also grow a beard by Opening Day. Finley didn't notice Reggie's new look until the middle of May, when he finally saw his first game. Never fond of seeing his players fall out of lockstep, he ordered manager Dick Williams to make Reggie shave it off. Reggie refused.

Finley never hesitated to confront players personally when they disobeyed, but Reggie required a different approach. Reggie cherished his individuality above all, so Finley privately ordered a couple of other players to grow mustaches in the belief that once it was no longer a point of distinction, Reggie would shave and things could get back to normal. Instead, Finley, to his own surprise, liked what he saw: a marketing opportunity.

Finley imagined his whole roster draped in hair and, thus, more closely resembling his northern California customer base. He also liked setting his team apart from the conservative remainder of Major League Baseball. Since many teams outlawed beards and mustaches and even placed limits on how long players could grow their sideburns, Finley's boys would do the opposite.

Soon he offered players $300 bonuses to grow mustaches, beards, and flowing locks. Almost everyone complied, even Dick Williams. Then Finley staged a "Mustache Day" promotion on Father's Day, in which he gave free tickets to any A's fan who wore a mustache. Eventually, each player on the Oakland roster except for two—Larry Brown and Mike Hegan—festooned himself with some kind of facial hair. But Reggie, contrary to Finley's strategizing, didn't mind the company. "People want to be like me," he thought.

By late May, the "Mustache Gang" clung to first place by a narrow margin over Dick Allen and the White Sox. They won, but nothing bred contentment when you worked for Charlie Finley. In the clubhouse during a trip to Texas, Reggie, the team's player rep, told his teammates about a new ticket policy. Mike Epstein, the dour, hulking first baseman, didn't care for Reggie's authoritative tone. Epstein was already put off because Reggie referred to himself as "Mr. B and B," or "Mr. Bread and Butter"—a reminder of how essential he was to Oakland's success. Epstein, like Reggie, was a left-handed power hitter, but according to the fans and media the A's had only one left-handed power hitter, and it wasn't Epstein.

Epstein asked Reggie for his allotted tickets, and Reggie asked to whom he intended to give the tickets. "It's none of your business," Epstein shot back. More harsh words followed, and soon the two men were in each other's faces. With one punch, Epstein, physically massive, Bronx-reared, and a former meatpacker and college football player, leveled Reggie.

It seemed to be typical Oakland stuff—two teammates brawl-ing—but Reggie's insecurities wouldn't let him move beyond it. Soon after, Reggie approached him. "You hate my guts, don't you?" he asked Epstein.

"I just don't want to have anything to do with you," Epstein said.

"It bothers me that you don't like me," said Reggie. It bothered Reggie when *anyone*, friend or foe, didn't like him, but Epstein was a special case. He was Jewish, and he was white. Reggie's fondness for and comfort around Jewish people traced back to his Wyncote days. He'd long had a better rapport with Jews than he'd had with blacks, and Epstein's disdain confounded him.

In September of that year, when Palestinian terrorists murdered eleven Israeli athletes and coaches during the Summer Olympics in Munich, Reggie joined Epstein and Ken Holtzman in wearing a black armband on his uniform sleeve. But even that gesture couldn't repair his relationship with Epstein. The gulf between them troubled Reggie until the day Epstein was traded. It wasn't so much Epstein as what Epstein represented—the kind of guy Reggie had grown up with. It seemed to Reggie a rebuke from the distant past.

On June 5, center fielder Angel Mangual made a critical misplay during the A's extra-inning victory over the Indians. Mangual's lapses in the field frustrated Williams, and he wasn't much of a hitter either.

So Williams moved Reggie from right to center and left him there for the remainder of the season.

Many fans remember Reggie as the somewhat lumbering slugger he was in his Yankees years, but earlier in his career he was a sleek, smooth, zipper-quick defender who could man center, one of the most demanding positions on the diamond.

Although Reggie's numbers declined modestly from the previous season, he received more All-Star votes than any other outfielder. During the game in Atlanta, a 4–3 NL win, Reggie went 2 for 4 and hit a first-inning double off Bob Gibson.

On August 2, the Royals plunked Bando, and a heated exchange with Kansas City catcher Ed Kirkpatrick turned into a brawl. Reggie played the peacemaker—he yanked bodies from the scrum and held back those late to the action. But he still managed to strain a muscle in his rib cage. Afterward, the team trainer told him it was a minor injury, but Reggie doubted him. He missed the next five games, of which the A's lost four. He tried to play again but couldn't. In Reggie's absence, Mangual again struggled in the field and went 4 for 45 at the plate. Soon enough, the White Sox whittled down the A's lead—six and a half at the break—to a single game. And then those same White Sox headed to town. Reggie's injury had worsened—cartilage had detached from his rib cage—and the club placed him on the disabled list. The A's won the epic opener 5–3 in nineteen innings and managed to split the four-game set.

Reggie missed sixteen of eighteen games, and the A's activated him on August 25. By that point Oakland had fallen a game behind the White Sox. Upon his return, Reggie keyed a five-game winning streak that lifted the A's back into first place.

The rest of the season brought more of the convulsions that typified the A's. Blue was hospitalized under mysterious circumstances. It may have been for nerves, a groin infection, major dental work, or something else. Then, during one game, the A's and Billy Martin's

Tigers engaged in a savage fifteen-minute brawl. Finley disabled second baseman Dick Green even though he wasn't hurt, and Epstein and Dick Williams almost came to blows in the clubhouse.

In early September, the A's visited Chicago for a determinative pair of games against the White Sox. In the two-game split, Reggie was a house afire: 5 for 9 with a home run and two doubles. After a split with Kansas City, the A's led the West by three and a half games with eight to play. On September 28, the A's came back from down 7–0 to top the Twins 8–7 and clinch the AL West title. For the first time since the early 1930s, the A's would go to the postseason in consecutive years. They'd been slowed by Blue's holdout, serious injuries to Reggie and Epstein, a disappointing season from Bando, and, as ever, the slings and arrows of Finley. Yet they won.

Their opponent in the ALCS was Detroit, the team they'd recently fought. Before the series, Finley and Martin traded insults in the press, so fans and media expected a hostile encounter. They would not be disappointed.

The A's opened the five-game series at home and with Blue in the bull pen. In game one, Oakland rallied from behind to win it in the eleventh. Reggie went 2 for 5 on the day, but he neither scored nor drove in any of the A's three runs. In game two, Odom flummoxed the Tigers all day long and notched a 5–0 shutout. Offensively, Reggie cinched it in the fifth with a two-run double off Fred Scherman—just after Scherman, on Billy Martin's orders, peppered him with consecutive brushback pitches. After the game, however, all eyes, ears, and microphones were on Bert Campaneris.

At the plate in game two, "Campy" was an auspicious 3 for 3 with a pair of runs scored; however, his quick-fire temper threatened to alter the series. In the seventh, Martin ordered his reliever, Lerrin LaGrow, to throw at the pestilent Oakland shortstop. LaGrow's pitch struck Campaneris on the left ankle. Campaneris picked himself up off the ground, stared angrily out at LaGrow, and then whipped his bat toward the mound. LaGrow ducked, and the bat narrowly missed the top of his head. The Tigers dugout, led by Martin, rushed onto the field and toward the A's dugout. The umpiring crew, on this day large and physically powerful men, restrained most of the players. Campaneris was carried from the field of play, and Martin, screaming for Campaneris to come out and fight like a man, was held back by two umpires. The rest of the A's knew they had nothing to gain, and they also knew that they'd lost the last rumble. They stayed in the dugout. Afterward, Martin said that Campaneris's actions were "as gutless as anything I ever saw in baseball."

And of the A's newfound pacifism, he sniffed, "They didn't want to fight us. Did you see anyone come out? If they had come out, they'd have got their heads knocked off."

Reggie had a different, oddly portentous take. "I hate Martin because he plays tough," he said in the clubhouse following game two. "But if I played for him, I'd probably love him."

Martin tried to turn a game into a feud. On one level, Martin's strategy worked: AL President Joe Cronin fined Campaneris $500 and suspended him for the remainder of the postseason. The series headed back to Detroit, the A's without their catalyst and starting shortstop and the Tigers with nothing left to lose.

Game three was all Detroit. Joe Coleman struck out a then–playoff record fourteen batters on the way to a 3–0 win. Reggie went 0 for 4 and dropped his series average to .231. For game four, Williams opted not to start Blue and instead went with Hunter on short rest. Hunter was Hunter—methodical, efficient, and befuddling. He gave up only one run in more than seven innings of work, but across the way Mickey Lolich pitched even better. Reggie managed two hits on the day, but the Tigers, thanks to a Gene Tenace misplay in the field, took the fourth game 3–2 in ten innings. A fifth and final contest would determine the pennant.

Odom, who made his second start of the series, gave up a run in the home half of the first. Reggie led off the second. He worked Woodie Fryman for a walk and swiped second base. Bando then smacked a fly ball to the right-field warning track, and Reggie tagged up and took third base. Mike Epstein took a pitch on the hand and jogged to first. Tenace followed. In the dugout, Williams put on the double steal. Tenace struck out as both runners moved. Detroit catcher Bill Freehan, unaware that Reggie had broken from third, threw to second. Epstein slid in under the tag, and shortstop Dick McAuliffe heaved the ball back home. Freehan had the plate blocked, so as Reggie approached home, he slid at an angle to complicate the tag.

Deep within his hamstring, something popped. The collision with Freehan was secondary and unimportant—Reggie, thanks to his deft slide, had already scored the tying run, and he'd already hurt himself. He writhed around home plate and had to be helped from the field.

Reggie, in pain and with the aid of crutches, returned to the bench. In the top of the fourth, his replacement, George Hendrick, reached first on a throwing error by McAuliffe. Bando then bunted Hendrick to second. Tenace stepped in. He was 0 for 15 in the series and, haunted by his failures, hadn't slept the night before. Fryman challenged Tenace with a fastball, but he whipped his bat through the zone and laced it to left field. In left, Duke Sims fielded it on one hop but failed to grip in cleanly. Hendrick slid home an instant ahead of Sims's throw. The A's led, 2–1.

Odom, meanwhile, pitched well but nervously. Aware that the game was freighted with importance, he felt the pressure. He overthrew and missed the zone with his fastball. After three hard groundouts in the fifth, Odom, breathing heavily, plodded into the clubhouse and vomited. Williams had seen enough. With a 2–1 lead, he turned to the disgruntled Blue.

Not long after Blue took the mound, a wind kicked up and blew in from left field at 17 miles per hour. Behind the plate, Tenace knew it would be hard to drive anything off of Blue in such a gale, so he called for fastball after fastball. The Tigers could do nothing. In four innings of relief, Blue permitted no runs and just three singles. In the ninth, the Detroit fans threw a smoke bomb at Ken Holtzman and pelted Hendrick with bottles, ice cubes, and rocks. In the end, the A's won the game 2–1 and claimed their first pennant in more than four decades. Reggie watched the final out—a routine fly to center, where he should have been standing—from the clubhouse. "We're champions," he said with no one around.

The first to greet Reggie was Gonzalo Marquez. Reggie rose unsteadily, dropped his crutches, collapsed into Marquez's arms and cried. His were not tears of joy—joy over his first trip to the World Series. "You're the biggest reason this club is here," Dal Maxvill reassured him.

Later, dressed only in flip-flops, a T-shirt drenched in champagne, and a bath towel at his waist, Reggie hobbled over to the Tigers' clubhouse. Billy Martin met him at the door. "You're a heck of a guy," Reggie said to the Detroit manager. "Believe me, I don't like playing against you guys."

"You showed me a lot of class," Martin said. "I like guys like you."

REGGIE FLEW WITH the team to Cincinnati that same night and cried through most of the trip. Upon arrival, he went to the nearest hospital. His leg felt better than it had earlier in the day, and he had taken a few uneasy steps without his crutches. However, doctors examined and reexamined Reggie and told him that he'd ruptured his left hamstring, twisted his knee, and pulled his calf muscle. Reggie's densely muscled legs had always been prone to pulls and strains, but never had it been so bad. He would miss the World Series.

The A's would get Campaneris back, thanks to Commissioner Bowie Kuhn's decision to overturn the initial ruling, but they'd be without their best hitter. Though Reggie knew the seriousness of his injury, hearing it from the doctors devastated him. His roommate for the trip, Dave Duncan, begged him to soldier on. "You gotta play,"

Duncan told him. "For me." He broke down in tears once again as Duncan helped him into bed.

The morning of game one, Duncan and Joe Rudi had to feed the inconsolable Reggie. Then Rudi helped him put on his shoes, socks, pants, and even his underwear. As much as his leg, Reggie's depression had immobilized him. Cincinnati's Johnny Bench said kind words to him during a pre-Series workout and took him to dinner the night before game one, but nothing helped. He had for the most part thrived thus far in his postseason career, and he'd already come to believe that he was hardwired to succeed in vital situations. Reggie badly wanted to prove himself in the World Series. He wouldn't get the chance. If he couldn't have his fingerprints on the championship, then, to a part of him, the championship barely mattered.

"A's VERSUS THE Establishment" blared an *Oakland Tribune* headline on the eve of the World Series. The contrasts tantalized fans and media. On one side, you had the Cincinnati Reds, the midwestern team with close-cropped hair and the dirty-uniformed approach that embodied the Protestant work ethic. On the other side, you had the Oakland A's, the team from the cradle of subversion—the team whose members sported beards, mustaches (nineteen of them), Afros, flowing locks, plunging sideburns, vulgar uniforms, and a collective slow burn. For most of the baseball world, the A's were interlopers of the worst kind—unwelcome, unanticipated, and menacingly unsatisfied.

On crutches and out of uniform, Reggie was as dutiful as his emotions would allow. Instead of the A's wedding-gown white, Kelly green, and Fort Knox gold, Reggie wore a cream-collared shirt, plaid bell-bottoms, and high-heeled leather boots. Just before the game, he told the Cincinnati writers that the Reds' speed might be the key to the Series, especially "with my arm out of the lineup." He went on to say that the National League had "more depth, better personnel overall, and more good, young black players."

His mood lifted momentarily when, during the pregame introductions, the Cincinnati fans gave him an ovation normally reserved for the home players. In the dugout, he cheered when he was supposed to, and he was quick with encouraging words. But it was theater on his part. Reggie wanted his teammates to succeed, but now he was far less invested in that success.

The A's took the first two in Cincinnati, and on the plane back to Oakland, Finley was as ebullient as Reggie was frustrated. Finley paraded through the aisle, saw the frowning Dave Duncan, put his hand on the catcher's shoulder, and said, "I know you, David Duncan."

Reggie, sitting nearby, pounced. "I don't think you really do," he told Finley. "After we lost that second game in Detroit, Dave and I went from room to room in the hotel telling everyone that we had to stop saying 'I' and start saying 'we.' The next day we really played as a team."

Finley began to say something, but Reggie cut him off. "No, no," he said, "what I'm trying to tell you is that sometimes it pays to think about other people, to be human." There was irony in Reggie's lecture. After his injury, the proponent of "we" thought mostly in terms of "I." But Reggie so rarely interrogated his own character.

The Reds took two of the three games in Oakland, and the Series shifted back to Cincinnati as the A's clutched a 3–2 lead. The A's arrived in a dour mood because Finley had squeezed his entourage onto the four-hour flight, which meant a plane stuffed with 163 passengers. Back in Cincinnati, things grew more bizarre.

Tenace was hitting as never before. That a player of such modest repute had been terrorizing the Reds didn't sit well with some of the fans back in Ohio. In the ticket line outside Riverfront Stadium, someone overheard a man threaten, "If Tenace hits another homer, he won't walk out of this ballpark."

Soon thereafter, police arrested the thirty-two-year-old man after they found a loaded handgun and a bottle of whiskey on his person. FBI agents in unmarked cars escorted the Oakland team bus.

News of the threat and the arrest shook Tenace in the clubhouse. "If you gotta go, Geno," Reggie said, as a sort of envy tinged his words, "at least it will be on national television."

The Reds dominated game six, but Hunter pitched the A's to a 3–2 victory in the deciding game seven. Reggie took part in the club-house celebration as best he could. It was, in his own words, a "pain-ful, ambivalent" time.

The injury frustrated him, but so did his own selfishness. The physical wounds he couldn't help, he told himself. But his ungenerous reaction to the A's championship also seemed beyond the reach of his will. "The worst feeling I've ever had, as an athlete and a human being," he said the following summer, "was the day we won the World Series."

EIGHT

"Superstar, My Ass"

NOT LONG AFTER the World Series, Dick Williams announced that Reggie would be moved back to right field for the 1973 season and beyond. He hoped that a less involving position might help Reggie stay healthy. Reggie preferred the prestige of center field, but he embraced any change that would help him avoid injury. To fill the hole in center, Finley dealt reliever Bob Locker to the Cubs in exchange for a speedy young outfielder named Billy North. Finley also traded away Mike Epstein, in part because of his inability to get along with Reggie.

On February 6, Reggie signed a $60,000 contract for 1973. It was the earliest he'd ever signed. That same month, Reggie, with divorce papers in front of him, phoned Jennie. "Are you sure you want to go through with this?"

Yes, she said. They had legally separated during the 1972 season, and in a real sense they hadn't lived as husband and wife for a number of years. He signed the papers. In the settlement, Jennie received only a modest cash payoff of $75,000.

She left Tempe and worked as a bilingual educator in Fountain Valley, California. In his most guilt-ridden and lonely moments, Reggie reached out to her. He'd occasionally phone Jennie's mother and press her for details on her daughter's private life. He'd call Jennie and invite her to ball games and to have dinner with him. She resisted, knowing, more than Reggie did, that they needed a clean break. At last she asked Reggie to stop writing and calling her. Reggie obliged, but not until a sense of rejection had replaced his feelings of guilt. Those old doubts—the ones seeded by his mother's abandonment of him—returned. With women, permanency would always elude him, Reggie believed. He was his father's son, with the heritable flaws to prove it.

REGGIE HAD PUSHED himself hard in the off-season—too hard. He worked out vigorously before his leg was ready, and he injured his other leg in the process. The A's feared those injuries would confine him to the designated hitter role for the upcoming season. American League owners had ratified the DH rule, one of Finley's more inspired concoctions, and it would be in effect for the 1973 season. Reggie, however, wanted nothing to do with such a diminished role. Instead, he talked of "projecting the image of a $100,000 ballplayer."

The next offense was Finley's decision to trade Dave Duncan during the final days of camp. It was a punitive measure on Finley's part. Duncan, like Reggie, openly criticized Finley and, come contract time, was too promiscuous with his grievances. Unlike Reggie, though, Duncan was expendable. Finley sent him and George Hendrick to Cleveland for catcher Ray Fosse.

As a result of Finley's maneuvering, the Oakland lineup looked quite different on Opening Day. On April 6 at home against the Twins, the A's featured Billy North at DH, Fosse at catcher, Dal Maxvill at short (as Campaneris served his carried-over ALCS suspension), and Billy Conigliaro in center. But Bando, Rudi, Tenace, and Dick Green were still in the lineup, and Reggie was still the cleanup hitter.

EARLY IN THE 1973 season, Reggie found a neighborhood Oakland kid and some of his cousins hiding in the right-field seats before a game. They'd hopped the fence well before game time, hoping to go unnoticed and see the A's play for free. They could get into serious trouble, Reggie told them. They were respectful and frightened. Reggie told them he'd get them tickets, which he did. He gave one boy tickets to other games, and after those games Reggie drove him home.

The boy was fifteen-year-old Dave Stewart, and those days with Reggie, mere months after Stewart's father died, turned him on to baseball and the promise of rising out of the Oakland ghetto. "He treated me like a human being," Stewart said. He would go on to become one of baseball's most dominating pitchers of the late 1980s.

ON MAY 31, Reggie, on a visit to Yankee Stadium, launched a massive home run that keyed a 6–0 win. In one of the luxury boxes, the new Yankees owner, George Steinbrenner, looked on in mounting contempt. He was entertaining several old college buddies, and this wasn't how he had envisioned the afternoon. Steinbrenner made countless phone calls to manager Ralph Houk in the dugout and berated him for perceived tactical errors and ordered him to make specific moves. Once the game was out of reach, Steinbrenner resorted to other displays of power. "I got to tell you," he declared to his friends, "I'm going to get Jackson, and I'm going to get Billy Martin."

IN LATE JUNE, Reggie mashed a pair of home runs off Chicago's Wilbur Wood, and the A's moved into first place. However, he then endured an 0 for 15 slump. On the Fourth of July against the Angels, he went hitless at the plate, misplayed two balls in right, and once lost track of the count and had to be told by the umpire to take first base after the fourth ball. He was distracted, almost sleepwalking at times, and Irv Noren, one of Dick Williams's coaches, told him so.

Reggie respected Williams, but he had less respect for the coaches on Williams's staff. He viewed them as hangers-on—figures at the margins who lacked the smarts and presence to become managers. If, as a rookie, he had ignored the teachings of Joe DiMaggio, then surely Williams's underlings had nothing to offer. "Who the fuck does he think he is?" Reggie said of Noren, loud enough for all to hear.

In the clubhouse following the 3–1 loss, the press asked Reggie about the run-in. Reggie spilled. "I am sick and tired of some fucking no-account coaches on this team who badmouth players and are a pain in the ass and aren't much good for this team. I don't care what they say to me. They can't do nothing. I'll be here long after they're gone."

The writers scribbled. Reggie looked around the clubhouse, forlornly and somewhat nervously. "You got all black guys on one end and all white on the other end," he observed, apropos of nothing.

During Reggie's Oakland years, he hadn't developed the racial consciousness that would characterize him in New York. When he appealed to race, it was usually a dodge. He realized midstream that attacking his coaches was unwise, so he brought up racial fissures in the clubhouse to make the writers forget what he'd just said. It was too late. When told of Reggie's remarks, Williams struggled to be diplomatic. "I suggest to Reggie Jackson that he do the best he can in right field and leave the rest of it up to the coaches and manager."

Williams was then asked whether Reggie was above instruction. "I don't see any superstars on this team, not yet," he said. "There's some good ballplayers here, but I haven't seen any superstars yet."

Reggie thought of himself as a superstar. He wasn't the captain, but he was the best player on the best team and one of the most popular players in all of baseball. By any standard, he was a superstar, and he saw Williams's refusal to acknowledge that fact as a direct attack.

On the plane to Baltimore following the 3–1 loss, Reggie passed Williams's seat in the aisle. Williams muttered to him, "Superstar, my ass." Williams had a direct manner and a voice hardened by a two-pack-a-day smoking habit. He would leave you alone so long as you did your job but bring hell down on you if you didn't. Most players feared him. Reggie didn't.

"Hey, man," Reggie said to him. "Who the fuck are you to be talking to me like that?"

Williams cut him a hard glare.

"I've followed the damn game my whole life, and I remember when you played, and you didn't do shit," Reggie said. "So don't lay any of your sarcastic superstar shit on me. You just leave me alone from now on. You write my name down on the lineup card and leave my ass alone."

At the break, he had twenty-three homers and a slugging percentage of .534, both league-leading marks, and he made the All-Star team for the fourth time. In that All-Star Game, Catfish Hunter took a Billy Williams grounder off his pitching hand and fractured his thumb. He missed the next month. But the team responded, went 18–10 without Hunter, and extended its lead in the West. In early August, Finley suffered a heart attack, but the A's continued to play well. They did not, however, play as well as Kansas City. By the time the A's headed to New York for a critical weekend series that began on August 10, they trailed by one game in the standings. Back in Oakland, Reggie regularly played in front of fewer than 10,000 fans. Over the three-game set in the Bronx, however, more than 100,000 turned out. He responded with his best series of the season.

In the first game, he homered twice, but the Yankees won 10–9 and dropped Oakland to two games back in the West. In the second game, a 7–3 A's win, Reggie went 3 for 4 with a walk and a double. In the series finale, he launched his twenty-seventh homer of the season and once again went 3 for 4. The A's erased a six-run deficit to beat the Yankees 13–12. "There's something about playing in this city that means excitement," Reggie said. "It brings out the best."

Near the end of the month, Hunter returned from the disabled list, and the A's kept fighting, often in the literal sense. Billy North touched off one brawl with the Royals' Kurt Bevacqua, and days later, before Reggie could intervene, he was almost pummeled by former Athletic Mike Epstein. North brought a fiery style to the A's that everyone appreciated, except for Reggie. Daring on the bases and an irritant to opponents, he made the A's a better team. But Reggie believed North had co-opted his way of playing the game. Reggie was the hard-charging igniter who played with "black style." He wanted no company. He appreciated North's contributions, but he resented what he thought was the derivative nature of his play.

Next came a trip to Texas and another low point for the A's. The Rangers swept the series, and Reggie once again pulled a muscle in his hamstring. He missed the next week, and he wasn't in the lineup on a regular basis until September 22. By that point, though, the A's had wrapped up a third straight division title.

As his injury healed, Reggie asked Williams to put him in the lineup at designated hitter so that he might stay within hailing distance of Willie Stargell and the major-league lead in RBIs. However, Finley, recovering from his heart episode but still calling the shots, forbade Williams to do so. Reggie took it personally. Soon, though, he had far more serious concerns.

In September, Reggie was summoned, cryptically, to the Coliseum to meet with a group of FBI agents. The agents told him that A's announcer Monte Moore had received a threat on Reggie's life. The letter said that if Reggie played in the ALCS or the World Series, he would be killed. The letter was signed by "The Weathermen." The Weathermen, or the Weather Underground, as they later became known, was a front group of Communist subversives. The group had formed during the Vietnam War and became an expert purveyor of domestic terrorism. The Weathermen had allegedly been involved in a number of high-profile bombings, including attacks on the Pentagon, the Capitol Building, and, earlier in 1973, the NYPD's 103rd Precinct. Later that same month, they attacked ITT corporate headquarters in New York and Rome, a response to the company's involvement with the U.S.-backed coup in Chile. None of that, however, explained why they'd want to take the life of a baseball player. The news harrowed Reggie. After the political assassinations of the 1960s, it took little to unsettle someone in the public eye.

At Reggie's urging, the FBI assigned to him a hulking bodyguard named Tony Del Rio, one of Reggie's neighborhood friends from Oakland. They also told him to be more vigilant in his daily activities—activities that included playing baseball in front of thousands of faceless fans. He was an easy target.

As the regular season drew to a close, Billy North tore ligaments in his ankle and missed the rest of the year. So Williams asked Reggie to man center field against Baltimore in the ALCS. However, Reggie, whose leg still wasn't fully healed, was stricken with flu before the series started.

While the rest of the A's worried about who would play center, Reggie worried about the death threat and the possibility of again missing the postseason. Reggie's status in doubt, Williams tabbed Angel Mangual as the starter in center field. However, Mangual, who hadn't played regularly since he'd fallen out of favor with Williams the previous year, took umbrage at being put in—as he saw it—a position to fail. He asked to be traded. As though that weren't enough discord, Finley bumped a number of players' wives—and his pitching coach and equipment manager—from the charter flight to Baltimore so he'd have room for his cronies.

The A's, angry and compromised, made it to Baltimore. In game one, Jim Palmer schooled them with a five-hit shutout. Reggie, who played despite his healing leg and a high fever, managed the only hard-hit ball. In game two, Catfish Hunter picked up the win after he allowed three runs over 7.1 innings. Rain delayed game three back in Oakland. Ken Holtzman spun a gem, and the A's won it in the eleventh on a Campaneris home run. In game four, the A's knocked out Palmer early, and Blue pitched well throughout the early innings. However, he fell apart in the seventh and frittered away what had been a 4–0 Oakland lead. Baltimore pushed another run across in the eighth and won 5–4. In the deciding game five, Hunter established himself as the star of the series. He struck out only one Oriole all day, but he went the distance in a 3–0 Oakland win.

In the clubhouse, the customary ebullience was mixed with relief. The champagne flowed, Finley's Dixieland band blared, and Reggie waxed joyful. "Fabulous, fabulous!" he said. "This is what life's all about, playing under pressure and producing, winning when you have to win."

Reggie had hit just .143 in the ALCS. His performance thus far in the play-offs stood at odds with the notion that he was a clutch performer. He'd pounded the ball in the 1971 ALCS, but the A's had lost. They'd won the ALCS the following year and in 1973, but Reggie had contributed little to the victories. The numbers needed to match the bluster, and Reggie knew it.

The rest of the night, he tooled around San Francisco's North Beach with his date and eventually wound up behind two slow-moving motorcycle cops. Reggie, restless from the events of the day, laid on his horn a few times. The cops checked him out, realized who it was, and motioned for him to pull over. They discovered that Reggie had two outstanding warrants for traffic violations, which, they told him, totaled $82. "I'm Reggie Jackson," he said. "I don't have to pay."

They placed him under arrest. Reggie argued, dangled his celebrity to no avail, and at last went peacefully, but not without some caustic words for the arresting officers. It was unwise for a black man in the early 1970s to stand up to police. Bay Area law enforcement had had a strained relationship with the black community at least since 1966, when the Black Panther Party had been formed in part to combat police brutality. However, even after his experiences in Birmingham, Reggie had quick limits with authority. After three hours in the city jail, he was bailed out and resumed his night.

THE NEW YORK Mets were unlikely opponents. They'd sneaked into the play-offs with a mere eighty-two wins, and in the NLCS they'd upset the ninety-nine-win Cincinnati Reds in five games. They'd won with starting pitchers: Tom Seaver, Jerry Koosman, and Jon Matlack. In 1973, Seaver had paced the NL in ERAs and strike-outs. "Blind people come to the park just to hear him pitch," Reggie said of him.

Reggie wanted to strike a blow against the organization that he claimed had wronged him, and he relished the chance to play against his baseball idol, Willie Mays, who drudged through his final season. Reggie and the A's were the better team, but the vagaries of the post-season so often got in the way of expectations.

The A's had only one day off before the Mets arrived in Oakland for the start of the World Series. The Oakland fans reserved their loudest hosannas for Mays, the fading luminary, but the sight of their beloved A's and the bicoastal hostilities made their allegiances clear.

In game one, Reggie played center field for the first time all sea-son. It was a pitcher's duel. Both bull pens dominated, and Reggie went hitless at the plate. But he announced himself through his glove work. In the fourth, with one out and the tying run in scoring posi-tion, the Mets' Jerry Grote smote a line drive to deep center. Reggie, relying on, as he said later, "no shortcuts, no science, no guessing," dashed as hard as he could and snatched the ball on the warning track. Ken Holtzman worked his way out of the inning, and the A's went on to win, 2–1.

With the A's, though, there was always a tempest. Fresh off the white-knuckled win over the Mets in the opener and unwinding in the clubhouse, Reggie and his teammates learned that their manager, wearied by Finley's heavy hand, might leave after the Series to manage the New York Yankees. Williams told them the rumors weren't true. But playing for Finley meant you were duty-bound to expect the worst.

WILLIE MAYS HAD once been the quintessence of boyish grace. But by 1973 he was nothing of the sort—he was lumbering, paunchy, unsure, methodical by necessity. In game two of the World Series, he fell several times in the field and once took an embarrassing spill while he chased a ball hit by Reggie. Reggie watched on as Mays soiled his memories of him, as did the fans who remembered Mays in the same sepia tones. Game two, though, was difficult beyond the struggles of a fading idol. During the contest, the two teams set World Series single-game records for game length (four hours, thirteen minutes) and players used (thirty-eight). The A's came back from two down to tie the game in the ninth, only to lose it 10–7 in twelve innings. Most troubling was that they lost the game in the field. Bando, Tenace, and Darold Knowles each made errors, and reserve infielder Mike Andrews committed two of his own. Reggie went 4 for 6 with a double and a triple, but his efforts were scarcely noticed that day.

The team's sloppy, lazy performance enraged Finley. He was especially angry with Andrews, whose pair of errors allowed the Mets to score three critical runs. Before the Series began, Finley had petitioned the Mets and the league to be allowed to add infielder Manny Trillo to the roster, but they had rebuffed him. Andrews's struggles in game two heightened Finley's sense of injustice.

Finley ordered the team doctor to examine Andrews. Dr. Harry Walker poked and prodded at Andrews and diagnosed him with "biceps groove tenosynovitis of the right shoulder." So serious was the injury that, according to Walker's signed statement, Andrews was "disabled for the rest of the year."

Andrews protested that he felt fine; he'd just screwed up. "I'm the goat, and I'm sorry as hell about it," he'd told reporters after the game. But Finley leaned on Andrews to sign the statement and told him that doing so was necessary to "help the club." If he didn't sign it, Finley admonished, he would never play another game in the major leagues. Andrews, stunned and fearful of what Finley could do to him, signed the piece of paper in front of him, even as he mumbled, "There's nothing wrong with me."

As the news crept through the clubhouse, Dick Williams called them together. "This is the last straw," he promised his players. Andrews's teammates were no less angry. His misplays had been critical, but they had committed three other errors, Blue had pitched poorly, and Campaneris and Fosse had combined to go 1 for 11 at the plate. Game two was a team loss, not a Mike Andrews loss.

When they boarded the plane for New York, Andrews's absence was conspicuous. As angry as the A's players were over the treatment of Andrews, Finley would soon raise their ire further. The Mets had traveled to Oakland on two charter planes, one for the team and one for families. The A's, however, journeyed to New York with players, staff, executives, and families all on a single 727. So crowded was the flight that Reggie sat in one of the flight attendants' jump seats. By the time the plane landed several hours later, the defending world champs were in a state of near mutiny.

As the union rep, Reggie was obligated to see to it that things changed. At his urging, the A's wrote Andrews's number 17 on strips of black tape and wore them on their sleeves during the off-day work-out at Shea Stadium. Reggie then told reporters he'd file a grievance with the Major League Baseball Players Association on Andrews's behalf. He wasn't done. "There is a possibility of refusing to play," Reggie told the New York *Daily News.* "There are a bunch of guys who are close to that point."

That night, Finley faced the media and told them that Andrews was indeed disabled and that he hoped to replace him on the roster. Specifically, he hoped to replace him with Manny Trillo.

Commissioner Kuhn, no ally of Finley, turned down his request and ordered Andrews to be returned to the World Series roster. Before game three, Andrews called Reggie in the A's clubhouse and relayed his version of events. "We'd love to have you back," Reggie told him. "Sometimes all of us have to be men and stand up to Finley on this kind of thing."

Dick Williams gathered the players and told them, on orders, Finley's side of the story. "I'm going to deny this if it leaks out of this room," Williams said in conclusion, "but I'm resigning after the Series, win, lose, or draw."

The A's players, though not surprised by the news, were crushed. In the view of Reggie and the others, Williams had taken them from unrealized potential to greatness. Considering the replacement who would surely follow—a Finley toady disinclined to resist him—Williams wouldn't be missed, he would be mourned.

More than 54,000 fans attended game three, which made it the largest crowd Reggie had ever played in front of. By then he'd also learned that New York was the city in which the Weathermen had perpetrated so much of their violence. With that fear lodged in the back of his mind and against the vintage Tom Seaver, he went 0 for 5 on the day. But the A's won thanks to the bull pen's five scoreless innings and Campaneris's RBI single in the eleventh.

After the game, Williams parried questions about his future, and Andrews, by then in New York, held a tear-sodden press conference and talked about what Finley had done to him. Reggie was asked whether Finley's recent actions had had anything to do with the A's win. "We win in spite of him," he said. "He's a financial empire and that's all. That's all I respect about him. It's too bad he doesn't use his money to help humanity."

A reporter then asked whether Finley had ever mistreated him on racial grounds. Certainly he had, Reggie believed. He ran the team like a plantation owner, he referred to black players as "boys"—Finley knew how to play racialist games. And Reggie, as the only player who had regular contact with the owner, knew that all too well. But Reggie resisted the urge to attack him, at least during the World Series. "To him, all people are the same color," Reggie said. "Green."

Game four belonged to Jon Matlack, the young Mets lefty who tamed Oakland for the first eight innings of a 6–1 win. The weather for game five was brutally cold, and the Oakland bats were in a similar state of chill. Jerry Koosman and Tug McGraw combined to limit the A's to three hits and no runs on the evening. For Oakland, the only highlight was when the flagellated Andrews was announced as a pinch hitter in the eighth. The capacity crowd at Shea greeted him with a standing ovation that lasted long enough to embarrass the light-hitting bench player. After Andrews grounded out, they again cheered him like a conquering hero as he returned to the Oakland dugout. Their sudden love for Andrews was really hate for Finley, but Finley, who cheered right along with them from his box, seemed oblivious to their true motives.

Reggie took joy in none of it. Koosman and McGraw held him hitless, and his average for the Series dropped to .238. Up to that point, he'd also abandoned seventeen runners on base. Besides the absurd strains and pressures that marked life under Finley, Reggie was failing in his first chance to play in a World Series. He labored to overcome the distractions as a critical matchup with Seaver loomed. "I'm a man split in two," he said upon the team's return to Oakland. "Half of me is trying to think about Mike Andrews, the other half is trying to think about Tom Seaver."

The sports pages back in the East Bay were mostly devoted to the A's familiar spot on the precipice, but they also relayed rumors that Finley planned to sell his team—rumors that Finley denied with biblical vigor. Even with the possibility of back-to-back championships, the city clamored for local ownership. It would never happen, Finley threatened. As the A's warmed up at the Coliseum, all about them—as much a part of the scene as the play-off bunting—were homemade banners that blistered Finley. KEEP A'S, TRADE

FINLEY read one. A'S FANS FOR OWNERSHIP. A MILLION FANS CAN'T BE WRONG blared another. WE LOVE OUR A'S BUT GO HOME FINLEY went still another.

Before the game, Reggie was the only Oakland player to refuse all interviews. Instead, he took extra batting practice with the Oakland reserves. Throughout his career, he hit much better in day games than he did at night. The light of day allowed him to pick up the seams of the ball much more easily, and the generally warmer temperatures helped his flexibility. As he worked to stay back and hit the ball up the middle, he felt better and sensed a new precision in his habits. The warm California sunshine renewed him.

Catfish Hunter bobbed into and out of trouble in the first but escaped without giving up a run. In the home half, Joe Rudi sprayed an outside fastball for a single. Reggie came up with two outs. With his first pitch, Seaver aimed inside with a fastball but left it over the plate. Reggie turned on it and lashed a sinking liner to the gap in left center. He steamed into second base, and Rudi scored the first run of the game.

Hunter settled down, and Seaver tamed the bottom of the Oakland order in the second. In the bottom of the third, Bando singled, and Reggie came to the plate once again with a runner on first and two outs. Seaver's first pitch tailed away from Reggie. But Reggie waited until the last instant to fire his hips. He went with the outside pitch and thumped it to right center. It landed in front of Rusty Staub. As Reggie dashed out of the box, he recalled the scouting report on Staub. The right fielder's shoulder was so sore that he had to throw underhanded. Bando had the same thought and chugged around the diamond without even looking up at the third-base coach. Staub all but rolled the ball to cutoff man Felix Millan, who bobbled the ball before he heaved it home. Bando slid under Jerry Grote's tag, and the A's were up 2–0.

Seaver gutted through the next few innings despite lacking his best stuff, and Hunter continued to dominate. In the eighth, though,

Hunter gave up a one-out single to pinch hitter Ken Boswell, and Williams beckoned Darold Knowles from the pen. Knowles surrendered back-to-back singles, and the Mets scored their first run. Staub, representing the tying run, came to bat. Knowles, mindful of Staub's crippled shoulder, pumped two fastballs on the outside corner and then came high and inside for strike three. Rollie Fingers came on to retire Cleon Jones with one pitch.

In the home half of the inning, McGraw took over for the Mets. Reggie lined a single to center, which Don Hahn overran. Reggie ran hard out of the box and wound up on third. Two batters later, pinch hitter Jesus Alou lifted a fly to left, and Reggie tagged up and hustled home for a crucial insurance run. Fingers worked a perfect ninth, and Oakland prevailed 3–1 to force a deciding game seven.

Jon Matlack, the Mets' starter in the finale, cruised through the first two innings, as did Ken Holtzman. In the third inning, Holtzman hit an unlikely one-out double, and Campaneris followed with a home run to deep right field. Rudi singled, and Bando popped out to second. Reggie was next. The afternoon sun all but blinded him, but Matlack hung a curveball. Reggie leaped at it. He stood at the plate and watched the ball for every moment of its flight. When the ball finally landed in the distant right-center-field bleachers, Reggie jogged around the bases. He reached home, jumped, and stomped on the plate. Oakland led, 4–0.

The Mets pushed a run across in the sixth and threatened again in the ninth, when John Milner walked to lead off the inning. Two batters later, Hahn singled to right. Tenace then misplayed a grounder, and the Mets cut the lead to 5–2. Williams lifted Fingers in favor of Darold Knowles. As Knowles warmed up, a man scurried over the outfield fence and snatched Reggie's hat off his head. The stunned Reggie gave chase, but then a female fan dropped into the outfield grass and stole his glove. Only after Reggie's equipment had been returned to him and he'd reclaimed his position did he remember the death threat. The chaos inside the Coliseum grew, and Reggie just wanted to get the final out and get off the field. Wayne Garrett lifted an easy pop-up. It settled into the sure glove of Campaneris in shallow left field, and the A's were champions again.

Seconds after the final out, Reggie's bodyguard rushed onto the field, dodged the Oakland fans who had poured in, and lifted Reggie off the ground. Fans tore off clumps of grass and unmoored the bases. Near the celebration at the mound, two fans attacked Holtzman and cut his chin and nose. Reggie and his bodyguard hustled to the safety of the clubhouse. Once there, he made for the nearest reporter. "Please don't give Finley credit," Reggie pleaded. "That takes away from what the guys in this dressing room have done."

Such uncommon pressures—the death threat, the Andrews controversy—made Reggie's performance against the Mets that much more impressive. He'd hit .310, slugged .586, and paced the Oakland attack in games six and seven. Still celebrating with his teammates, Reggie was told he'd been named MVP of the Series by *Sport* magazine. "I was just trying to live up to what you guys were writing, to what you guys said I should be doing," he said. "Superstars are supposed to hit, and I wasn't."

As part of the honors, Chrysler gave Reggie a new Dodge Charger, which he later donated to a Chicano and Yaqui Indian community organization back in Arizona. Yet some believed the honor should have gone to Campaneris. Among them was the influential columnist Dick Young. "In this phony commercial world of ours," he wrote in the pages of the New York *Daily News*, "Reggie Jackson, who had two good games, wins the MVP car instead of Bert Campaneris, who had seven good games. Do you know why? Because Reggie Jackson is great copy."

Diplomatically enough, Reggie agreed with Young. "Hell, I've got six cars now," he said. "I'd have voted for Campaneris." In reality, Reggie had outproduced Campaneris in the Series and was a worthy MVP selection.

Soon enough, though, Reggie focused on his outgoing manager.

Good-byes made a saccharine lump of Reggie, and he quickly pardoned—or forgot—all the things he didn't like about Dick Williams. "You taught me how to win," he gushed and then planted a kiss on Williams's cheek. "I'm sorry you're leaving."

"He doesn't play favorites," he then said of Williams to the media, who recognized it might not be a compliment coming from a player like Reggie. "But he likes you better if you are hard-nosed. If you are a candy-ass, you may have trouble making this team."

Candy-asses were indeed nowhere to be found on the Oakland A's. The night of the clinching victory, the alcohol flowed, and Reggie and the drunken and combative Blue Moon Odom had to be pulled apart at a late-night Oakland diner.

NOT LONG AFTER Reggie won World Series MVP, the writers voted him MVP of the American League for 1973. His selection was unanimous and made him just the sixth player in AL history to sweep the balloting. Appropriately, he succeeded Dick Allen as the AL honoree.

In 1964, Reggie's senior year in high school, he'd followed the nearby Phillies as they had barreled toward one of the most agonizing stretch drives baseball would ever see. The city was still reeling from riots in the city's black neighborhoods, and the team blew a six-and-a-half-game lead with twelve to play. In the torture of it all most of the city's fans and writers would blame the team's young, black, and vocal star, Dick Allen.

As the Phillies' hopes died, the hometown fans ritually called Allen a "monkey," a "darkie," and a "dirty nigger," and in later seasons they threw trash, coins, and batteries at him as he took his position in the field—to the extent that Allen wore a batting helmet at all times. Some of Reggie's father's customers' North Philadelphia businesses were looted and burned to the ground in the riots, and Reggie heard his white friends mourn the entangled fates of Dick Allen and the Phillies and lament that the blacks in the city were allowed to run wild. Eventually, Allen's circumstances, skills, and complicated bearing would invite comparisons to another rising black star: Reggie Jackson.

The comparisons persisted, sometimes on their merits and sometimes as a way to impugn both of them. "I like Allen as a person and admire him as a ballplayer," Reggie once said of the man he'd once watched from the left-field bleachers—the "colored" section—of Connie Mack Stadium. "But I'm not trying to be like him."

Early in Reggie's career, Allen had counseled him to "not let anyone fuck with your ability" and to "get your money from them." Reggie was already living Allen's advice, but hearing it from the man he called "the boss among blacks" riveted him to those principles.

Both Reggie and Allen were accomplished black sluggers who hailed from Pennsylvania. Both had grown up relatively uninjured by prejudice, both had been seared by their time in the Jim Crow South as minor leaguers, and both had the reputation of being combative and—in the racist parlance of the day—"uppity." During his days with the Phillies, Allen clashed with his managers, traded barbs with the racially callous Philadelphia media, smoked cigarettes in the dugout, missed games because he was drunk, and came to blows with a white teammate, Frank Thomas. Not until Allen landed in Chicago and played for a manager, Chuck Tanner, who didn't attempt to "tame" him, did he achieve a psychic calm. He won the MVP in 1972, and Allen's White Sox finished with the second best record in the AL. Still, the narrative in the press was that black individualism, of which Allen had plenty, harmed the team dynamic.

Reggie, like Allen, became a nationally recognized superstar, but, unlike Allen, his teams won. While Allen had broken from the old black models just as furiously as Reggie did, Reggie's success and his team's success in the World Series truly changed things for black ballplayers. Reggie conquered the idea that a black man, in order for his team to win, must be grateful, obliging, and content to remain in the shadows. The A's not only won it all, but they won it all helmed by a black leader who, as Reggie would say of himself a few years later, didn't know how to be subservient. The comparisons with Allen, a great player victimized early in his career by the times and by an unenlightened city, held up no more. Neither did the effort to make black ballplayers conform to the molds of the past.

Reggie Jackson was baseball's New Black Man.

NINE

"My Objective Right Now Is Money"

DIVORCED FROM JENNIE and living alone, Reggie spent the winter of 1973 in Tempe. He and Gary Walker worked tirelessly on their real estate business. Most major-league players whiled away their winters fishing, working out, and spending time with their families. Reggie, though, had no family, and after being at the mercy of Finley for so long, he was determined to build wealth outside of baseball.

By 1977, his share of United Development, the company he founded with Walker, would be worth roughly $9 million, and the company would have more than $40 million in landholdings. In his Oakland days, he boasted six cars (one of them a cherished Porsche with plates that read "MVP 73"), two hundred sport coats, more than two dozen leather jackets, a hundred pairs of shoes, a jungle of exotic houseplants, paintings, a personal secretary, more than $100,000 in annual income from United Development, and regular cash from endorsements and a pair of car dealerships he'd opened in California. It wasn't enough.

Back in Oakland, Finley announced that his failing health would force him to get out of the business. He was entertaining offers not only for the A's but also for his hockey team, the California Seals, and his basketball team, the Memphis Tams. Reggie delighted in the news. He could now envision the end of his days under Finley, and he also saw an opportunity. As he matured, his interests drifted from the playing side of sports to the business side. He wanted to own a team. Now that Finley was apparently headed for divestiture, Reggie might have his chance. But Finley turned down his offer for the Tams. There would be other chances, Reggie told himself.

Instead, he bought a new home. It was a luxurious condo that covered almost 3,000 square feet. Positioned above the Bay, where hardscrabble Oakland locked eyes with tawny San Francisco, Reggie's latest digs afforded gaping views on the rare clear days. It sat on "Yankee Hill."

AS EVER, REGGIE was ready for a contract fight. Finley had already agreed to terms with most of the roster, but Reggie once again proved to be a difficult sign. Finally Reggie and Finley took their cases before an arbitration panel.

In 1974, salary arbitration was new to baseball. After a player had accumulated two years of major-league service time, he was eligible to have salary impasses resolved by an independent arbitrator. In baseball, the process was binding: each side presented a figure, and the arbitrators chose one or the other—no splitting the difference or choosing some other number. The idea was to give both sides an incentive to negotiate and, failing that, to force them to submit realistic salary proposals. As with most innovations, some consequences were unintended. In particular, the exercise—defending the proposed salary to the arbitrators—forced ownership to denigrate its own players. To make the case that his offer was the fairer of the two, the owner had to prove why the player didn't deserve the money for which he was asking. Doing so added even more acrimony to a process already sodden with it.

A number of A's headed to arbitration with Finley, and Reggie, the freshly minted World Series and AL MVP, was foremost among them. Reggie defined himself by his salary, and now he had new heights in mind. "One hundred Gs is like the sun coming up. It's sure. I'll go past it," he said of his upcoming hearing against Finley. "My objective right now is money. I want money because I want the titles that go underneath: leader, professional, man, and winner."

Finley submitted a figure of $100,000 for the 1974 season, while Reggie asked for $135,000, which constituted a $65,000 raise over his 1973 salary. Reggie's side—which was comprised of his two New York–based advisers—pointed to his undeniable statistical accomplishments and his pair of MVP awards. Frank Robinson, Jim Palmer, and Dave Duncan also testified on Reggie's behalf. Finley, meanwhile, showed up alone and unprepared. He rebutted that *someone* had to win those awards and that Reggie was "a lousy MVP." In the end, the panel that had convened at the Sheraton Palace Hotel in San Francisco sided with Reggie, presumably with little deliberation.

Afterward, Finley ignored questions about Reggie's historic victory, easily the largest sum to date awarded in arbitration and one that made Reggie the most highly paid player in franchise history. Instead, Finley reiterated that his doctors were imploring him to sell the team. "It will break my heart if I have to get out of baseball," he said. "But if I have to get out to live, I will."

Soon after, Finley learned that a federal judge in Oakland had sided with him in a breach-of-contract suit he'd filed against Dick Williams. The judge enjoined Williams from managing any other team until his contract with the A's expired in 1975. The verdict vindicated Finley, but he was still without a manager.

Early on, the press floated Frank Robinson's name as a possible replacement for Williams. Reggie had fond memories of his time in Puerto Rico under Robinson, and he knew it was long past time for

baseball to have a black manager. Robinson, like Williams, was exacting and tough but aware of the personalities in play. A manager was
as much psychologist as tactician, and few were adept at both roles.
Robinson, Reggie thought, was one of those rare men.

Yet Reggie feared for him in Oakland. Robinson was poised to
become baseball's first black manager, and Reggie wanted him to have
the best chance for success. In Oakland, he'd be following Williams
and his triumphs, and he'd be striving for the impossible and mutable
standards of Charlie Finley. It was the wrong place for Robinson,
Reggie determined. "Robby has too much class to manage for Charlie
Finley," he said.

The more he mulled it over, though, the more Reggie came to
believe that even an imperfect opportunity should not be squandered.
The important thing was breaking through—getting baseball past
the notion that a black man wasn't equipped to manage. He changed
course. "Both Frank and Dick [Williams] are similar in personality
and in handling people," Reggie said while the managerial search carried on. "Now I think all the class he has might be what he needs to
manage our club."

Robinson belonged to the Angels at the time, but Finley angled
to acquire him as player-manager. "Knowing Charlie Finley, it's possible that Frank Robinson could be hired," Reggie, with barely concealed optimism, told a reporter for *Black Sports* magazine. "Finley
wants to be first in everything, and the fact that he likes publicity
wouldn't hurt, either."

Eventually, though, Finley settled on the uninspiring Alvin
Dark. Dark had managed for Finley before, unsuccessfully, and he
had a complicated history when it came to working with players of
color. Dark had once had a rather famous temper—he'd once torn off
a finger in the midst of a clubhouse tantrum—but in the intervening
years, he'd left his wife for a comely young flight attendant and found
religion. Previously one to rage at things beyond his control, Dark
was now a scripture-quoting study in equanimity. More important

to Finley was that he knew his place. "Yes, he was hired by me to manage the A's in 1966. Yes, he was fired by me in 1967," Finley said at Dark's introductory press conference, with his new manager at his side. "Yes, I hired him again at midnight last night. Yes, he expects to be fired again someday."

When asked about the prospect of working for a tyrant like Finley, Dark summoned biblical wisdom. "Exhort servants to be obedient to their own masters," he intoned, "and to please them well in all things, not answering back."

Finley had found his man.

Meanwhile, Finley's decision to pass over Frank Robinson disappointed Reggie, and he was grimly aware of Dark's history. "We have trouble because we have so many Spanish-speaking and Negro players on the team," Dark had told Stan Isaacs of *Newsday* when he managed the Giants in the early 1960s. "They are just not able to perform up to the white ballplayer when it comes to mental alertness."

Dark claimed that his comments had been distorted. But Orlando Cepeda said Dark had banned Spanish conversation from the clubhouse, assigned lockers based on race, and often blamed black and Latin players for the team's struggles. In 1967, when Dark had first managed the A's, Blue Moon Odom had accused him of racism after he demoted the young pitcher, seemingly without cause. Justified or not, Dark's reputation followed him like a shadow.

Above all, though, the reconstructed Dark obeyed. "Charlie Finley is the owner and general manager of this team, and he'll be calling me and telling me things he wants me to do," he told his players early in spring training. "I'll put up with the phone calls as long as I can, and I'll do what he wants."

Reggie had heard it all before. "Fuck Charlie Finley," he said, loud enough for all to hear. "We'll win it again anyway."

Within days, Reggie and the A's had other things to grouse about; namely, their championship rings. The new rings, unlike their predecessors in 1972, were adorned with small, synthetic gemstones, not a diamond to be found. Finley had promised them better rings if they repeated in 1973. Reggie told the press that the rings were "trash" and accused Finley of exacting revenge for their "protest over the Mike Andrews thing." His teammates were similarly uncharitable. Finley said Reggie and the others were "ingrates."

"Screw 'em," Finley said. "The next time we win, I won't give them a thing."

The rings controversy faded when, just prior to Opening Day, the issue became shoes. Adidas paid Finley a handsome sum to make his players wear its baseball cleats. However, Reggie, who had worked hard to cash in on endorsements after his double MVP season, had his own shoe contract with Puma, one that paid him $30,000 to wear Pumas on the field for three seasons. Finley called Reggie and ordered him to wear Adidas. Reggie said no. Reggie then offered free Pumas to any teammate who agreed to wear them. A few of the A's took him up on his offer.

Once Finley learned of the insurrection, he phoned Dark and told him to order the players to wear Adidas or suffer his punitive wrath. "This is both trivial and typical," Reggie said. "I'm not going to wear Adidas under any circumstances."

Reggie had taken the care and feeding of his personal fortune seriously, and as wealthy as he was thanks to his baseball salary, his endorsements, and his real estate business, it all felt tenuous and fleeting to him. His father's struggles with money and stories of the Depression had made Reggie fear he'd lose it all in an instant. He had side opportunities in Oakland—pitching General Mills products on occasion, a yearly free car from Doten Pontiac, an offer (not accepted) to pose nude in *Playgirl*—but Reggie knew he'd earn substantially more if he played in L.A. or New York. That's why he took Finley's money games so seriously. As he came to see it, when Finley haggled with him over his contract or showed little regard for his private business arrangements, he was trying to force Reggie back into a state of need.

When the season opened on April 4 in Texas, Reggie wore his Pumas. Finley lied that he'd decided to allow Reggie to wear his shoes of choice for this one game. After Reggie went 4 for 5 with a home run, two doubles, and a stolen base, Finley relented. "He has my permission to play barefooted if he wants to," he said.

Once the A's returned to Oakland for the home opener, the mutual pettiness continued. Reggie disparaged the groundskeeping at the Coliseum, and Finley told the players that when they responded to fan mail they must pay for their own postage. As well, the A's comely, hot-pants-wearing ball girls, many of whom Reggie had casually dated, were no more. Finley even refused to hang a banner recognizing the championship his players had won the previous season. And then he concocted a money-saving plan to have resting pitchers provide color commentary on the A's television broadcasts.

Their opponents in the home opener were, once again, Billy Martin's Texas Rangers. In the second game of the series, Reggie homered early and came up again in the eighth with the A's down 2–1. With Billy North on third and Bando on second, Reggie expected to be walked so the right-handed Steve Hargan could face the right-handed Joe Rudi. Instead, Martin ordered his pitcher to challenge Reggie. Reggie's responded with a three-run homer that proved to be the game-winning hit. "I don't know whether they don't respect me or whether they don't think I'm that good," he wondered after the game.

Reggie ended the month of April with ten homers and a slugging percentage of .872. He was hitting, but the team was losing. Some of Dark's early managerial bungles—he'd shown an untimely touch with the bull pen and a disregard for structure—provided a convenient target. Reggie, still mindful of Dark's comments while in San Francisco, also saw an opportunity to strike a blow for those Dark had offended. "I don't think we're executing the fundamentals well," he said. "There has to be some discipline on this club, and Dark doesn't do it."

No mastery of basic baseball and a lack of order—it was the most ruthless way to assail a manager. Reggie continued, "He could give us all hell sometimes, right out in the open. If you screw up, he should let you know it right away."

Pleased with his own performance but frustrated with the state of things in Oakland, Reggie made a jarring announcement: the New York franchise of the forthcoming World Baseball League had made overtures to him. A desire to prove himself in a larger environment, to give full expression to his gifts, was growing in Reggie. That meant playing in New York. Nothing came of Reggie's threat to jump to the fledgling league, but his longing persisted.

In early May, Dark discussed with Reggie whether he should return the injured Sal Bando to the lineup. Dark said he hesitated to use Bando right away, even as the DH. "Hell, Alvin," Reggie said, "I'm coming back from an injury, and you've been using me as a designated hitter."

"Well, look, I can talk to you, and you understand," Dark said to Reggie. "Just between you and me, we know black boys heal faster than white boys."

Reggie was less shocked by the words than he was by Dark's comfort in saying them to him. *I can talk to you. You understand.* Dark saw him as some sort of fellow traveler. *Why can you talk to me about this? Why do you think I understand?* he wanted to ask. Instead, he looked blankly at Dark, walked away, and allowed the awkwardness to speak for him.

In the middle of May, Reggie suffered yet another leg injury, and he missed the next six games. In his absence, the A's slipped from first place. While he healed, Reggie took note from afar of the new dynamics at play. The core of the A's was still there and still behaved in character: Bando, Rudi, Hunter, Blue, Odom, and the rest. However, Dark had brought lawlessness to the team. It wasn't so much freedom granted as freedom pilfered—pilfered from a leader who lacked the guts to resist. Reggie sensed in some of the newer A's—Billy North in particular—a lack of deference to the ones who'd been in the organization since the leaner years.

Not until early June did Reggie's healing leg allow him to return to right field. On his first day back, he clouted a pair of home runs. Appropriately, the latest issue of *Time* magazine—one with his face on the cover—was released, adorned by the headline "One-Man Wild Bunch: Oakland's Reggie Jackson." A week later, *Sports Illustrated* made Reggie its cover model, and called him, in the most authoritative of fonts, a "SUPER-DUPERSTAR."

It should have been a good time to be Reggie Jackson. He was building another exceptional season, the A's were back in first place, and he'd earned national attention. Yet the mood in the clubhouse troubled him. Mostly, Billy North troubled him.

When Finley had acquired North prior to the 1973 season, Reggie had felt an affinity for the younger black outfielder. North had grown up poor in Seattle. He'd picked beans to help his family get by and played pickup baseball in supermarket parking lots. When he'd hit the majors, he'd been a speedy, slick-fielding center fielder and, like Reggie, a malcontent. He'd previously been with the Cubs, but after he'd threatened to quit and become a schoolteacher unless he received more playing time, Finley had swooped in and traded for him.

Reggie and North became fast friends. They hung out socially after games and spent time together during the off-season in Arizona, where they both lived. In spring training, they'd have breakfast together each morning and carpool to the ballpark. In time, though, North noticed that Reggie dated exclusively white women—Finley's white ball girls, white "bunnies" from the Playboy Club in San Francisco, and on occasion a white editor from a television station in Phoenix, among others. "Living black, sleeping white," other players said of Reggie.

Reggie also consorted for the most part with white friends and surrounded himself with white business associates. He even shared his apartment and his clothes with a white teammate, John Summers.

Whereas in later years other black teammates, particularly players such as Willie Randolph, Chris Chambliss, and Roy White on the Yankees, saw Reggie as merely an overpaid loudmouth who hurt their standing by association, North came to regard him as something more noxious: a racial compromiser who refused to invest in his own blackness.

By this time, blacks were well established in the major leagues, but a certain level of segregation still existed. Black, Latin, and white players generally consorted with their own kind, so North was upset to find that Reggie shunned his teammates of color, even openly criticized them. This was tantamount to betrayal. "There are 200 million people in this country and 180 million of them are white," Reggie once said. "It's only natural that most of my friends are white."

Reggie needed to be liked, and when he wasn't it confused and obsessed him. So it was with North. Early in the season, he scolded North, loudly and in full view of the rest of the team, for not hustling. "You're not Number Five," North spat back, referring to manager Alvin Dark. "I only take orders from Number Five." Later, North told Reggie never to speak to him again. After each of Reggie's next ten home runs, North refused to shake his hand.

The disloyalty of it all bothered North the most. He was not alone. The other black players on the A's—Blue Moon Odom and Vida Blue, specifically—harbored occasional resentment toward Reggie. But they kept quiet. For a while, so did North. But after weeks of privately boiling, North told Reggie how his black teammates really felt about him.

The criticisms stung—they called to mind the servility he'd shown in Birmingham and his failure to assimilate back at Arizona State. He thought about Alvin Dark's comfort in telling him that "black boys heal faster than white boys," and he thought about confessing to Catfish Hunter that he wanted to *be* white. He wondered if he really was derelict in his obligations to blacks.

But Reggie cast himself as the victim. "I've made a special effort to help my own kind," he lamented. "But it has backfired. I'm having trouble communicating with them, and that upsets me. I know they mistrust me because I spend so much time with white people."

In early June, just before a game in Detroit, Reggie, according to most contemporary reportage, was fully naked in the clubhouse regaling his teammates with tales of the "gorgeous white chick" he was dating. North, weary of the tension between them, reached out. "She got a friend for me?" he asked.

Reggie still wanted acceptance from North, as he wanted from everyone. At the same time, he resented North for divining his weaknesses, for knowing that often Reggie didn't feel black at all. "Nah," he said to North. "She doesn't go out with niggers."

If indeed Reggie called North a "nigger," he did so not out of concord, as some blacks did with one another to subvert and take ownership of an ugly word. Rather, he used it to draw a distinction between North and himself: *you're a nigger, but I'm not.*

North punched Reggie in the jaw. It took three teammates to separate them, and in the violence catcher Ray Fosse wrenched his back. While Blue and Odom, the other peacemakers, tended to Fosse, Reggie and North went at each other again. Reggie crashed into a metal dressing stall, fell to the ground, and clutched his shoulder. This time Bando and Tenace broke up the fight.

Reggie went 0 for 3 and played just five and a half innings of a 9–1 A's win. After the game, Fosse went back to Oakland and wound up in traction at a local hospital. The A's moved on to Milwaukee, where Finley waited for them. He caucused Reggie, North, and Dark, scolded them for "acting like a bunch of flipping kids," and ordered them to shake hands. Reggie, who never had patience for lectures, offered a terse "no comment" afterward. North had more to say. "I don't have to love anybody," he said. "As long as I do my job, everything will be all right."

Around that time, Reggie became the first player ever to receive

2 million votes for the All-Star Game (he wound up with almost 3.5 million). It also meant that for the fifth time in six full seasons as a major leaguer, Reggie would be a part of the Midsummer Classic. Yet he remained bothered. North's assault troubled him, but so did his teammates' refusal to blame North for the whole thing. When the reporter Ron Bergman told Reggie that North said he had no use for him off the field, Reggie replied, "But nobody else on the team said that, did they?"

He withdrew. In the days following the fight, his performance suffered—partly due to his shoulder injury and partly due to his self-imposed isolation—and the A's lead in the West shriveled to a single game. Reggie directed his anger toward Finley.

Ever since Birmingham, stances not taken and words not said haunted Reggie. This time, he regretted bowing to Finley when the owner had blamed him for the fight with North. Late one night, sleepless after another frustrating game, he called Finley. "I have tried to figure out why I didn't punch you in the mouth," Reggie said. "I have decided it was because I have respect for my teammates and didn't want to cause any more trouble than you had already caused. As much as I love them, that's how much I hate you."

Reggie's glowering mood hurt the team, and Finley knew it. The owner hastily assembled a "Reggie Jackson Day" at the Coliseum in the hope that he would be pacified. But another death threat against Reggie—one, like the first, signed by "The Weathermen"—marred the occasion.

Again, the broadcaster Monte Moore received the threat, and again the FBI investigated. It matched the handwriting to the previous threat and discovered that both had been mailed from South San Francisco. Reggie pondered canceling the event, but the FBI agents said it wouldn't be necessary. "Reggie Jackson Day" went ahead as planned.

The opposing Tigers gave Reggie a clock, and Finley gave him a new entertainment center and an autographed glossy photo. As well, the A's gave Reggie both of his MVP trophies from 1973. Nothing came of the threat.

Not long after, Gene Autry fired Bobby Winkles, Reggie's college coach at Arizona State, as manager of the Angels. An opportunity followed: Autry considered naming Frank Robinson, still toiling for Autry's miserable team, as Winkles's replacement. Robinson phoned Reggie to get his advice. Robinson wanted to take the job and become the first black manager, but he feared that it was a less-than-ideal situation. Reggie agreed that it shouldn't be with the Angels. "They can't give you the job because they got the team in Orange County, and that's John Birch country," Reggie said. "There's too many who hate niggers there, and you're a nigger."

Robinson quietly considered what Reggie had said. "If I had a team in Orange County," Reggie went on, "I wouldn't bring in a black man to manage." If Reggie had been in charge, he would've passed up the chance for progress in favor of safety and acceptance. It said much about Reggie's racial consciousness. Robinson didn't get the job.

Finley at last released Dick Williams from his contract, and Autry hired him to manage the Angels. Not long after that, Finley made sweeping changes to his coaching staff. Among other moves, he fired third-base coach Irv Noren and replaced him with the recently deposed Winkles. Finley didn't want Winkles for his major-league experience; he wanted him to control Reggie.

The fight with North proved to Finley that Reggie was disrupting the team. With a meeker man like Dark in charge, Finley believed he had to do something to keep Reggie under control. Reggie saw Winkles's hiring for what it was. He was also angry at Winkles because, he believed, his former coach had ordered an Angels reliever to throw at him earlier in the season. Reggie welcomed him to the team, but he was wary.

The team's fortunes continued to rise. By late July, Oakland had extended its margin in the West to nine games, its largest lead of the year. Reggie crafted another fine season, but on occasion his temper took over. On August 20, he struck out in the late innings and hurled his bat into the stands, narrowly missing Alvin Dark's wife and a pair of eleven-year-old boys.

The Royals began to chip away, but after the A's took two of three in Boston, they maintained a four-game lead with a month to play. On the twenty-eighth, Reggie stung two long homers in Milwaukee to help Catfish Hunter win his twentieth and push the lead to five and a half.

With the A's closing in on a fourth straight division title, Dick Williams and his last-place Angels came to town. The A's won the series opener 6–4, and as the game drew to a close, Finley ordered a message to be run on the Coliseum's leviathan of a scoreboard. It read GOOD NIGHT, DICK. Williams shrugged off the childish jab, but the A's players, even more loyal to Williams in his absence, were outraged. "If they ever do that again," Reggie seethed afterward, "I'll walk off the field and they can fine me. That was disgusting."

On September 20, the White Sox, on the strength of Bart Johnson's pitching, blanked the A's. The surging Rangers pulled within four games of first place. Two days later, Reggie fell down chasing a line drive and wrenched his hamstring. He missed the next three games, all of them crucial. It was a familiar malady. Reggie's heavily muscled legs contributed to the problem, but one of his Oakland trainers suggested at the time that Reggie wasn't committed to running sprints. Hard runs would've prepared him for those vigorous dashes in the outfield and on the bases, but Reggie didn't take the advice. This time, it cost him with Texas closing fast.

Without Reggie in the lineup the A's were still able to clinch the flag on the occasion of Hunter's twenty-fifth win. Reggie returned in time to play in four of the final five games of the season, ending what had been another campaign of distinction: a .391 on-base percentage, good for fifth in the league; a .514 slugging percentage, good for second in the league; twenty-nine home runs, also good for second in the AL; as well as top-10 finishes in total bases, extra-base hits, and times on base.

For the third time in four seasons, the A's would play the Baltimore Orioles in the ALCS. The Orioles had been a game better in the regular season—ninety-one wins to Oakland's ninety—but the A's standing as two-time defending champs made them the favorites.

In game one, Baltimore battered Hunter, so brilliant all season long, for five innings. Reggie went hitless, and the A's never caught up. However, Ken Holtzman shut out Baltimore in game two with a little help from North's brilliant defense in center. Homers by Bando and Fosse provided more than enough offense.

Before game three came a cross-country flight to Baltimore and a day off. Reggie, hitless in the series up until that point, would face right-hander Jim Palmer, one of the toughest pitchers in the game. He reached on an error early in the game and managed a hard single to center in the ninth. However, the day belonged to Palmer and Blue, his Oakland counterpart. Palmer was flawless other than a Bando solo home run in the fourth. Blue was even better. On the day, Blue gave up just two hits, struck out seven, walked none, and worked a complete-game shutout to give the A's a 2–1 lead in the best-of-five series. Reggie was hitting .091 in the ALCS, but the A's were on the brink of a third straight pennant.

Pitching was again the story in game four. Catfish Hunter, ritually abused in game one, came back to pitch seven dominant innings, but Mike Cuellar was almost as good, if perilously so. Through four and two-thirds innings, Cuellar surrendered only one run, but he walked nine batters. Three of those walks went to Reggie. He came up again in the seventh. With Bando on first and the A's holding a tenuous 1–0 lead, Reggie went the other way and laced a double to left. Bando scored and gave Oakland a critical second run. The Orioles worked a run out of Rollie Fingers in the ninth, but the A's held on to win, 2–1.

The typical clubhouse celebration it was not. The mood was

restrained, and the liturgies of celebration—the champagne spray-
ing, the hair mussing, the trophy hoisting—seemed forced at best.
"It's getting to the point where the A's are supposed to win and be
champions," Reggie explained. "And if we don't, we're bums."

IN THE INTERIM between the ALCS and the World Series, the
Chicago Sun-Times reported that Finley had failed to pay Catfish
Hunter's contract in full. Hunter's contract called for $50,000 of his
compensation to be established as an annuity with a North Carolina
insurance company. Finley, though, had belatedly realized that such
payments wouldn't be tax-deductible and refused to make them.
Hunter's attorney repeatedly asked Finley to comply with the terms
of the contract, but Finley would not. Hunter then informed Finley
that he would become a free agent shortly after the conclusion of the
World Series.

Finley declined comment on the story, but privately he tried to
pay Hunter the money owed him. Hunter, who knew he might have
already won his freedom, refused to accept it. Reggie followed the
story with interest. Like so many other players, he had long coveted
free agency, which, under the rules of the day, was allowable only
when an owner cut a player or breached his contract. For a player like
Reggie—gifted, accomplished, marketable—the idea of open bidding
was beyond alluring—and beyond possible.

Notwithstanding Hunter's unfolding drama, the real story was
the World Series. For the first time in baseball history, two California
teams would play in the Fall Classic. There were the A's, of course,
and opposing them were the Los Angeles Dodgers, who had won
102 games during the regular season. Yet the A's weren't all business,
even as such a formidable opponent awaited them. During a pre-
Series workout, Rollie Fingers and Blue Moon Odom began some
good-natured banter that, in A's fashion, devolved into something
uglier. Odom mentioned Fingers's looming divorce, and the two

soon brawled. After they were pulled apart, Odom had a limp, and Fingers needed six stitches in his scalp. "It means we're mean again and ready," Reggie said of the latest Oakland scrape. "Those Dodgers are in deep trouble now."

Though the Fingers-Odom fight didn't unsettle Reggie, his ailing leg did. The hamstring he'd injured in September again nagged him, and he took cortisone shots before game one. Using a DH wasn't at that time permitted during World Series play, so Reggie would be forced to play the field. Despite his pain and listless performance in the ALCS, he refused to miss a single moment.

He'd also gone to great lengths to involve his family in the World Series. He had shelled out thousands of dollars for premium seats and offered to fly his father and brothers from Philadelphia to Oakland. They'd distract him from the task at hand, but Reggie wanted them there. Somehow, though, Reggie and his father, Martinez, failed to communicate leading up to the Series, and Martinez felt excluded— so excluded that he aired his grievances to the *Los Angeles Times*. Martinez told the *Times* that Reggie hadn't been particularly generous with him over the years and that his promises to fly him and his other two sons to the World Series had gone unfulfilled. "You be sure to put that in the paper and let him read it," Martinez told the *Times*. "That'll knock him on his can. You be sure to put in there that his father and his brothers were all set to leave, but they didn't hear from their Most Valuable Player."

Reggie, who had indeed made reservations for Martinez and his two brothers but had failed to return a phone call, was livid. Being painted as disloyal angered him, but it bothered him even more coming from the man who'd caused him so much pain. Reggie didn't call his father and instead forced himself to concentrate on the Dodgers.

The Series opened in L.A., and Holtzman opposed Andy Messersmith. To lead off the second, Reggie adjusted to a Messersmith fastball and sprayed it for a homer to left. It proved to be the winning hit, as the A's never lost their lead and went on to win the opener

3–2. Game two provided another compelling pitching matchup: Vida Blue versus Don Sutton. Once again Reggie was the hitting star, as he went 2 for 3 with a double and a walk. However, his teammates managed just four hits off Sutton and reliever Mike Marshall. The Dodgers took the second game 3–2.

The day of travel back to Oakland brought another round of rumors. This time, Finley was prepared to move the A's to Seattle or New Orleans. Within hours, an Alameda County supervisor filed suit against Finley in an attempt to block any relocation. Finley blamed the press for what he claimed were falsehoods. He didn't divulge that his lease with the Coliseum contained an escape clause, one that would allow him to move the team or sell it to out-of-town buyers.

The players had learned to tune out such noise, but Reggie would not ignore the presence of a writer named Murray Olderman. Olderman had written a story for the October issue of *Sport* magazine titled "Reggie Jackson: Blood and Guts of the Fighting A's." In the article, Olderman took readers on a mostly benign tour of Reggie's Oakland apartment. In one part, though, he told readers he had seen Reggie's Bible placed alongside a pistol and a stack of pornographic magazines. Olderman also told them of the comely young blonde who was lounging around Reggie's place.

Reggie sensed in the piece some whiff of condemnation, that his occasional Christian pieties were at odds with his bachelor's lifestyle. Gary Walker had introduced Reggie to Christianity just after the A's had drafted him, and he'd considered himself a practicing Christian ever since. Still, he struggled to reconcile his religious views with his sexual appetites. Along the way, some—like the A's team chaplain who had once told Reggie that God was not opposed to casual sex so long as people were not "using each other and abusing each other"—had helped him get past his hang-ups, but Olderman's story made him feel judged and ridiculed. Not long after the magazine hit the clubhouse, Reggie blustered about what he'd do to Olderman if the writer had the guts to show up again.

While Reggie took batting practice on the off day before game three, Blue told him that Olderman had indeed turned up. Reggie left the cage, found Olderman on the field, and stomped toward him. He shook his fist at Olderman and berated the fifty-two-year-old writer in front of players, journalists, and even the writer's sixteen-year-old son. In a profane and childish tirade that lasted almost ten minutes, Reggie accused Olderman of making up much of the story he'd written about him. "You better not get around me," Reggie threatened. "I want to embarrass you. I'll punch you in your fucking mouth." Olderman, frightened and taken by surprise, beat a hasty retreat.

The next day, Reggie received a call from the commissioner's office. One of Bowie Kuhn's PR flaks told Reggie that the commissioner "doesn't want anything like this to happen again" and then threatened him with a suspension. Reggie told him he got the message. Afterward, though, he fumed. "They are not going to do anything to me," he said. "They know it, and I know it."

He felt wronged by Olderman, and he felt doubly wronged that the commissioner would threaten him for, as he saw it, merely defending himself. Then along came Finley. The owner, who hated Kuhn, asked Reggie whether, once they'd won the Series, he'd pour champagne over the commissioner's head during the televised trophy presentation. "I'll have a bottle of champagne for you," Finley schemed. "When they call for you, go up there and spray that whole fucking bottle over that son of a bitch." It was the perfect opportunity to embarrass the staid, image-conscious, and conservative Kuhn. Reggie thanked Finley for the great idea.

IN GAME THREE, Dodgers lefty Al Downing failed to tame the A's in the early innings. By the time Walter Alston lifted him in the fourth, Oakland led 3–0. Catfish Hunter cruised until the eighth, when Bill Buckner homered to deep right. In the final frame, Willie Crawford touched Fingers for another solo home run, but then the

A's reliever settled down. Oakland prevailed, 3–2. Reggie went hitless in the game, but a crucial run was scored when he reached base on an error in the third.

In game four, Ken Holtzman limited the Dodgers to two runs in 7.2 innings, and, much more improbably, he hit his third career home run en route to a 5–2 Oakland win. Reggie contributed a single and a walk, which left his average for the Series at .333.

Game five presented the A's the chance to clinch the Series at home. With the A's clutching a one-run lead in the eighth, Dark called on Fingers. The first batter of the inning, Buckner, ripped a single to center, but North overran the ball and allowed Buckner to romp around the bases. Reggie backed up North on the play. He darted after the ball, scooped it up, and hit cutoff man Dick Green with a perfect throw. Green spun and heaved the ball to Bando, who made a sweep tag of the sliding Buckner. Out.

The Dodgers went quietly the rest of the way, and for the fourth time in five games the final score was 3–2. The A's had joined the Casey Stengel– and Joe McCarthy–era Yankees as the only teams in baseball history to win at least three consecutive World Series. Reggie, Bando, Rudi, Blue, Hunter, and, yes, Finley—they had their dynasty at last.

In the clubhouse, Reggie remembered his promise to Finley. He popped a champagne bottle and poured its contents over the unsmiling and relentlessly composed Bowie Kuhn. Reggie then kissed him sloppily on the cheek. Fingers reveled in winning Series MVP, and Dark praised God. Even Finley was uncharacteristically gracious. The fighting, brawling, scrapping, occasionally fratricidal Oakland A's were happy. So happy that they couldn't feel the foundation crumbling beneath them.

TEN

"Isn't My Name Reggie Jackson?"

THE WINTER OF 1974 brought customary drama. Finley jousted with city leaders over the future of the team, and rumors of the manager's fate made the Oakland sports pages. As well, Finley sent Darold Knowles, Bob Locker, and Manny Trillo to the Chicago Cubs in exchange for the aging outfielder Billy Williams, who would become Oakland's regular designated hitter.

At the winter meetings in New Orleans, Finley, fretting over his payroll, shopped Reggie's name around. He got serious with Baltimore, talking about a deal that would've sent Reggie its way in exchange for Bobby Grich and Ross Grimsley. Then he angled for a deal with Philadelphia—Reggie for Mike Schmidt—but the Phillies balked. The Dodgers, Mets, and Yankees also asked about Reggie, but none met Finley's steep price.

Then Catfish Hunter made his play for free agency. The Players Association had filed a grievance in October and asked that Hunter be able to shop his services to the highest bidder. Mere days before an arbitrator heard Hunter's case, sportswriters voted to give him the American League Cy Young Award for 1974.

On December 16, the arbitrator, Peter Seitz, ruled that Finley had breached his contract and Hunter was a free agent. He ordered Finley to pay the disputed $50,000 plus compounded interest. Had Finley known the consequences of his graft, he never would've tried it. But his regrets came too late. At first Reggie looked on with disappointment and envy—disappointed because losing Hunter would weaken the A's, envious because Hunter was about to become a wealthy man.

Winning and winning often, which the A's had done, bred a state of presumption. Without Hunter, though, the champions faced fresh challenges. The loss of their ace would allow Reggie to prove that *he* was the true core of the team and that *he* was the one most essential to the team's fortunes. In those ways, Hunter's departure revived Reggie.

On New Year's Eve, Hunter agreed to a five-year, $2.85 million pact with the New York Yankees. The dollars involved stunned fans, observers, media, players, owners—anyone having anything to do with the game of baseball. The owners were left believing that the freedoms Hunter enjoyed must not be extended to his peers. The players were left desperately wanting their share.

REGGIE SPENT THE rest of the winter focused on his business interests. He shaved off his beard for fear that it frightened white customers, and he sold land in Oakland. He also purchased shares of the Phoenix entrant into the World Team Tennis league. Reggie had no particular interest in tennis, but it was an incremental journey toward team ownership. One day, he might be Charlie Finley.

As spring training approached, he was reminded that he wasn't yet Charlie Finley. Finley presented Reggie with a contract for 1975 that would pay him precisely what he had made in 1974. Reggie told the media that his contract offer was "too depressing " to discuss.

He called Finley and asked to be traded. "If I can sell you for two million dollars," Finley said, "I might not give you some of the money, but I'd at least send you a box of candy."

Reggie, stunned that Finley might trade him, went to Hawaii to fulfill his duties as host of the *Team Superstars* television show. There he met with Dodgers executive Al Campanis. Reggie told him he could be a Dodger if they met Finley's asking price of $2 million. Campanis said it was a possibility. Reggie then phoned Finley and told him the Dodgers were interested. "I can't play money," the owner said. He explained to Reggie that unless he received a king's ransom in talent, he couldn't trade his best player and still manage to sell tickets. Parting with one of baseball's biggest stars in a cash grab simply wouldn't play with the fans. Reggie knew that, but he also knew what Finley had told him earlier. Reggie called him a liar and hung up.

Then he battered Finley in the press over the Catfish Hunter situation. "They say Charlie is a smart businessman, a baseball genius," Reggie said. "You call that smart? You call that good business? I could tell you what I think it is, but you couldn't print it in a newspaper."

Some of his frustrations were real, but mostly he used the entire affair as a cudgel against Finley. As spring progressed, Reggie's optimism rose to the surface. "Without Catfish, we just have to look at new horizons and new goals," he mused. "We can win it again, and we will."

Then the story that Reggie had attempted to engineer a trade to the Dodgers made the rounds in the Oakland press. Finley confirmed the rumor and said that he'd been shocked by Reggie's actions. He didn't mention that he had given Reggie permission to seek out a deal, and he didn't mention that he had discussed trading Reggie to the Phillies, Indians, Yankees, and Orioles, among other teams. When Reggie learned of Finley's lies, he called the Oakland beat writers and told them that Finley was willing to sell him for $2 million. They went back and confronted Finley with Reggie's version of events. He laughed it off. "The Oakland fans would run me out on a rail," Finley said.

Shortly thereafter, Finley defeated Reggie in their arbitration hearing in Los Angeles. Reggie had hoped to make $200,000 for 1975, but the arbitrator chose Finley's figure of $140,000. Freshly embittered, Reggie went back to Arizona for spring training.

THE A's WERE dealing with a bottleneck in the outfield. Finley wanted the talented youngster Claudell Washington in the lineup every day, but Washington's natural position was right field: Reggie's domain. Dark and Finley discussed moving Reggie to first base, in part to spare his legs but mostly to ease Washington's transition. But Reggie refused.

Finley decided to play Washington in left and shift Joe Rudi, one of the best left fielders in baseball, to first base. Reggie didn't like this, either. Rudi was one of the old guard, and Reggie had never forgotten Rudi's faithful presence in Birmingham. He was loyal to Rudi, and he didn't like to see his friend, a Gold Glove winner in 1974, displaced and frustrated because of a rookie, even if that rookie was a young black man in need of tutelage and acceptance. "Claudell should be taught how to play first," Reggie said, "or play part-time this year."

Even when acknowledging Washington's obvious skills, Reggie resorted to backhand compliments. "He knows he's not articulate, he knows he's no financial genius or mathematical wizard," Reggie said. "But he knows he can play baseball." His dismissal of Washington in some ways validated what Billy North had said of him the previous year: he was disloyal to his black teammates.

Finley, meanwhile, failed to see what the stink was about. "If I were twenty-five years younger," he said, "I probably could come out of retirement and play first base myself because it's that easy." It affirmed what many of the A's had long suspected: Finley thought he could do the manager's job better than the manager, and the breadth of his delusions led him to believe he could play the game better than the players, save for the wastage of age.

So without Hunter and the retired Dick Green and stoked only by Finley's slogan ("Keep It Alive in '75!"), the jaded, angry A's set about defending their titles. Meanwhile, Billy Martin, back at the helm in Texas, promised, "We will win the American League."

Against those Rangers, Reggie made his first statement of the season. On April 11 in Arlington, he crushed a pitch from Bill Hands to deep right field. Roughly 450 feet later, the ball landed in the bleachers and gave Reggie one of the longest home runs ever hit in that ballpark. The A's went on to win the game 7–5. By the end of the series, Reggie's A's were in first place, and Martin's Rangers were in last.

Things went well until Dick Williams's Angels shut down the A's 2–0 on April 25. Reggie struck out three times and committed a crucial error in the field. Afterward, he threw a rack of bats onto the field, and as he made his way to the clubhouse he smashed every lightbulb in the visitors' corridor under Anaheim Stadium. Alvin Dark said Reggie was depressed from medication he was taking for a case of the hives—something that afflicted him in times of stress. In reality, Reggie was depressed, medication or no. Since his divorce from Jennie, he'd been into and out of psychotherapy, and much about him—his vacillations of mood, his need to withdraw, his outbursts, his sulking—suggested that he was a man in a clinical state. To his credit, he knew he needed help and, going against the athlete's code of stoic suffering, sought it out. Every so often, though, his emotions dominated him, as they did that afternoon in Anaheim. He sat out the rest of the series.

The time off didn't help him rein in his temper. On May 6, he was hitting just .250. Oakland still clutched first place, but it won for reasons other than Reggie. In the fifth inning, Reggie came up with the tying run on base, but home-plate umpire Nick Bremigan called him out on strikes. Reggie screamed at Bremigan and bumped him with his chest. He earned a two-game suspension and a $350 fine.

He returned in time to play on May 11, on Catfish Hunter's return to Oakland. Before the game, he was asked whether he would hit a home run off his former teammate. "Sure, I will," he said. "Isn't my name Reggie Jackson?" The presumption was unwise. Reggie went 0 for 3 with a strikeout as Hunter shut out the A's by a score of 3–0. "Batting against Catfish was weird," he said after the game. "It was the strangest thing I've ever experienced in baseball. The first time up I couldn't believe I was looking at Hunter out there. It was like a bad dream."

He was as dazed as he sounded. That Hunter had shut him down bothered him, but seeing him free of Finley's grip was even harder to take. Only a serious error on Finley's part had allowed Hunter to gain his freedom, and Finley was far too savvy an operator to let that happen again.

A few days later, Finley traded Blue Moon Odom to Cleveland. It was Cleveland that, at long last, had made Frank Robinson Major League Baseball's first black manager. Odom was out of Oakland and playing for Robinson, and Reggie envied him on both counts. In particular, playing for a black manager like Robinson had fast become irresistible to him. "I guess color means more to me than I'll admit to myself," he said.

A week later, the A's were in New York facing Hunter once again. And once again Hunter dominated them. When Reggie came up against him in the sixth, he was 0 for 2 with a pair of strikeouts, and the A's were down 9–1. Angered by his own fecklessness against Hunter, Reggie scooted a surprise bunt down the third-base line for a single. It was a pointless departure for Reggie, but at least he could say he got a hit off Hunter. The A's then moved on to Boston, where the Red Sox brutalized them in a three-game sweep. They fell into a first-place tie with Texas.

In the first game of the series, Reggie failed to tag up from third on a deep Bando fly ball. After the inning, Bando blasted Reggie for his lack of hustle. Within seconds, the two veterans shoved each other and raised their fists. Dark stepped between them.

For most teams, a brawl between their captain and their acknowledged leader would unsettle them. But for the A's it was a sign of health. Four days later, they shut out Cleveland and reclaimed first place for good.

In early June, though, Reggie slumped and ached from yet another leg injury. "Jackson will start hitting again soon," he promised. "You can count on it."

Days later he hit a game-winning homer in Milwaukee, beginning a streak that raised his batting average more than twenty points in a fortnight. Finley shopped him once again, this time to the Angels and Orioles.

ON JUNE 16, in an eventual loss to Minnesota, Reggie launched a mammoth home run, one that tied him for the league lead, but he had a terrible day in the field. On one misplay, he charged in on a sinking line drive, tumbled, and allowed the ball to carom around the outfield. Billy North, who should've backed up the play, stood by as a playable ball turned into an inside-the-park home run. After the game, Reggie, to the disappointment of the writers, said nothing about North's lack of effort. "I didn't play too well in the field, did I?" he offered.

North intimidated him. Despite his smaller stature, North had beaten him up, and North's accusations still perplexed him. Reggie believed, wrongly, that North had failed to back up the play in order to make him look bad, but he let it pass. He simply didn't have the will for further discord. But more discord was on the way, and it was of Reggie's own making.

A chronicle of the 1974 season that he'd coauthored with Bill Libby—which opened with the line "My name is Reggie Jackson and I am the best in baseball"—was about to be released, and the *Oakland Tribune* had run a handful of salacious excerpts. In one of those excerpts, Reggie insulted a number of his teammates, called out Dark and Finley, and spoke candidly about players' use of "pep pills," or, more commonly, "greenies." He confessed to taking them himself and puffed that he would "continue to take them unless I get so much shit over this I am forced to stop."

Greenies were amphetamines, drugs that had been a part of the game since the 1940s. In 1970, however, amphetamines, or "artificial adrenaline," had been reclassified and declared illegal to possess without a prescription. Baseball players beset by fatigue or age-related decline continued to use them with impunity. Their illegality, though, meant you didn't speak of such things. Jim Bouton, in his book *Ball Four*, had angered the baseball world with his frank talk of amphetamine use. Yet in Bouton's day greenies had been legal. They weren't during the season Reggie chronicled, and that's what made his revelatory moments so dangerous to baseball. When the excerpt in question hit the newsstands on June 18, Reggie knew he had underestimated the consequences of his words.

When Finley learned of the evolving scandal, he phoned Playboy Publishing, the publisher of Reggie's book, and demanded that it cancel the excerpts. It refused. Then he called Reggie in Minnesota hours before the A's took the field and berated him for his loose tongue. Reggie hated following orders from Finley, but when Finley informed him that the league might take action against him, he knew he had no choice. Reggie then cornered Ron Bergman of the *Tribune*, the lone beat writer who traveled with the A's, and begged him to see that the second excerpt was killed. Bergman said he couldn't do that.

As a last recourse, Reggie joined announcer Monte Moore in the booth before first pitch and retracted what Libby had written for him. He was most adamant (and least believable) when he addressed the topic of amphetamine use. He claimed his words had been taken out of context, trumped up for sensationalist purposes, and otherwise made to take on a greater heft than he'd intended—all moves straight from the chastened athlete's playbook. "The connotation is much worse than the facts," he said to those who were listening back in Oakland. "A diet pill gets twisted around, and somebody calls it dope or heroin. When you're eighteen or nineteen, you do things you'd never do later."

Then he played the naif: "I feel like I've been used and abused," Reggie said. "It's not right to use people like that."

Reggie's campaign of dishonesty didn't mollify Bowie Kuhn. Kuhn had warned players before the 1971 season that they must comply with all drug laws, and that same year he'd threatened Chuck Dobson, Reggie's former roommate, after the right-hander had admitted he'd thrown a shutout in 1970 while charged up on greenies. In Kuhn's eyes, the A's had a history.

AL President Lee MacPhail called Reggie and imparted to him the seriousness of what he'd done. Genuine fear set in when Kuhn sent a former FBI agent to investigate Reggie's own drug use. Reggie's on-field production remained steady, but inside he agonized. He'd always been confessionally inclined—often to his own detriment—but now he'd talked his way into *serious* trouble. How much trouble depended upon Kuhn's whims. Reggie entertained the grimmest possibilities.

But then Reggie's coauthor fell on his sword. Bill Libby told the Associated Press that he'd distorted Reggie's comments to wring "something explosive out of the book." He assured everyone that Reggie had long ago stopped taking pills and that he'd even stolen a glance inside Reggie's medicine cabinet and found nothing untoward. Kuhn was satisfied.

Mere days after the drug controversy passed, broadcaster Monte Moore sorted through his Friday mail and uncovered yet another threat on Reggie's life. The letter promised that Reggie, along with Vida Blue, would "be assassinated one of these days: June 20, 21, 22." It was signed, "Xavier, World Liberation Movement."

For the third time in less than two years, Reggie's life had been threatened. Kuhn put the former FBI agent, the very one who'd investigated Reggie's amphetamine use, on the case, and the A's ramped up security at the ballpark. Both Reggie and Blue said they would play despite the threats. Reggie confessed that the death threat and drug scandal on top of the usual Oakland Sturm und Drang were almost too much to bear. He looked and sounded exhausted far beyond his twenty-nine years.

On Sunday, the final day of the threat, Reggie's play was defiantly brilliant. He homered to deep center and went 3 for 6 in an Oakland win. In the field and in the dugout, he vetted the crowd for suspicious, angry faces. The A's swept that day's doubleheader against the Royals, and, presumably, the threat passed.

The pair of victories over Kansas City sent the A's on an eight-game win streak, and by the end of it they'd extended their lead in the West to seven and a half games. All was not well with Reggie, though. He wanted out of Oakland but still fiercely protected his standing and station with the A's. Again in Claudell Washington he saw a threat.

On July 1, Washington keyed a road win over the White Sox with a couple of hits, a stolen base, and a run scored from second base on a wild pitch. Washington's performance so enthused Finley that he called a press conference in the sixth inning. He announced that he would give Washington a $10,000 raise. "This young man is the A's next superstar," he gushed. "He can't miss ending up as one of the game's greats."

Finley led a coterie of reporters down to the visitors' clubhouse to give Washington the good news. "That man has done a lot for me," Washington said of Finley. "He brought me up last year when he didn't have to."

Washington went on to predict that he might go on to lead the league in steals, hits, runs scored, and total bases. A few lockers away, Reggie looked on in anger. Finley was nuzzling up to Washington just as he had with Reggie when *he* was a young player. Yet he'd given Washington an impromptu bonus, which he'd never done for Reggie.

Then Reggie had to listen to Washington pontificate about his own abilities. He played Reggie's role and attempted to dislodge him as the soul of the team. All of it would've come as a shock to Washington, but in the haunts of Reggie's imagination it made perfect sense.

THE A's WERE hot to start the second half of 1975, and so was Reggie. From the time play resumed on July 17 until the end of the month, he tallied eight home runs. His efforts pushed the A's to an eleven-game cushion in the division, the largest lead they'd enjoyed since the franchise left Philadelphia.

On the twenty-fifth, they won an interminable four-hour, thirteen-inning game against the White Sox the night after they played the Tigers and flew from Detroit to Oakland. A blast from Reggie won the game for the exhausted A's, but he wasn't too tired to stay in the clubhouse until well after midnight and explain his second-half surge to the press. He told them he'd adjusted his swing and been inspired by comments from Johnny Bench, Joe Morgan, and Dave Cash at the All-Star Game. "You've got no business hitting .240," Cash had said to him. "With your talent, I'd hit a million."

It was good for Reggie to have the beat writers once again interested in him and not Washington. Within days Reggie tied Philadelphia's Greg Luzinski for the major-league lead in home runs, and Oakland moved closer to a fifth straight division title. But the A's began to wear down in the heat of August, and on three different occasions the Royals pulled within five and a half games of the lead. Rudi, North, and Washington all sustained injuries, and in their absence Reggie slumped.

The nadir came when the lowly Tigers, who had just lost an unthinkable nineteen straight, came to Oakland and took the opening two games of the series. The veteran, battle-tested A's, whom the Boston lefty Bill Lee had days before dismissed as "emotionally mediocre," were falling apart. Blue obliterated a watercooler after a tough outing; Reggie, after whiffing twice with runners in scoring position, smashed his batting helmet to bits and accused his teammates of giving less than full effort; and Dark called a closed-door meeting in the hope of forestalling a historic collapse.

On the final East Coast road trip of the season, Reggie tumbled into the dugout and once again injured his leg. The A's would have to fend off the tireless Royals with a skeleton crew of a roster and a clubhouse of percolating frustrations. In Boston, though, the A's ended the month with vigor. Umpires threw out the mild-mannered Dark for arguing a call at second base, and after his ejection he hurled the third-base bag into the Fenway seats. Inspired or perhaps amused into action, the A's won the game. The next day, Reggie hit his first home run in almost three weeks and plated five runs in a to-and-fro Oakland victory. A week later, the A's swept the Royals at home to stretch their lead back to eight games and all but clinch the division title.

For the first time under Finley, they'd drawn more than a million fans to the park. Reggie clouted five homers over the final two weeks of the regular season and earned his second home-run crown in three years. Two of those home runs came on September 24 against the White Sox—the game that sealed the AL West title.

The champagne flowed in the clubhouse. Reggie and North, still mostly chilly toward each other, embraced and laughed together. Dark thanked "all the Christians out there who prayed for us," and the rest of the team celebrated yet another triumph over circumstance, expectations, and Charlie Finley.

NATURALLY, CONTROVERSY PRECEDED Oakland's ALCS matchup with the Red Sox. That season Blue had won twenty games and ranked in the top 10 in the AL in ERAs and strikeouts. By all rights, he should've been the game one starter against Boston. However, Finley was angry at Blue over some of his recent comments, and he ordered to Dark to start Ken Holtzman instead. Dark, on Finley's orders, even floated the risible idea of using Blue out of the bull pen in the ALCS. The news miffed Reggie, who believed Finley had hurt the team's chances. But he feared they had enough distractions and kept quiet about it.

Game one at Fenway was an ugly, torpid affair for the A's. Boston trounced them 7–1, and the A's committed a play-off-record four errors. Reggie managed one of just three Oakland hits on the day. Immediately after the debacle, Finley ordered Dark to shuffle his defensive arrangement.

In game two, Reggie did his best to reverse the team's fortunes early. In the top of the first, he sent a Reggie Cleveland pitch 435 feet on a line, deep into the right-field stands. His blast gave Blue, whom Dark had graciously named the starter, a 2–0 lead. However, Boston, thanks mostly to a Carl Yastrzemski home run, chased him in the fourth. In the fifth, Reggie cut down Cecil Cooper at the plate to preserve the tie score, but the Red Sox battered an Oakland bull pen that Dark had ridden hard all season. Boston won 6–3. The champs were one game from elimination.

Back in Oakland, a crowd of almost 50,000—the second largest crowd in postseason history—turned out to cheer the A's back from the ledge. Part of the draw was the fear that the A's were bound for Chicago or some other far-off new city. It would be perhaps a final farewell.

As in game one, the A's came out sluggish and distracted. Ken Holtzman, pitching on just two days' rest, gave up singles to Denny Doyle and Yastrzemski in the first, but then Carlton Fisk grounded into a double play. On the other side, Rick Wise, fresh from nine days off, pitched more briskly and less perilously than Holtzman. The game remained scoreless until the fourth, when Claudell Washington dropped a fly ball from Fred Lynn. Lynn made it to second, and Rico Petrocelli followed with an RBI single.

In the home half of the inning, Reggie slashed a base hit down the third-base line and dug for two bases out of the box. The calm and deliberate Carl Yastrzemski, playing left field instead of first base because of an injury to Jim Rice, fielded the ball and made a crisp throw to second, an instant ahead of the sliding Reggie. He was out. "Reggie," Yastrzemski said to him as the teams changed sides, "you know you can't do that to me."

"Yes, sir," Reggie said with a grin.

The Red Sox then battered Holtzman in the fifth to take a 4–0 lead. By the eighth it was 5–1, but the A's pieced together a threat. Cesar Tovar led off the inning with a single and advanced on Campaneris's grounder to short. Washington's hard ground ball handcuffed Doyle at second, and the A's had runners on first and third. Bando singled, cut the lead to 5–2, and moved Washington to third with one out. It was Reggie's turn.

Wise threw Reggie a fastball on the inner half, and he crushed it to the gap in left center. Immediately, Reggie saw that Lynn in center was shading him too far to right field. *Triple*, he thought as he charged out of the box and curved toward first base. Then Yastrzemski, with an impossible sense of anticipation, sprinted and flopped to his left, noosed the ball in the last inch of webbing, leaped to his feet, and hit the cutoff man before Reggie could stretch the hit and, more critically, before Bando could score from first. Reggie kicked the dirt as he stood on first base.

Had Yastrzemski not played it perfectly—had Jim Rice not broken his hand on September 21, had manager Darrell Johnson not defied his first instincts and allowed the thirty-six-year-old Yaz to patrol the outfield in Oakland—it would've been a 5–4 game with the tying run 90 feet from home. Instead, it was 5–3 with runners on first and third. Johnson called Dick Drago from the bull pen.

The crowd rose. The outfield scoreboard flashed DINGER POWER! Fans rang cowbells and stomped their feet, and some dropped smoke bombs into center field. At the plate, Joe Rudi looked for a first-pitch high fastball—Drago's specialty. Instead, the right-hander, hoping to tease a grounder out of Rudi, shook off Fisk until his catcher called for the pitch he wanted. Drago fed him a hard sinker low and away. "I gave it all I had," Drago would say later. If Rudi took or missed the pitch, Drago would come back with the fastball that Rudi wanted. But Rudi bit and flicked his bat just as the ball dived. Somehow, he hit it solidly, but he also hit it straight to Rick Burleson, who smothered it and began a 6–4–3 double play to end the inning.

In the ninth, the A's went quietly. A Billy North walk and reams of trash thrown on the field by the Oakland fans prolonged the inning. After Jim Holt grounded out to second, the game, the Series, and the Oakland dynasty were over.

Reggie had batted .417 and slugged .667 for the Series and manned his position with aplomb. "I'm not sad," he said in the clubhouse after the final out. "Hell, we just got beat. It's not the end of the world."

Reggie Jackson poses during his rookie campaign in 1968. He hit twenty-nine of Oakland's ninety-four home runs that season.
(National Baseball Hall of Fame Library, Cooperstown, New York)

For much of his career, Reggie was more than just a power hitter. He ranked in the top 10 in stolen bases in 1970, 1971, and 1973.
(National Baseball Hall of Fame Library, Cooperstown, New York)

"The worst feeling I've ever had...was the day we won the World Series." Reggie, on crutches and in street clothes, missed the 1972 World Series because of a serious leg injury. *(Associated Press)*

"I was just trying to live up to what you guys were writing, to what you guys said I should be doing." Reggie sits on the hood of his new Dodge Charger—his reward for being named MVP of the 1973 World Series. He would also win the AL MVP Award for 1973. *(Associated Press)*

Reggie stands alongside Alvin Dark, who replaced Dick Williams as manager of the A's before the 1974 season. To hear some tell it, the A's won in spite of Dark's leadership. *(Associated Press)*

"Fuck Charlie Finley," Reggie said of the owner, pictured below during the 1974 World Series. "We'll win it again anyway." After a tense five games against the Dodgers, the A's did indeed "win it again anyway." *(Associated Press)*

Reggie and his parents smile for the cameras on November 29, 1976—the day Reggie became a New York Yankee. *(Associated Press)*

Thanks to Reggie's three home runs in game six, the Yankees topped the Dodgers in the 1977 World Series. The stadium—and the city—exploded in celebration. *(Associated Press)*

"Anyone fights you, skip, he's got to fight both of us." Reggie and Billy Martin, after winning the 1977 World Series, share a moment together. The two would soon resume hating each other. *(Associated Press)*

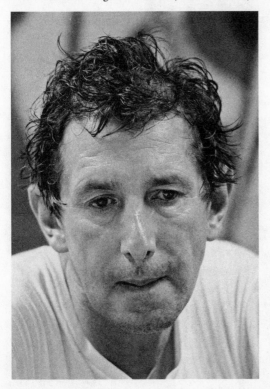

"I've never been angrier in my life," Martin said, after Reggie ignored orders to swing away during the 1978 season. Reggie was suspended, but Martin would soon be fired. *(Associated Press)*

Reggie's relationship with Bob Lemon, Martin's replacement and polar opposite, was far less strained but still contentious at times. *(Associated Press)*

Reggie's "calculated anticipation" at the plate leads to one of his 563 home runs. *(National Baseball Hall of Fame Library, Cooperstown, New York)*

Reggie and Catfish Hunter, pictured here during the 1978 World Series, were teammates for eight seasons in Oakland. Then Reggie followed him to the Bronx. (*Associated Press*)

Reggie and Thurman Munson butted heads in New York, but eventually each developed a grudging respect for the other. Here, they celebrate a second-straight World Series triumph over the Dodgers. (*Associated Press*)

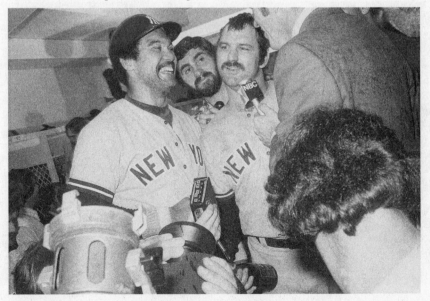

Reggie with Angels owner Gene Autry, the man he called his "second father." (*Associated Press*)

By turns friends and enemies, Reggie and George Steinbrenner helped define each other for more than thirty years. They reconciled in 1993, not long after Reggie was voted into the Baseball Hall of Fame. (*Associated Press*)

ELEVEN

"I Ain't Going"

SINCE 1879, A ballplayer had been bound to one team for life unless that team traded or released him. It was a consequence of the "reserve clause," which had begun as a gentleman's agreement among teams and evolved into a sanctioned ruse to tamp down labor costs. Rule 10A stated, "If prior to March 1 . . . the Player and the Club have not agreed upon the terms of such contract, then on or before 10 days after said March 1, the club shall have the right . . . to renew his contract for the period of one year."

That rule, wielded in tandem with another that barred players from suiting up without a contract, made players, in essence, property. The owners believed that the "period of one year" was a contract option they could renew in perpetuity. Thus players couldn't peddle their services to the highest bidder, they couldn't choose where they worked, and, according to the owners' parsing of the rules, they couldn't do anything about it.

The slow march toward change began in earnest back in 1969,

when Curt Flood challenged the reserve system after his trade to the Philadelphia Phillies. Flood's efforts came to grief in 1972, when the Supreme Court ruled against him by a 5–3 margin. But his sacrifice and resolve united the players.

Late in 1975, union head Marvin Miller readied for another assault. Miller believed that if a player played an entire season without signing the contract offered to him, he would have exhausted the owner's option on him and would become a free agent. From time to time, a frustrated player would report to camp unsigned, and Miller would wonder whether this was his long-sought "test case" that would go before an arbitrator and overturn the reserve system. Whether that would be the eventual reality depended upon two things: the player's willingness to play the entire season unsigned and the arbitrator's willingness to see things Miller's way.

By persuading pitchers Andy Messersmith and Dave McNally not to sign their 1975 contracts, Miller forced an arbitrator to rule on the viability of the reserve clause. That arbitrator, Peter Seitz—the very one who'd ruled in favor of Catfish Hunter a year earlier—concurred with Miller's reading of Rule 10A. He declared Messersmith and McNally free agents. As a result of the Seitz decision, all a player had to do to be granted free agency was play out his option year without signing a contract.

Coincidentally, baseball's collective bargaining agreement was up for renewal, and the issue of how to structure this new system dominated the process. Seemingly, just two people involved in the talks grasped the supply-and-demand dynamics in play: Miller and Finley. Finley knew that if the supply side of the market were flooded, salaries would remain depressed. So he proposed to make all players free agents after each season. This worried Miller, who knew that if available free agents were kept at a relative trickle, salaries would escalate beyond the players' hopes. He proposed that only players with six years of major-league service time be eligible for free agency.

Fortunately for Miller and the players, Finley's fellow owners either lacked his understanding of basic economics or so loathed the Oakland crackpot that they refused to receive his wisdom. They went for Miller's plan, which to them sounded like a stunning capitulation. The aftereffect, just as the players had hoped, was an increase in salaries of unthinkable dimensions. A new era of baseball had arrived.

As things unfolded on the labor front, Reggie and Finley talked about his contract for 1976. Reggie wouldn't be a part of the first class of free agents, so for one more winter he was at Finley's mercy. "I'd like to offer you a raise, Reggie," Finley told him. "But I can't. Your batting average is embarrassing. You still strike out too much. I know you drove in 104 runs, but I don't feel they were important runs. Maybe if we'd made the World Series, I could give you a raise. But we didn't. So I can't. I'm sorry, I feel bad about this."

In 1975, Reggie had led the AL in home runs and ranked sixth in the league in slugging percentage. He'd also battered Boston pitchers in the ALCS. Finally, Finley offered him $140,000 for 1976. Reggie and Gary Walker, emboldened by the prospect of free agency, countered with a three-year, $525,000 proposal that included a substantial amount of deferred money. Finley turned them down. Instead, he unilaterally reduced Reggie's salary to $112,000—the maximum allowed cut of 20 percent.

In spite of Finley's latest assault, Reggie went to spring training with a sense of optimism. Finley had fired Alvin Dark during the World Series and shortly after named Chuck Tanner, the former White Sox manager, as Dark's replacement. Tanner handled players without regimentation and with an awareness of the personalities involved. In his own words, Tanner had "25 sets of rules" for the men on his team—one set for every player on the roster. He pandered to each player's sense of self, and they loved him for it. Most notably, Tanner's easygoing style in 1972 coaxed an MVP season out of Dick Allen, the player with whom fans and writers so often compared Reggie. "There are a lot of good kids who go to bed at eight P.M. every night, are no trouble at all, are great to be around, and hit .180," Tanner once said. "Give me the outspoken good player."

Reggie, outspoken and good, knew he would thrive under the permissive guidance of Tanner.

ON APRIL 2, with the start of the regular season a mere six days away, Gary Walker called Reggie at the A's spring training facilities. "Charlie just traded you and Holtzman to Baltimore for Don Baylor and Mike Torrez."

Reggie was silent. "It's true, Reggie," Walker said. "He's traded you."

To hear Finley tell it, the structural changes in baseball had forced his hand. At season's end he'd lose Reggie to free agency. Better to trade him now, he reasoned, and get something in return. So Finley sent his star slugger to the Orioles along with the lefty Holtzman and the minor leaguer Bill Van Bommel in exchange for Baylor, Torrez, and right-hander Paul Mitchell.

Reggie had become comfortable in northern California. He liked the climate and the lifestyle, and he'd formed lasting bonds with many of his teammates. He was as weary as ever of Finley's yoke, but the misery in the A's clubhouse galvanized them. To Reggie, his A's teammates constituted a family—haphazard, surrogate, and dysfunctional in the extreme at times—but a family just the same. He enjoyed being the biggest star on a championship team, and he feared the uncertainty that waited for him in Baltimore. He'd begged Finley to trade him time and again, but now he didn't want that. "I ain't going," he told Walker. "You tell Charlie and you tell Baltimore and you tell anybody else who cares to listen that I am about to go on vacation."

He left the A's clubhouse in tears. Too overcome to drive himself, Reggie called Walker back and asked him to take him home. After Reggie had time to process the changes ahead, Walker called him once more and asked what it would take to make him an Oriole. "Two hundred thousand dollars," Reggie said. "If I'm going to get jerked around, then they're going to have to damn well pay me to get jerked around."

He went back to Oakland to put some things in order. Then he flew to Hawaii, checked into the Hilton Hawaiian Village, and rifled through his thoughts. He lay in the sun. He ate room service alone. He took long jogs on the shore.

When he got back to Tempe, Reggie hid away at Walker's house. Earl Weaver, Brooks Robinson, and Jim Palmer called and begged him to join them in Baltimore and help them win a World Series. Bowie Kuhn and Lee MacPhail phoned to remind Reggie that the game of baseball needed him. The hard sell failed. This trade—Finley's final betrayal—had finally taught Reggie that baseball was more business than game, and that business was, as Tennyson said of nature, "red in tooth and claw." Now more than ever, the money mattered.

Around this time, Reggie reached out to Finley and offered to put together enough investors to buy the A's. The more Reggie suffered under the system, the more he craved Finley's power. Finley told Reggie he'd get back to him. He took the offer seriously and even mentioned it to Bowie Kuhn, the Players Association, and rival executives. Reggie waited. He then ordered Walker to tell the Orioles that he'd sign a one-year contract for $200,000 or a five-year contract for $250,000 per. Unless they'd meet his conditions, Reggie would shanghai the trade. He had money, and his real estate business was blossoming. If he needed to walk away from the game at age twenty-nine to prove a point, he would. Orioles players began to lose patience. Jim Palmer sarcastically referred to Reggie as "the Messiah" and wondered, "Do you think it ever occurred to Jackson that there are twenty-four other guys over here counting on him?"

Negotiations dragged on into late April. The Orioles foundered in last place, and the team sent GM Hank Peters to Arizona to meet with Reggie and Walker. Peters told him they could win a World Series with him. He told him the fans in Baltimore would adore him, that he'd relish the intensity of East Coast baseball, and that he'd be reunited with his old friend Dave Duncan, who was now the Orioles' regular catcher. He also told him that he'd be able to spend more time with his mother and sisters, who all lived in Baltimore. It was, Peters reminded him, the same city in which Reggie, eleven years younger and eyes on fire, had left them awestruck as the first black player in the city's amateur summer league. "I understand all that, Hank," Reggie said. "But I'm not moving on the money."

Reggie walked away and sipped a beer while Walker and Peters continued to talk. In the end, they agreed upon a $190,000 pact for the remainder of the 1976 season and the option for Reggie either to sign a 1977 contract for $200,000 or test the free-agent market.

On April 30, the Orioles introduced Reggie, dressed in tailored jeans and a leather jacket, to the Baltimore media at Memorial Stadium. He took batting practice after the game. Hundreds of Orioles fans stuck around after an 11–1 loss to boo Reggie as he took his swings. He hit until his hands cracked and bled. Two days later, he made his Orioles debut in the second game of a doubleheader against, coincidentally, the A's. He went 0 for 2 in an Orioles win.

In the clubhouse, Reggie was detached and uneasy. New teammates such as Mark Belanger, Bobby Grich, Lee May, and Brooks Robinson had welcomed Reggie and tried to absorb him into the team's culture. Others, like Palmer, were miffed that his holdout had dragged into the season. During that long period of inactivity, Reggie had slipped out of baseball shape. He would struggle, at least for a while, but the Orioles didn't have time for a learning curve.

————

By June 7, Reggie's batting average had slipped to .205. He pressed, hoping to make up for weeks of frustration with a single blow that kept eluding him. The fans and many of his teammates resented him. The only way to win their favor was to hit, but going from casual workouts at the Arizona State campus to major-league game action left him unprepared. With each strikeout, with each pop-up, the dollars slipped away. The more he struggled, the less he would make on the market. He hadn't felt such pressure since he'd chased "Ruth Maris" seven years earlier. Yet he could find no sympathy among his teammates. As Palmer later said of Reggie, "He wanted us to concern ourselves with his needs."

They didn't. Instead, they worried about rescuing the season. Mostly because of the excellent pitching of Palmer and Wayne Garland, the Orioles had climbed into second place. That only made the fans in Baltimore angrier. If Reggie had trained properly and reported on time like the nine other unsigned Orioles, they would have been a first-place team. To the fans, Reggie's greed was distasteful enough, but he was also having the worst season of his career. Outwardly, he didn't seem to care.

Later in June, the Orioles made their first trip to Chicago. Finley sent word to Reggie that he wanted to see him. Reggie hoped he was ready to sell the A's. They met at a bench in Grant Park, just across from Finley's Michigan Avenue offices. "You doing all right in Baltimore?" Finley asked him. "You comfortable?"

Reggie told him he was and that it was a thrill to play for Earl Weaver. But he also told him that he missed Oakland. Finley asked about Catfish Hunter. Reggie told him he was doing just fine in New York. "We had some time, didn't we, Reggie?" Finley said, almost reading Reggie's thoughts at the moment. Back to his fatherly role, he continued, "You're going to do all right. And every time you hit a home run, or Sal or Joe or Cat wins another game, it's going to be a feather in my cap."

They were quiet for a moment. "You should be proud of yourself, Reggie," Finley said.

As Reggie walked back to his hotel in perfect weather, it didn't occur to him that Finley had said nothing of his offer to buy the A's.

A FEW DAYS later, the Orioles traveled to Texas as Reggie rode a modest four-game hitting streak. Not long after he arrived in Arlington, Reggie received a phone call from Everett Moss, one of his business associates back in California. Moss told him that his two-story Oakland condo had burned to ruins. The garage, which housed a Porsche and one of Reggie's most prized cars, a 1940 Chevrolet, was the only thing spared. Many in Oakland would whisper arson, but the evidence retrieved at the scene revealed little.

The loss of his home and so many cherished personal items unmoored Reggie. The girl he was dating was away in Europe, he had no friends on the team—even Duncan had drifted away from him—and now his home had been destroyed. He was as unhappy as he'd been since the trials and struggles of 1970. One Baltimore acquaintance who sensed Reggie's solitude offered to introduce him to "some outtasight blacks."

"Why don't you just introduce me to some outtasight people?" Reggie said.

On the day he received word of the fire, he arrived late at the ball-park. Weaver waited for him. "Goddammit, you're not bigger than this team, Reggie," he hissed. "I am not going to let you get away with this shit. Who the fuck do you think you are?"

Reggie was too numbed to fight back or even tell Weaver why he was late. That numbness, though, concealed what Reggie really was: desperate. His life was different. He spent nights alone at the Cross Keys Inn. Instead of taking in the Bay Area nightlife, he ate meals at his mother's house and spent more time with young nieces and nephews than with friends and female conquests. And the Baltimore fans still couldn't forgive him. They'd given up two talented players, both still in their prime, to get Reggie, and it appeared that the trade wouldn't net them even a division title. Anything short of a pennant meant they wouldn't forgive Reggie for holding out through the first fifteen games of the season and for—they were certain—leaving them once the season ended.

They threw hot dogs at him as he stood in the on-deck circle. After games, they loitered near the players' parking lot to shout profanities at him. They kicked in the door of his car. One night at the Pimlico Hotel, 138-pound Irvin Weinglass insulted Reggie, and Reggie attacked him. "This is a business," Reggie said. "I can't worry about the fans."

Finally he hit. By the end of June, he'd lifted his average to .225. He told Weaver, "By next month, I'll take over this league." He did just that. By the All-Star break he had lifted his average to .242, and in the second half the power followed. Starting July 18, Reggie homered in six straight games, which tied an American League record. The Orioles climbed back into second place.

Near the end of the month, Dock Ellis of the Yankees struck Reggie in the face with a pitch, and he missed the next three games. In his first time back at the plate, he homered off Detroit right-hander Dave Lemanczyk. "That's why you are who you are," teammate Terry Crowley told him back in the dugout.

But the beaning by Ellis left Reggie in a defensive state of mind. A few nights later, Ken Brett of the White Sox brushed him back. Later, he hit a grand slam off Brett, and as Reggie circled the bases he shouted at him, raised his fists, and gestured wildly. As one game story put it, Reggie "went berserk on the base paths."

He feared being struck in the face again. Ellis had left him with numbness around his right eye and for a while he feared he'd lose his sight. In the same game against Chicago, reliever Clay Carroll came inside again, and Reggie flung his bat at him and earned an ejection. After the game, Reggie called Brett to apologize and explain that the

Ellis beaning had left him fearing for his career. Reggie said he would fight any pitcher who came inside on him again. Brett said he'd kill Reggie the next time they faced each other.

THE ORIOLES HELD strongly to second place in the East, but the Yankees' lead over them stayed at nine, ten, eleven games for most of the September stretch drive. Despite missing several games, Reggie was contending for the AL home-run title. He'd also been the league's hottest hitter in the second half. The timing meant he was bound for a legendary payday.

As the Orioles' hopes dimmed, the media focused on Reggie's future. Where would he go? He didn't know. What mattered to him, besides money and rapt attention? Lifestyle, Reggie told a writer from *Sports Illustrated*. "When I talk about lifestyle, I mean I want to go to a place with a liberal attitude," he explained. "I don't like sectarian living . . . I don't necessarily mean segregated living, I mean certain people living among themselves: Jews here, Poles there, blacks over there. I'm not interested in playing in any town that has that."

He ruled out the South because of his past there and the Midwest because his business interests were nested on the coasts. He ruled out the A's, and then he ruled out the Mets and Dodgers because he wouldn't fit in with teams "that emphasize organization over individual personality." When the Orioles visited Cleveland, they asked him whether the Indians were a possible suitor. "Not enough papers here to carry my quotes," he said.

The season ended with the Orioles in second place, a healthy ten and a half games behind the Yankees. For Reggie, though, there were measures of satisfaction. Without him, the A's failed to make the play-offs for the first time since 1970, and attendance had dropped by 300,000 (the Orioles, in contrast, drew almost 70,000 more fans than they had the previous year). Reggie had played in just 134 games in 1976, but he still finished second in the league in home runs (twenty-seven) and tenth in RBIs (ninety-one), and he also paced the AL in slugging percentage. Moreover, the Orioles had gone 77–57 when Reggie played but a paltry 11–17 when he hadn't.

Shortly after the Yankees eliminated Baltimore from contention, ABC hired Reggie to broadcast the ALCS alongside Keith Jackson and Howard Cosell. During the deciding game five, Yankees outfielder Mickey Rivers tallied a base hit. Then Cosell recounted that the night before a certain member of the Yankees front office had given Rivers a pointed lecture on his efforts. Reggie waited a beat. "It always amazes me how someone who's never played the game can tell someone how to play," he said. "Don't come into the Oakland or Baltimore clubhouse and tell me how to play."

That certain member of the Yankees front office, the man who'd never played the game, was George Steinbrenner.

TWELVE

"We Are Going on This Venture Together"

HE HAD GROWN up in a family of wealthy Cleveland shipbuilders, and he would wield that privilege when he needed it. But George Steinbrenner *had* to be more than just his birthright. It was inevitable that he would turn to sports.

Henry Steinbrenner, George's hard-driving German father, had been a track star at MIT, had set an AAU record in the 220-yard high hurdles, and had even made the U.S. Olympic team in 1928. George, though, lacked the old man's talent.

George ran track and played football at the exclusive Culver Academy in Indiana, but he made the teams only because his father donated generously. He was an especially bad football player—he didn't relish the contact as the best players did—but his desire to be known as a football player trumped the bodily demands. He joined the athletes' fraternity and tried desperately to ingratiate himself, but the jocks mocked him to cruel extremes. On the outside, George seemed unfazed by their taunts and bullying. Inside, though, he took care to remember each and every humiliation. Those humiliations left him with a will to dominate straight out of Nietzsche.

George enrolled at Williams College in Boston and joined ROTC so as to avoid service in the Korean War. However, the war was still going on when he graduated from Williams. As a young, single man with ROTC training, he was prime fodder for local draft boards. Once again, though, his privileged origins bailed him out.

After basic training, Steinbrenner's commanding officer recommended that he be dispatched to the front lines, mostly because he couldn't stand the young man. However, a high-ranking official in Washington had arranged for George to be stationed as close as possible to his mother back in Ohio. George became a special services director at Lockbourne Air Force Base in Columbus, Ohio, far from the perils of Inchon, Pusan, and Pyongyang.

That high-ranking official was Charles Edward Wilson, President Harry Truman's secretary of defense and an old friend of Henry Steinbrenner. Not only did George avoid combat or any sort of foreign deployment (most Lockbourne airmen flew reconnaissance missions over the Soviet Union), but he also led a life of uncommon ease at Lockbourne. An understanding grew out of Secretary Wilson's involvement: if the base commander, Colonel Charles "Bo" Dougher, made things easy for George during his time at Lockbourne, the colonel would became a general. He accommodated the secretary's wishes.

George's "war service" consisted mostly of coaching the Lockbourne baseball team. He told his fellow soldiers that he had recently tried out for the Cleveland Browns. After taking one look at the awkward and gangly Steinbrenner, they knew he was lying. All the while, though, he cultivated a passion for coaching. He enjoyed strategizing, using his wits, and instilling discipline and order. He also saw coaching as a way to bend athletes to his will—athletes like the ones who had tormented him at Culver.

In 1956, George married Elizabeth Joan Zieg, the daughter of a successful Ohio real estate baron and the girl he'd dated since his early days at Lockbourne. That same year, he took a job coaching freshman ends for the Northwestern University football team. Then he jumped to Purdue, where he helped mold a young quarterback named Len Dawson.

Steinbrenner rose fast within the profession, and anyone who saw his quick mind for football and his tireless work habits figured he'd one day become a head coach in the Big Ten. Yet the patriarch, Henry Steinbrenner—the one who'd made George's life so easy for so long—would soon squelch those dreams.

Henry gave his son an ultimatum: come home at this moment and join the American Ship Building Company, or be shut out of the family business—and the family fortune—forevermore. The decision bruised George. He believed he had found his life's work, but his passion for football was outdone by the certainty of family money. He told his father he would bring Joan to Cleveland and join the third generation of Steinbrenner shipbuilders. The desire to structure, manage, plot, and make tactical decisions unique to the job would always be with him, as would his zeal for subordinating athletes. Perhaps someday, George told himself, he'd find an outlet for those desires.

GEORGE WANTED TO take risks with the company, while Henry was cautious to a fault. Henry closely monitored George's work hours, while George believed he worked better with less oversight. Swinging wildly between rage and remorse, Henry fired and rehired his son on occasions too numerous to chronicle. Like the jocks back at Culver, George's father made him feel powerless.

He compensated by lording it over Joan. He humiliated her to the point of tears at dinner parties and told her what she could wear and when she could wear it. In 1962, Joan filed for divorce, citing gross negligence, but she relented when George promised he'd treat her better. They did, however, agree to lead separate lives. The distance—emotional and physical—suited George. In Joan's absence, his thoughts turned back to sports.

He gambled on Notre Dame games, but that failed to sate his desires. So after shaking down his friends for cash, Steinbrenner purchased the Cleveland Pipers, a franchise in the semiprofessional Industrial Basketball League, in 1961. As the Pipers' owner, Steinbrenner displayed his dictatorial side to the fullest. At the outset of one game, he chose the uppermost seat in the arena so as to prevent himself from interfering. But as the game went on, he scooted his way down through the stands, closer and closer to the court. In the fourth quarter, he was called for a technical foul while sitting on the bench.

In later years, Steinbrenner would be credited with making John McLendon the first black professional basketball coach in history. In reality, though, Steinbrenner inherited McLendon when he purchased the Pipers, and he tried to fire him despite his unassailable record of success. Asked whether his treatment at the hands of Steinbrenner had been racially motivated, McLendon said, "He isn't antiblack, he's antihuman."

In his final power play as the Pipers' owner, Steinbrenner signed Ohio State star Jerry Lucas. To pry him away from the Cincinnati Royals, who had also drafted him, Steinbrenner took Lucas to all of Cleveland's hot spots and, at just the right moment, offered him a base salary, a stock portfolio, and enough bonus money to pay for the rest of his education. Steinbrenner went to such lengths to make the Pipers—and himself—more appealing to the NBA.

The NBA at the time yearned for a white star, and Lucas had the potential to be just that. The league, according to Steinbrenner's plan, took notice and invited the Pipers to become the league's tenth franchise. By that point, though, Steinbrenner was broke and couldn't afford the entrance fee. His bid to become a big-time owner and Cleveland's bid to join the NBA were snuffed out.

Chastened and shamed in his hometown, he still wanted in. His next chance came in 1971, when Cleveland Indians owner Vernon Stouffer decided to sell. Steinbrenner called in enough markers and pressed enough flesh to cobble together a $9 million offer. He also established a powerful internal ally when he told Indians president Gabe Paul that he'd keep him on to run the team. For a time, it appeared that Stouffer would accept Steinbrenner's bid. First, though, Steinbrenner angered Stouffer when he leaked news of the deal to the local media. Then he reopened old wounds over his treatment of Stouffer's son during his days as an investor with the Pipers. Stouffer, in harsh language, told Steinbrenner that his deal wasn't good enough.

Before long, Steinbrenner sniffed out his next chance. Gabe Paul, grateful for Steinbrenner's earlier gesture of faith, told him that Mike Burke, who helmed the New York Yankee front office for CBS, was angling for the team and looking for investors. When it came to power, status, and recognition, the New York Yankees stood above all. Moreover, after years of listless caretaking on the part of CBS, things could only get better for the once-proud franchise. The sale price was the best news of all: CBS was asking for a mere $10 million—well below any sensible valuation of the club.

In December 1972, CBS accepted Burke and Steinbrenner's offer. "We plan absentee ownership as far as running the Yankees is concerned," Steinbrenner promised. "We're not going to pretend we're something we aren't. I'll stick to building ships."

Despite assurances that Burke would remain in control and that the new owner would be neither seen nor heard, Steinbrenner forced the holdovers first to the margins and then out of the organization altogether. In April 1973, Burke, humiliated by Steinbrenner's treatment of him, resigned. By the end of the year, Steinbrenner had shoved out general manager Lee MacPhail and everyone else with ties to the CBS regime. The Yankees, in the realest sense, now belonged to George Steinbrenner.

And then he imperiled all of it. In an attempt to curry favor with the Nixon administration, Steinbrenner funneled money to the odiously corrupt Committee to Re-Elect the President. It was risky, but Steinbrenner had good, if unsavory, reasons. To wit, he wanted to win government contracts for his shipping company, for the Department of Labor not to press him on safety violations, to avoid paying millions of dollars in cost overruns on a previous government contract, and to skate around antitrust laws that were impeding his takeover of two rival firms. Nixon could help, but only if Steinbrenner met his price. The challenge was to meet that steep price while evading campaign contribution laws.

To those ends, Steinbrenner issued phony bonus checks to several carefully selected workers and then had those workers funnel the money to various politicians. He'd pay the rest of the tab himself. However, Steinbrenner's plan caught the attention of the feds, and soon enough the media picked up the scent. Steinbrenner begged them to exercise restraint. He told one reporter that his wife was terminally ill and that the scandal would surely be too much for her. He was lying.

Only after he forced his terrified employees to lie for him and claimed that political operatives had duped him did Steinbrenner admit to himself that he'd been caught. On Opening Day 1974, the feds indicted him on five counts of making illegal contributions, four counts of obstructing justice, two counts of obstructing a criminal investigation, and two counts of encouraging false statements. Steinbrenner's highly priced legal team hammered out a plea agreement. He would cop to a pair of the charges, and the rest would be dropped. That meant he would be a convicted felon and likely face jail time. However, the civic and business leaders of Cleveland wrote more than seventy letters extolling Steinbrenner's sterling character and kind heart. In the end, the judge fined him $20,000. But there was still baseball to deal with.

Commissioner Bowie Kuhn, who, like Steinbrenner, cherished

order and discipline, mulled over what to do with an owner who had sullied the game so soon after he joined the exclusive fraternity. Steinbrenner, meanwhile, brayed his innocence to anyone who would listen.

A team of investigative reporters for the *Cleveland Press* was to run a lengthy exposé that refuted Steinbrenner's version of events. Worst of all, the story would run before Kuhn had meted out his baseball punishment. Steinbrenner begged the *Press* to hold off, at least for a little while. His wife, he told them, was in a New York hospital battling what doctors feared was stomach cancer. His son, he told them, had been in a serious automobile accident and was fighting for his life in Massachusetts General Hospital. On both counts, Steinbrenner appears to have lied.

A timely newspaper strike spared Steinbrenner the indignities of the truth, and the story didn't run for several months. Meantime, Kuhn delivered his verdict: he suspended Steinbrenner from baseball for two years. Notionally, that meant no say in the day-to-day operations of the club and no contact with those who would make decisions in Steinbrenner's stead. Reality, though, was something else altogether.

Steinbrenner never showed up at Yankee Stadium during his suspension, but he ran the team from a discreet remove. He phoned Gabe Paul regularly, and on more than one occasion he tape-recorded speeches—rousing speeches, in his mind—for the players. In one of his boldest decisions during this time, he named as his manager the combative Billy Martin, who'd just been fired in Texas.

On March 1, 1976, Kuhn announced that he'd shortened Steinbrenner's suspension and he could now resume his duties as team owner. Kuhn was grateful because Steinbrenner had blocked his fellow owners from ousting the commissioner. After Kuhn got his seven-year contract extension, Steinbrenner got his team back.

The 1976 season, the first under Martin, brought the Yankees a pennant, but the Cincinnati Reds spoiled Steinbrenner's greater hopes when they swept his team in the World Series. The team was good. It needed to be great.

To most New Yorkers, Steinbrenner was a corrupt interloper, a fat loudmouth from Cleveland who had the stench of Nixon all about him. Steinbrenner knew this, but he also knew that nothing remade a reputation quite like winning. With another, sexier crop of free agents now on the market, Steinbrenner had a chance to demonstrate his commitment to the team and to the city. But it would take something big.

REGGIE WAS, BY a sturdy consensus, the most coveted of free agents. But he didn't make sense for the Yankees. With Graig Nettles, Chris Chambliss, Mickey Rivers, and Oscar Gamble already on the roster, the Yankees had a surfeit of left-handed batters. They needed pitching, an upgrade at shortstop, and power from the right side. Despite his gifts and despite his longtime yearning for New York, Reggie became an afterthought.

In 1976, the free-agent process worked much differently than it would in later years. Teams drafted the right to negotiate with specific free agents, and in most circumstances the rules barred them from signing more than two. The draft provision mattered—just the first thirteen teams to claim a player could negotiate with him. Steinbrenner wanted Cincinnati lefty Don Gullett, who was just twenty-five and had tamed the Yankees in the World Series. Gabe Paul wanted Bobby Grich, who could hit and had the defensive skills to shift from second base to shortstop. They both liked Don Baylor. Billy Martin wanted Joe Rudi, but Steinbrenner never asked for his opinion.

At the Plaza Hotel in New York—the very place where Finley had drafted Reggie out of college more than a decade earlier—Steinbrenner and Paul chose, in order, nine players: Grich, Baylor, Gullett, outfielder Gary Matthews, right-hander Wayne Garland,

Reggie, shortstop Bert Campaneris, second baseman Dave Cash, and infielder Billy Smith. Steinbrenner told the press, "Grich, Gullett, Baylor, and Jackson are the players we're most interested in." He didn't want Reggie at the time, though. He bandied his name about merely to prove to Yankees fans that he would chase the high-dollar talents. Besides, twelve other teams also drafted Reggie, and that meant high demand for his services.

Straightaway, the Yankees focused on Gullett and Grich. By the middle of November, they'd signed Gullett, but the Angels closed in on Grich. Grich's agent had promised Steinbrenner the opportunity to top any offers. In topping those offers, though, Steinbrenner offended Grich. Grich left their meeting and within hours signed with the Angels. Thereupon, almost everyone else on the Yankees' list came to terms with other teams. That left Reggie as Steinbrenner's last redoubt against the team's demanding partisans.

Before he pursued Reggie in earnest, Steinbrenner revised recent history. He told Murray Chass of *The New York Times* that the Yankees had been angling for Reggie the whole time and that only recently had he persuaded Gabe Paul to come around to his way of thinking. The more Steinbrenner thought about it, though, the more he liked the idea of bringing Reggie to the Bronx. The more he thought about it, the more he believed that signing Reggie would distinguish his team from the crosstown Mets, especially on racial terms.

In spring training of 1975, south Florida police arrested Cleon Jones, the Mets' accomplished black outfielder, after they found him passed out in the back of a van wearing nothing but socks. Next to him lay a white woman wearing even less. Jones was a married man, and police found a small amount of marijuana in the van. The Mets, though, were less concerned about adultery and drugs than they were about finding their black star in compromising straits with a white woman.

Although the criminal charges were dropped for lack of evidence, the team fined Jones $2,000 and forced him to read a public apology to his wife, employers, and fans. Manager Yogi Berra proceeded to play Jones sparingly until the Mets released the popular veteran in August.

Steinbrenner, ever since he had bought the Yankees, had been ferociously competitive with the Mets. The Boss took it as a personal affront whenever the Yankees lost—or even won without the proper aesthetics—the annual Mayor's Cup exhibition against the Mets. Worse, the Mets had outdrawn the Yankees every year since 1963 and had more than doubled their attendance figures as recently as 1971. In 1972, the Mets' television ratings in the New York area were more than twice that of the Yankees. In the just-completed season, when the Yankees had won ninety-seven games and the pennant, they had finally topped the Mets in home attendance. But Steinbrenner wanted more.

Perhaps he thought back on how the Mets had passed on Reggie because, as the lore of the day went, he dated white women. Then perhaps he thought of the racial currents of the Cleon Jones situation, which were still fresh in the minds of many New Yorkers. There was something there. It was hardly a mission of conscience for Steinbrenner. When he'd owned the Cleveland Pipers, he'd tapped into the racial dynamics of the day by signing Jerry Lucas. Now he'd do the same with Reggie.

Yet the Yankees had a racial history even grimmer than that of the Mets. In 1938, Yankees outfielder Jake Powell had touched off a controversy when, on live radio, he remarked that he spent his off-seasons "cracking niggers over the head" as a police officer in Ohio. While the outcry over Powell's comments helped along baseball's glacial march toward integration, the Yankees were among the bitter-enders until they finally added catcher Elston Howard in April 1955. "When I finally get a nigger," manager Casey Stengel said upon seeing Howard play for the first time, "I get the only one who can't run."

They'd had slick-fielding first baseman Vic Power, a black Puerto Rican, in the system, and in 1952 Power had won the minor-league batting title. However, the Yankees had declined to invite him to spring training, mostly because he dated white women. In December 1953, the Yankees, at the behest of the racist George Weiss, traded Power to the Philadelphia A's.

When it came to black players, the Yankees wanted the frame to be more compelling than the portrait inside. They wanted their black players to be like Elston Howard or Roy White or Willie Randolph—quiet, workaday, nonthreatening. Reggie was nothing of the sort.

REGGIE HAD LONG desired to play in New York, and the portents of his doing so weren't hard to find. But Reggie and Gary Walker entered the process with open minds. The Padres offered $3.4 million spread over five years, but because they wouldn't include a $250,000 business loan in the deal, Reggie passed. He traveled to Montreal, and Expos owner Charles Bronfman offered him a package worth almost $5 million. But Reggie feared the relative anonymity that would come with playing in Canada. The Dodgers and Orioles were slow to act and thus failed to cater to Reggie's ego.

Steinbrenner, meantime, told Reggie that though the rest of the Yankees' brain trust wanted Grich, he'd known all along that Reggie was his man. Those words moved Reggie. That Steinbrenner, this wealthy, white industrialist, saw something in him when those who had his ear did not spoke powerfully to Reggie. After the serial betrayals by Finley, he pined for fatherly trust again.

In New York, a charm offensive awaited him. Steinbrenner met him at LaGuardia Airport with a limo. The Yankees owner looked impressive in his customary blue dinner jacket and pleated gray pants. He locked Reggie into a firm handshake. "Welcome to New York," he said. "Let's have lunch."

He took him to the exalted "21" Club. As they waited for their meals, Steinbrenner spoke to Reggie in language the slugger himself could've scripted. "You can own the town, Reggie," he rhapsodized. "There will be so many business opportunities for you out there, you'll be able to pick and choose like you're at a long buffet table."

As for Reggie's concerns about the rapacious New York media, Steinbrenner assured him that, for a man of his rhetorical gifts, dealing with the writers would be "like eating ice cream." Steinbrenner wrapped up his pitch: "You and I are going to make a great team."

The insular nature of his promise—you and I, not everyone else—was what Reggie wanted to hear. The assurances of quick wealth were important to him, but so was his sense that Steinbrenner was treating him like a superstar and, better still, a son.

After lunch Steinbrenner suggested they take a walk around the city. "I've been here before," Reggie told him.

"Not with a chance to be a Yankee," Steinbrenner said with a wink.

It was an unseasonably warm, bright November day. Traffic choked the avenues, countless New Yorkers surged over the sidewalks, vendors barked, cops shouted, horns blasted—the bustle peculiar to the great city coursed about them. All around Reggie teemed purpose and promise.

Steinbrenner had stage-managed everything about the day, right down to the street scenes outside the club. "Reggie, you gotta play for the Yankees!" bellowed a passing cabbie.

"Hey, Reggie!" another yelled. "Come on, man. This is your kind of town!"

A group of black schoolchildren spilled around them and begged Reggie for autographs, and a horse-and-carriage driver offered him a ride. "See," Steinbrenner told him, "everybody knows and loves you already in this town."

He and Reggie walked back to his Upper East Side brownstone. Along the way, Steinbrenner pointed to the luxury apartments along Fifth Avenue and asked Reggie to imagine living there. He'd make the easy drive to Yankee Stadium, dine in upscale restaurants, drink deeply of the New York nightlife, and finalize lucrative endorsements on nearby Madison Avenue. Money and glory—on this day, their lingua franca.

After they arrived at Steinbrenner's sumptuous home, they talked money. "You know Gary and I want three million dollars," Reggie said.

"I can't pay you that much," Steinbrenner replied and countered with an offer of $2 million over five years.

"Guess I'll be on my way," Reggie said. "We can't do business together."

Steinbrenner promised he'd make another offer.

Reggie left New York the next day and informed his suitors that he'd accept final offers at the O'Hare Hyatt in Chicago on November 24.

On the twenty-fourth, Steinbrenner, in Indiana to visit his son at Culver Academy, chartered a plane and flew to Chicago to meet with Reggie and Gary Walker. He arrived at the hotel by 7:30 A.M. He sketched out the parameters of his final offer and stressed not only the dollars involved but also the opportunities, thrills, and gratifications of playing in New York.

He waited in the lobby. Walker called the Dodgers to see whether they'd match the existing offers. After a final discussion, they paged Steinbrenner, who returned to the suite. "You're it, George," Reggie told him.

In 1973, Steinbrenner, the new Yankees owner, had boasted that he'd one day have Billy Martin and Reggie Jackson on his team. He'd made good on his word. His eyes welled up, and he and Reggie embraced.

Reggie scribbled the terms of their agreement on a piece of hotel stationery: $2.66 million over five years, another $270,000 in alternative compensation, another $63,000 for the purchase of a luxury automobile, and a $1 million interest-free business loan. Reggie had left better contracts from San Diego and Montreal on the table—the latter an offer that Walker had begged him to accept—but ultimately what Steinbrenner, Yankees tradition, and the New York market offered couldn't be matched. Reggie handed Steinbrenner the piece of stationery. At the bottom of the page, he had scrawled to his latest father figure: "We are going on this venture together. I will not let you down. Reginald M. Jackson."

THIRTEEN

"Reggie Challenged Him in Every Way"

"REGGIE JACKSON," GABE PAUL told Steinbrenner, "will be a destructive force on the New York Yankees."

His wisdom penetrated. Paul knew that if they paid the going rates for Reggie it would disgruntle other veterans on the team, veterans who would suddenly feel unappreciated and underpaid. The 1976 team had enjoyed a famous rapport. As Dock Ellis, a former Pirate and a key member of that 1976 club, said, "In all those years on the Pirates, not one of those teams had the camaraderie that the Yankees had in one year." Reggie would upset things. Paul also knew a player like Reggie under a manager like Martin might tear the team apart.

Steinbrenner's refusal to listen to Martin outraged the manager. He cherished his relationship with his owner, as volatile as it was, and he wanted desperately to be closer to Steinbrenner. "We should have been the best of friends," Martin lamented years later.

To Steinbrenner, though, Martin was a drunk, an unrefined scamp who would only embarrass him in social settings. Reggie, in contrast, was cultivated and worldly enough to be more to Steinbrenner than just a foot soldier. Martin sensed the new arrangement from afar, and he resented it. He'd won a pennant the year before, and he deserved more consideration. But the onset of free agency brought out a new, unseen side of Steinbrenner. Never before had the Yankees' owner *romanced* anyone to the extent that he had Reggie. From Martin's standpoint, signing Reggie was the worst of all possible outcomes.

Martin could manage black and Latin players—in his days as a coach with the Twins he mentored a young Cuban shortstop named Zoilo Versalles and helped turn him into an MVP—but he also believed unfortunate things about them. In Martin's eyes, they lacked the personal courage and fortitude of white players. He often told his pitchers to throw at the heads of black and Latin hitters, in an effort to cow them. During Reggie's Oakland days, Martin had on a number of occasions ordered him brushed back for that very reason. He forbade his pitchers to throw first-pitch strikes to Latin hitters because he believed they lacked the discipline to resist a pitch off the plate. Martin also disdained "college boys"—as a minor-league manager he'd refused to play them at times—and Reggie was one of those, too. Then there was the money.

Fatherless and achingly poor, Martin had grown up in a tough section of West Berkeley, just across the line from Oakland. As a consequence, he resented the wealth of others. Even in his moneyed days as a coveted, championship manager, Martin schemed to make ends meet and never stopped feeling like a street punk who had trespassed his way into someone else's world. In that sense, he was uniquely ill equipped to manage a player like Reggie. Reggie boasted about his money and was about to become one of the richest ballplayers in the history of the game. He swaggered, he revolted, and he did things his own way.

The divide that separated baseball's generations gaped between Martin and Reggie. Martin's era was scarcely integrated and almost feudal in terms of player salaries. Reggie's, in contrast, was one of thoroughgoing change and empowerment. Martin had once, at the behest of Casey Stengel, swapped uniforms with Phil Rizzuto because the Yankees' star shortstop had received death threats. If the manager wanted a player to risk life and limb, a man of Martin's time and breeding would've done so. But not a coddled star like Reggie Jackson.

Millions of fans remembered Martin fondly as colorful, passionate, and intensely competitive. During his playing days, he was a modestly talented second baseman who made a career out of guile and doggedness. He was smart enough and driven enough to figure out what he needed to do to stay in the major leagues. His cornucopia of personality flaws—the heavy drinking, the paranoia, the smoldering envy, the spring-loaded temper—was well known around baseball. He assaulted strangers, players, reporters, and, on one occasion, an elderly traveling secretary. Still, as the manager of the Twins, Tigers, and Rangers, he got the most out of limited talent, just as he had as a player. Success came quickly and against all odds to Martin's teams. But it disappeared just as suddenly. So Martin was hired—and fired—with tidal regularity.

In his worst moments, Martin was prejudiced and vindictive. He peppered his speech with racial epithets; spoke in a faux southern drawl (an affectation from his days in Texas); and often referred to Elliott Maddox, one of his players in Detroit, as the "downtown nigger." In the years to come, Martin, when in the company of certain writers, would also refer to Reggie as a nigger. Long after the hell between Martin and Reggie had broken loose, Elston Howard would say that Martin "can get along with blacks if they don't challenge him. But Reggie challenged him in every way."

An old-school Yankee if ever there were one, Martin believed that the pinstripes were an honor a man sweated to earn. They were not to be used to entice a black player who seemed too comfortable in the new moneyed environment. He couldn't stand that this black braggart would make more in a month than he had in his entire career.

News of Reggie's signing descended upon Martin at the worst possible time. Less than two weeks prior, Martin's daughter had been arrested in Colombia for smuggling cocaine in her panty hose and was facing a lengthy stint in a third-world prison. Martin and his second wife had also separated, and she had custody of his only son. That left Martin alone and drinking at a modest hotel in Hasbrouck Heights, New Jersey.

He needed guidance and sympathy. The only man who could give that to him was busy wining and dining Reggie Jackson, across the Hudson River in glimmering Manhattan.

THREE DAYS AFTER coming to informal terms with Steinbrenner, Reggie arrived in New York. His introductory press conference was to be held at the Americana Hotel, and he arrived there the night before with a white, blond girlfriend on his arm.

They went up to their room and found twin beds. Reggie called the front desk, and the clerk told him they had nothing else available. He threatened to leave. He'd been given the Americana's most sumptuous suite—one in which President-elect Jimmy Carter had once stayed—but he didn't care. Reggie demanded a room in which he and his girlfriend could sleep comfortably and together. There was no such room, the clerk assured him.

Perhaps, Reggie thought, it was because he was with a white woman. This was New York, not Birmingham, yet as a grown, rich man he couldn't share a bed with his girlfriend. He sent for his bags. Then he phoned Steinbrenner and told him he was headed back to Oakland and wouldn't sign the contract.

Soon, Yankees public relations director Marty Appel called Reggie and told him that everything would be fine. He pleaded with Reggie not to go anywhere; then he hung up and secured a suite at the Plaza. By the time Appel called back, the desk manager told him that he'd located a room with a foldout double bed and that Reggie had taken it.

The next morning, Appel bustled into the Americana hours in advance of the 11 A.M. press conference. An hour beforehand, he phoned Reggie's room and told him he was coming up to brief him on the events of the day.

Reggie was dressed sharply in a tailored Geoffrey Beene suit— one of many he had received as part of his endorsement deal with the clothier. However, when Appel knocked, Reggie sent his naked girlfriend to answer the door. Reggie's romantic arrangements didn't trouble the Yankees, but he needed to make a point: Reggie Jackson wouldn't hide his taste for white women.

After Appel composed himself and they talked for a few minutes, they went downstairs for the press conference. Surrounded by his father, mother, brother, retinue of friends, and blond girlfriend, Reggie signed his contract. Steinbrenner beamed all the while.

Looking on were a few of Reggie's new teammates, including Thurman Munson, the AL MVP for 1976. Reggie held up his new Yankees jersey, numbered 42 in honor of Jackie Robinson. (Weeks later, he'd change it to 44, in honor of Hank Aaron and Willie McCovey.) "I'm not coming to New York to become a star," he told the assembled media. "I'm bringing my star with me."

Even the *New York Times*' editorial page recognized the magnitude of what had happened. "By choosing New York," the page read on December 6, "Jackson has become the Yankees' first black superstar, not to mention their first black millionaire."

FOURTEEN

"I'm the Straw That Stirs the Drink"

HE'D TAKEN HIS long-lens camera down to the water's edge. He snapped pictures of shorebirds in flight, people fishing off piers, children running through the deep sand. Then he stood on a pier and talked to an old man from New York. The man told Reggie that he had wandered as a child through the South Bronx turnip fields where one day Yankee Stadium would stand. He told Reggie he'd make it back there and come see him play. "Sit in right field," Reggie said. "I'll say hello to you."

Despite the simple, contemplative pleasures of that day, Reggie was depressed. He had arrived in Fort Lauderdale for his first Yankees spring training overweight and with an injured elbow. As well, after he had signed with the Yankees he had hosted a "Superstars" event for ABC, and two of his new teammates in attendance, Graig Nettles and Sparky Lyle, had been cold to him.

Many of the holdover Yankees envied his contract. Lyle wanted a new deal; Steinbrenner had promised Thurman Munson that he'd always be the highest-paid Yankee; Roy White and Chris Chambliss, among others, had yet to sign; and Nettles, coming off a year in which he had led the AL in home runs, wanted a pay raise. "It seems the guys who make the money are the flamboyant, controversial guys," Nettles said. "At least on this club."

When Reggie arrived—conspicuously, of course—at the Yankees' facilities for the first time, only Catfish Hunter bothered to walk over and greet him. Reggie worried that the Yankees players wouldn't accept him, even if the old man from the Bronx had.

The fear of failure consumed him. With all the dollars, his championship renown, and the bold talk came expectations—expectations heightened by the man who shouldered them and the city in which he was to play. If he failed, he would need someone else to blame. Society, he decided, would be his stooge. "The East Coast is not philosophically or socially as liberal as the West Coast," he said early in spring training. "I don't think the East is used to the black man standing up and saying what he thinks. Out of the ordinary." If those expectations went unmet, it would be because New York didn't know how to handle a man like Reggie. It wasn't true, but maybe people would believe it.

Reggie was still in a vulnerable state when Robert Ward of *Sport* magazine approached him for an interview. After the Murray Olderman story about him during his Oakland days, Reggie had sworn off ever talking to *Sport* again. But Ward persisted. Finally, Reggie agreed to meet Ward at the Banana Boat Bar in Fort Lauderdale.

When Ward asked him about the dynamic with his new teammates, Reggie gave no quarter: "I've got problems the other guys don't have. I've got this big image that comes before me. . . . I used to just be known as a great black athlete; now I'm respected as a tremendous intellect.

"You know, this team, it all flows from me. I've got to keep it all going. I'm the straw that stirs the drink."

He paused and sipped his drink. He thought about Munson, the captain. On the first day, Munson had ordered Reggie to run laps each day before he went to the cage to hit, as every other Yankee did. Reggie had refused. "Maybe I should say Munson and me," Reggie went on. "But really, he doesn't enter into it. He's being so damned insecure about the whole thing. I've overheard him talking about me."

Another pause. "Munson's tough, too. He's a winner."

Ward asked him whether some common ground could be reached with Munson. Reggie thought again about the captain, barking orders at him as though he were a rookie. "No, he's not ready for it yet. He doesn't even know he feels this way. . . . No, I'll wait, and eventually he'll be whipped. There will come that moment when he really knows I won, and he'll want to hear everything is all right, and then I'll go to him and we will get it right.

"I'm a leader and I can't lie down. But 'leader' isn't the right word . . . it's a matter of presence. Let me put it this way: no team I am on will ever be humiliated the way the Yankees were by the Reds in the World Series. That's why Munson can't intimidate me. . . . There is nobody who can do for a club what I can do. There is nobody who can put meat in the seats the way I can. Munson thinks he can be the straw that stirs the drink, but he can only stir it bad."

Finally, he said that if he chose, he could "snap" Munson and that he'd soon "have New York eating out of the palm of my hand."

Ward, taken aback, asked Reggie if he was speaking on the record. "Yes," Reggie said. "I want to see that in print. I want to read that."

He'd learned from his time in Oakland that candor was always acceptable. "On some teams, you might look into a corner of the clubhouse and think, that son of a bitch is loafing, that son of a bitch isn't carrying his load . . ." Catfish Hunter, Reggie's teammate in Oakland and New York, once explained. "But on the Athletics, you didn't just think it, man. You fucking *said* it."

Reggie lived that credo. This time, taking full flight from common sense, he had assailed Munson, the first Yankees captain since Lou Gehrig. Worse, Munson had done nothing to provoke him.

Worse still, Reggie had attacked a player beloved by teammates and fans alike.

Munson was a mulish sort, frumpy, built like a street-corner mailbox, and veneered with a reputation as a tireless worker and fierce competitor. The Yankees of the mid-1970s were Munson's team. And Reggie, the interloper who had yet to play a game as a Yankee and who had set off a rash of shared jealousies over his contract, had broadsided him.

"WE PRAY THIS year," a local pastor boomed to the Opening Day crowd at Yankee Stadium, "that from your great Heaven we receive the world championship."

Reggie was nervous. The calm he had felt that day on the beach in Florida was no more. Some of his teammates were already against him, and the *Sport* magazine article had yet to hit the newsstands. And then there was Martin.

Early in spring training, Martin had held him out of a game against the Mets. He'd done so, Reggie believed, because the game had been televised back in New York and Martin wanted to do everything he could to blunt Reggie's appeal. When Reggie did play, Martin batted him sixth in the lineup.

Martin drank heavily in spring training and ignored Steinbrenner's lineup mandates. As manager, he believed he deserved a power-sharing arrangement, but Steinbrenner, as owner, believed otherwise. Following the loss to the Mets, Martin and Steinbrenner screamed at each other in the clubhouse and almost came to blows. "If you want to fire me, fire me!" Martin screamed. "But leave me the fuck alone!" Steinbrenner did fire him, but he rehired him the next morning. Their struggle, with Reggie lost in the middle, continued.

Martin posted the Opening Day lineup, and Reggie was in the five hole and not, as had been customary for years, batting cleanup. Martin had once batted Munson second, but he had been returned to the third spot after he objected. The manager would accommodate most of his players—maybe just his white players—but definitely not Reggie. In Detroit, Martin had treated Willie Horton, another accomplished black hitter, similarly. Martin had platooned him, Horton had complained, and Martin had then questioned Horton's hustle, dedication, and toughness. It was his playbook for black players who defied him.

Reggie's mood lifted briefly when his name was announced to deafening calls of "Reg-gie! Reg-gie! Reg-gie!" He went 2 for 4 on the day with two runs scored in a win over the Brewers, and the chants didn't stop. But his anxieties soon took over, and he played distractedly.

In the third game of the season, he misplayed a ball in the outfield and was picked off first base in a Yankees loss. A few days later, though, Martin rewarded him for a home run and moved him from the sixth spot in the order to the coveted third spot—still not cleanup, though. Frustrated over the move, Reggie spent his off day shopping with Catfish Hunter, Lou Piniella, and Don Gullett. Afterward, Reggie insulted Piniella by telling a reporter that he'd never lower himself to purchasing a $26 shirt, as Piniella had, and that he wouldn't even consider a $50 pair of shoes. He then sorted through the thick roll of $100 bills in his wallet for all to see.

Within days, Reggie angered Martin once again by telling reporters he'd seen a doctor about his elbow. Martin said little about medical matters, and above all he was the one who decided what to tell the press. The next day Reggie wasn't in the lineup. "His arm is bothering him," Martin explained with Reggie nearby. "He told all the press it's bothering him. A couple of days' rest and he can come back strong. Right, Mr. Jackson?"

"Right," Reggie said.

The tight-lipped atmosphere bewildered him. Finley, for his multitude of faults, had let the A's talk. Reggie needed that. When he said he liked writers better than baseball men, he was currying favor, but he was also hinting at a larger truth—that Reggie was oftentimes an outsider in his profession. To an extent, he relished that status. But Martin pushed him too far outside, too far beyond the boundaries of comfort. The following weekend, he had dinner with a couple of writers in Milwaukee. For the first time, he talked openly about leaving the team.

He missed the camaraderie he'd enjoyed in Oakland. There he'd had deep histories with his teammates, and that made for a social ease. That ease was plainly lacking in New York. When he'd attempt to banter with guys like Mickey Rivers, Munson, and Nettles at the back of the bus, he came off stilted and uncomfortable. Heavy silences followed what he thought were his best one-liners. Reggie didn't know whether he was misfiring or his teammates were ostracizing him (he suspected the latter). Eventually, he started sitting at the front of the bus.

In those days, he had few friends, but Fran Healy was one of them. Healy and Reggie hit it off early. Some writers speculated that Healy, a nomadic backup catcher of little consequence, had befriended Reggie on Steinbrenner's orders. In truth, they had met a few years earlier, when Reggie had been in Oakland and Healy in Kansas City. After one game, they had lingered at the players' gate and talked about baseball, life, women, and aspirations. They had hit it off, and Healy would become one of his rare allies on the Yankees.

Some other Yankees, however, failed to appreciate the friendship. They thought Healy cozied up to Reggie for some other purpose—self-serving reasons or, as the rumors went, to please Steinbrenner. More than once, teammates called Healy a "nigger lover." But according to Healy, he and Reggie merely liked one another. He could tell that Reggie needed a friend.

Sometimes they'd have dinner at Reggie's apartment. Other nights, they'd dine together at Oren & Aretsky, Jim McMullen's, or Rusty Staub's place on Third Avenue. On the road, Healy would pick out an expensive restaurant and make reservations for two. Reggie would always pick up the bill.

Another friend to Reggie was nineteen-year-old Ray Negron. One afternoon in 1973, Negron, two of his brothers, and two cousins were spray painting graffiti on Yankee Stadium. Steinbrenner happened upon them, grabbed Negron by the collar, and dragged him inside. The others got away. Negron pleaded for mercy, and Steinbrenner, in one of his charitable moods, let him do penance by working as a batboy. Steinbrenner then gave him a job performing menial tasks around the clubhouse. Later came a brief stint in the Pirates' minor-league system, and then he returned to the Bronx to work for the Yankees, which he did on and off for much of his adult life. Over the years, Negron's brothers and cousins, the ones who had gotten away on that day in 1973, would suffer the perils of street life. "You were lucky you got caught," one cousin, then dying from AIDS, once told him.

He survived by befriending the right people. When Reggie came along, Negron was already close to Martin and Steinbrenner. Initially, Reggie and Negron bonded because they both spoke Spanish and could have private conversations even in a crowded clubhouse. Then, to keep Negron close to him (and away from Martin), Reggie made him his factotum. He paid him to pick up his dry cleaning, answer fan mail, take phone messages, and be his spotter in the weight room. In essence, Reggie paid him to be his friend.

In spite of those moments with Healy and Negron, the early days of the 1977 season were lonely. Then Munson reached out to him. At first his gestures were small—a pat on the back, a few words of idle talk during batting practice—but then he told Reggie that he hadn't realized how sensitive he was. He told Reggie to relax and focus. "We need you," Munson said.

For a man of Munson's reserved mien, it was an outreach to behold. Reggie appreciated it deeply and told the writers that Munson was "a good human being." But his attack on Munson had yet to come to light.

On April 25, Reggie returned to Baltimore for the first time as a Yankee. The Orioles fans threw beer at him in right field. They threw heavy lug nuts, rocks, and even a bucket of water. A couple of white fans just beyond the outfield fence lynched him in effigy. Reggie, with two doubles and a game-winning homer, lifted the Yankees to their sixth consecutive win. "The more pressure, the more I respond," he said afterward.

In early May, Reggie attended a luncheon in his honor at the "21" Club, the very place where, the previous November, Steinbrenner had seduced him. This time the occasion was the Reggie! bar. Reggie had said years earlier that if he played in New York "they'd name a candy bar after me." Now that was coming true.

Standard Brands would pay Reggie up to $3 million over the next decade to lend his name to its 25-cent candy. It would be the first candy bar named after a baseball player since the Ty Cobb decades earlier. It was also one of the three most valuable endorsement contracts ever bestowed upon an athlete.

Reggie's corporate presence was indeed on the rise. Before his deal with Puma Shoes in 1973, no black athlete had been part of an extended national advertising campaign. Then came the Reggie! bar and, around the same time, O. J. Simpson's deal with Hertz. Not long after, Joe Greene's iconic Coca-Cola commercial aired during Super Bowl XIV, and Walter Payton became the second African American to appear on the Wheaties box. Reggie, more than anyone else, proved that a black athlete could pitch products to white America.

He went on to sign lucrative contracts with Panasonic, Volkswagen (in one famous VW television spot, Reggie beamed at the camera and said, "The only person I have to please is me"), Pony Shoes, Nabisco, Murjani jeans, Ellesse sporting wear, Pentax cameras, and Remco Toys. Locally he struck deals with the furrier Ben Kahn and the jeweler Ralph Destino, among many others. Later would come movie roles and guest appearances on popular television shows such as *The Love Boat*, *Diff'rent Strokes*, *Archie Bunker's Place*, and *The Jeffersons*. Reggie also did off-season work for ABC Television and developed a children's show for Warner called *Reggie Jackson's World of Sports*.

Reggie's rising business fortunes pleased him, but on the field things took a turn for the worse. He slumped in mid-May. On a road trip to Oakland, Martin benched him against Vida Blue. Reggie was eager to face his old teammate, but Martin worried about the Yankees' struggles against left-handers. The game went fifteen innings, and Martin never called on Reggie. Even in the final frame, Martin turned to Dell Alston—a recent call-up from the minors—and not Reggie, to pinch-hit. "I'm a mediocre ballplayer, and I'm overpaid," Reggie said after the game.

Soon after, the *Sport* magazine article he so dreaded came out.

The Yankees were in Boston for a series against the Red Sox, and before the game a few copies of the magazine were passed around the Yankees clubhouse. The players who read it were agape, some with disbelief and some with anger. "That prick," one player muttered. "That dirty son of a bitch," said another. Two others moved their lockers away from his.

Rather than explain his heresies or deny the contents of the article, Reggie said nothing and dressed as quickly as possible. After a few teammates had gone out of their way to walk by his locker and kick his equipment bag across the floor, he went out to take batting practice.

Fran Healy suggested that perhaps Ward had misquoted him or taken his comments out of context. "For three pages?" Munson shouted. "Three fucking pages?"

Munson was a famously jealous ballplayer. He resented that Boston's Carlton Fisk was regarded as the better player, and he suspected that Fisk's prep school good looks had something to do with it. But when he surveyed what it meant to be Carlton Fisk and what it meant to be Thurman Munson, his consoling knowledge was that he was the one and only Yankees captain. Reggie had struck at the heart of that consolation.

Reggie would insist that his words in the *Sport* story had been twisted. Then he would claim that Ward had revealed off-the-record portions of their conversation. And then he would say that Ward had made things up out of whole cloth. To this day, Reggie denies referring to himself as "the straw that stirs the drink." However, years after the story came out, he admitted to Ira Berkow of the *Times* that he had made, as he called it, the "straw remark" about Munson.

That same night, on ABC's *Monday Night Baseball*, Reggie went 2 for 4 with an RBI and two runs scored, and with one out in the seventh he homered to right off a Bill Lee sinker. He admired the shot as it carried deep into the outfield stands, and then he rounded the bases. His teammates—angered yet dutiful and aware of the leering cameras—thronged at one end and prepared to greet Reggie with outstretched hands. Reggie, though, made an abrupt turn and entered the opposite end of the dugout. He took his seat on the bench without touching a single hand. Afterward, Reggie said his hand had hurt too much for such vigorous handshakes and high fives. Munson called him "a fucking liar."

The next day the fans in New York gave Munson a blaring ovation and booed Reggie every time he batted and every time the ball settled into his glove in right field. No one, save Healy and Negron, spoke to Reggie in the clubhouse or in the parking lot after games. Before a doubleheader against Texas, Reggie asked Willie Randolph four times when batting practice began. Each time, Randolph ignored him. "Did you ever see anything like this?" Reggie asked a writer. "Thank God I'm a Christian. This stuff doesn't bother me."

But it did bother him. It particularly bothered him that Randolph, one of the Yankees' black players, was taking Munson's side. Panicked, Reggie went to Martin and asked him whether he could address the team. Martin said no. The manager wanted Reggie to apologize first to him and then to each individual on the team. Reggie had no choice but to agree. Before Martin allowed the press into the clubhouse, Reggie went to each locker and made his apologies. Most, including Munson, didn't acknowledge him.

Days later, Munson was on base when Chris Chambliss homered. Waiting at home plate, Reggie put out his hand. Munson ignored it. "I don't think he saw it," Reggie said.

"I saw it," Munson said.

When Reggie again homered off Bill Lee, Munson waited for him, hand coolly extended. Reggie touched it.

Healy then summoned the pair to dinner in the hope of repairing the relationship. Munson, though, had made as much peace as he could. "Tell me, Jackson," he said at one point. "Tell me one thing you have that I'd want. I have three beautiful children and a lovely wife. I have a happy home life. What do you have? You have nothing."

For once Reggie had no answer.

FIFTEEN

"I'm a Nigger to Them, and I Just Don't Know How to Be Subservient"

As June 1977 dawned, Reggie authored solid numbers, and the Yankees were just one and a half games out of first place. Yet Reggie's depression reached new depths. First, Finley told a gathering of reporters in Chicago that Reggie was "a disruptive influence" on the A's and that Oakland had "won in spite of Jackson and Holtzman, and not because of them."

Finley's comments dumbfounded Reggie. Less than a year before, they'd spoken kind words to each other on a Chicago park bench. They had, Reggie thought, overcome their lingering resentments. In his solitary moments in New York—which were all too frequent—he had nothing but his sugary recollections of how things had been in Oakland. Now Finley had sullied those memories.

Reggie spoke openly of leaving New York. After games and on off days he avoided friends and spent lonely evenings on his Fifth Avenue balcony, drinking wine and vacantly watching the more purposeful human traffic below. He had a nineteenth-floor corner apartment with a view of Central Park. He was neighbors with Gloria Vanderbilt, Cicely Tyson, Anne Bancroft, and Mel Brooks. Around him, he had imported rugs, exotic plants, and portraits of himself. Yet so much was missing.

Reggie raised his batting average by forty-four points in the span of twenty-three days, but his relationship with Martin worsened. Martin still refused to bat Reggie in the cleanup spot and still found other ways to needle his star. Following a Friday game in Boston, a 9–4 Yankees loss, Martin worried to the press about the safety of Mickey Rivers, who had worn a batting helmet in the outfield because fans in the Fenway bleachers hurled trash at him. "How come I've had things thrown at me all season and he's never said a thing?" Reggie wondered aloud.

The next morning, Martin read Reggie's comeback and fumed. Later, Martin sat on the bench alongside Reggie and Bucky Dent, and he and Dent discussed Martin's somewhat controversial—and unsuccessful—decision to have Dent lay down a squeeze bunt the night before. "Reggie," Martin said, looking for validation but also offering Reggie a chance to suck up, "don't you think it was a good play?"

Reggie's eyes never left the field in front of him. "No," he said.

The next day, the Yankees played the Red Sox again in the nationally televised Game of the Week. In the home half of the sixth inning, with the Yankees down 7–4 and a runner on first, Jim Rice, Boston's fearsome slugger, stepped in. He lofted a check-swing fly to shallow right, which fell in front of Reggie. Rice's hustle in tandem with Reggie's casual throw back into the infield yielded a double. From Martin's perspective, it looked as though Reggie had been loafing. Indifference never played well with Martin, particularly while losing to Boston. In the dugout, Martin said to Munson, "I'm going to go get the son of a bitch."

In the middle of the inning, Martin sent out Paul Blair to replace Reggie in right field—an unusual step and one taken only to embarrass a player. As Blair jogged to his position, Reggie pointed at himself and asked, "Me?"

Blair nodded and told him he'd have to ask Martin about it. Reggie made his way to the dugout, and when he reached the top step, he flung his arms wide. "What did I do?" he screamed at Martin.

"Nobody who doesn't hustle plays for me," Martin spat back at him.

Reggie took the virtue of hustling seriously, but a sense of mission didn't drive him. Instead, he feared being labeled a "lazy" black ballplayer. In his play, Reggie had always lacked the mellow richness of a Willie Mays or a Curt Flood, but he believed deeply in the appearance of effort. "They mean nothing," Reggie once said of those appearances. "It's all eyewash, and I've mastered it."

On that day in Boston, Reggie had shaded Rice to right center, and the location of the hit meant that Willie Randolph, normally the cutoff man on any ball hit to right field, pursued the ball and was out of position. When Reggie fielded it, he had no cutoff man to throw to, and his failing elbow (three cortisone shots since March) made the throw less than firm and direct. As well, because Fred Lynn charged into third, Nettles wasn't free to back up a strong throw. So Reggie played it, in his own words, "cautiously." It was a tough and confusing play for Reggie, and it laid bare his declining skills in the field. It was not, however, an act of laziness.

"Why did you take me out?" Reggie shouted at Martin. "You have to be crazy to embarrass me in front of fifty million people!"

It was just what Martin didn't want to hear. Reggie worried more about the television lens than anything else. "I don't give a shit," he said. "When you decide to play, then you play right field. Not until."

Nearby, Ray Negron sensed the rapidly deepening crisis. He lobbed a towel over a nearby television camera and threatened to crack the cameraman over the head if he continued shooting. Negron's actions spared the Yankees an invasive close-up, but another NBC camera, this one in center field, channeled the showdown back to, as

Reggie estimated, 50 million viewers across the country. The broad-caster Joe Garagiola narrated the action. "Billy," Reggie said, "nothing I can ever do would please you. You don't like me. You don't think I can play ball. You never have from the first day. "

"I treat every player the same," Martin shot back. "I ought to kick your fucking ass."

Elston Howard, one of Martin's coaches, got between the two men. But then Reggie said, "Who the fuck do you think you're talking to, old man? Don't you ever dare show me up again, mother-fucker."

"Old man?" Martin screamed back at him. "I'll show you who's an old man."

He charged Reggie once more. Yogi Berra stepped between them and wrestled Martin down to the bench. Reggie took off his glasses. "Let's go, old man!" he shouted. "Come on, old man . . . let's get it over with, old man!"

"Let me go!" Martin yelled at Berra. "I'm gonna break his fucking ass!"

"There they go!" Garagiola blared over the airwaves.

Berra's grip was firm, though, and Jim Wynn secured Reggie and shoved him up the hallway to the clubhouse. Once there, Wynn, Mike Torrez, and Healy tried to persuade Reggie to leave and go back to the hotel. But Reggie wanted more. He'd done nothing wrong, and he wanted a final confrontation with his overreaching foe.

Despite their visceral dislike for each other, Reggie and Martin had more in common than either cared to admit. Each cherished his relationship with Steinbrenner, and each had been betrayed by a father figure. For Reggie, it was Finley. For Martin, it was his manager, Casey Stengel, who had allowed the painful trade that had sent Martin from the Yankees to Kansas City in 1957. Growing up, they had resented the wealth around them, and they had bullied the neighborhood rich kids. Back in Wyncote, Reggie and his friends would park their muscle cars at a nearby church and drink beer and razz people as they came out of the Sunday worship services. When they'd hear about a party they hadn't been invited to, Reggie and his buddies would crash it and beat up any kids who didn't act properly deferential. If it was winter, they would steal their jackets. To compound the humiliation, Reggie would wear the jacket to school the next week, all but daring his victim to say anything. Reggie, though, had turned that envy into a drive, whereas Martin had held on to it and let it derange him.

Reggie wanted to face down that ugliness. He was in the trainer's room, a haven off limits to the media, resisting Torrez's entreaties to leave the ballpark. Then Negron showed up. "Come on," Negron said to Reggie. "Let's go back to the parking lot. There'll be a cop out there, and he'll get you a cab."

Something about Negron at that moment calmed Reggie in a way his teammates could not. His senses returned to him. He was not Martin. He was not a street thug who needed to settle things this way. He was smarter and more calculating. He was better at this game. Reggie left the park.

After he returned to the Boston Sheraton, he summoned a handpicked group of writers to his suite. He'd already divided up the New York scribes into "Reggie guys" and "Billy guys." He invited the former group up to his room. This was his catharsis—airing his feelings, sometimes in a calculated manner and sometimes not calculatedly enough, with an honesty that could frighten. Few on the Yankees would listen to him or even talk to him. So he turned to his writers.

When they arrived, Reggie was shirtless. A gold cross dangled in front of his chest. He sipped wine and thumbed through a copy of the Bible. "You cut me off if I go too far," Reggie told Mike Torrez, who stood nearby.

He hadn't been loafing, Reggie told them. Then he dropped to his knees and threw his arms theatrically apart. "I play right field when they let me. I hit anywhere from third to seventh," he wailed. His voice rose like a street preacher's. "I do anything they tell me to do. I'll continue to play well all year. I won't ask to be traded. Thank God I'm a Christian. Christ got my mind right. I won't fight the man. I'll do whatever they tell me.

"It makes me cry, the way they treat me on this team!" he bellowed. "The Yankees are Ruth and Gehrig and DiMaggio and Mantle. I'm a nigger to them, and I just don't know how to be subservient. I'm making seven hundred thousand dollars a year, and they treat me like dirt. I've got an IQ of 160, they can't mess with me. They've never had anyone like me on their team before." But Reggie spared Steinbrenner. "I love that man, he treats me like I'm somebody," he said of the Boss. "The rest of them treat me like dirt."

Torrez finally kicked everyone out of the room. After the writers—frantic with their career-making quotes—scurried away, Reggie continued his hysteria. It was Reggie in all his pathos, contradictions, and insecurities. It took the civil rights leader Jesse Jackson, whom Reggie had called to his hotel room, to calm him down. He told Reggie how important he was to the black community, what a visible reminder he was of the possible. He mattered to too many people to let Martin run him off. Buck up and fight, the reverend told him.

Reggie spent the rest of the evening drinking with George Scott of the Red Sox. He stumbled into the lobby about eleven o'clock. "The Yankees have never fucked anybody like I've been fucked!" he screamed at the guests and hotel workers. "It's you people I feel sorry for. You're the ones who are going to miss out when I'm gone next year."

Rarely had Reggie been a tribune for his race—he was, after all, the man who had admitted to Catfish Hunter that he wanted to be white. And when he did invoke his blackness, he usually did so to deflect blame. On that evening in Boston—when he said things that other black ballplayers dared not—it seemed as if race were once again his armor.

Perhaps, though, there was some sincerity in his words. Earlier in the year, when other obligations had forced him to leave an autograph session with people still waiting in line, an older black woman had scolded him: "We helped make you. You owe black people something."

Her words had given Reggie pause. Others had said similar things to Reggie before, but hearing it from this woman, who was motherly in appearance and manner, struck him in a new way. He may have thought about that woman when he spoke out against the strains of racism on the Yankees. Or it may have been a cynical dodge. The country's preeminent black newspaper, the *Amsterdam News*, thought it was just that.

Shortly after he arrived in New York, Reggie had talked about committing himself to the redevelopment of Harlem—"I'm rich," he'd said, "I want to give something back to blacks"—but according to the *News* he wasn't living up to his promises. Major Robinson, one of the most venerable black journalists, said that Reggie had refused invitations to do a walk-through in Harlem and meet with a black civic group. "What has the 'rich nigger' done for the 'poor niggers' before he arrived in New York?" Robinson wrote shortly after the Boston meltdown.

Robinson then quoted Huel Washington, the editor of a black weekly in Oakland, who was equally unsparing. "He screamed black when it was to his advantage," Washington said of Reggie's Oakland days. "But otherwise he lived on the other side of town. . . . He was all for Reggie, riding around in his $27,500 car and living in his $175,000 house. When he left town, not a black tear was shed."

Yet Reggie, mixed motives and all, made a difference. In the coming months and years, black Yankees such as Willie Randolph would occasionally reassure Reggie that he was "speaking for a lot of the black guys around here." Even Roy White would encourage Reggie's activism from time to time. In the full light of Reggie's history, what happened in his Boston hotel room may have been false and dishonest pioneering. But it mattered.

The next morning Gabe Paul, on Steinbrenner's orders, summoned Reggie and Martin to his office. Paul listened to each man's version of what had happened. Reggie explained that he had, in fact, hustled. Martin exploded again. "Boy," he said, "what you think you're doing and what my eyes tell me you're doing are two different things."

Whether it was the old woman at the autograph signing or Martin— his bigotry, his intemperance, and the tense environment he created— who brought out Reggie's latent racial consciousness, he wasn't going to let Martin call him a boy. He told him so.

"Nobody's restraining me now, motherfucker!" Martin shot back. "You thought I was an old man yesterday. Let's see how old I am right now."

Paul calmed them down, and the meeting continued, albeit with more harsh words. In the end, Reggie and Martin agreed that they should hide their contempt for each other. Reggie's sense of persecution, though, remained intact.

Boston completed the sweep and gutted the Yankees 11–1 in the final game. They had come to Boston in first place, but they left two and a half games out and caught up in a devitalizing feud. They moved on to Detroit.

By the time the Yankees arrived, the fallout from Reggie's hotel suite comments was being fully realized. The press wanted more from him. When they probed him, though, he struck back. "They can't accept the idea of a black man being as smart as they are," Reggie said of the media in a televised interview. Some of those who covered the Yankees were appalled that Reggie had summoned them to his room, delivered a blistering diatribe on the subject of race, and then ridiculed them when they reported his words. Other writers knew from experience his vaporous sense of accountability.

Scathed though they may have been, the writers had something else to chase down: rumors that Martin would soon be fired. Steinbrenner joined the team in Detroit, and before the first game of the series he called Reggie. The Boss asked him whether Martin should be let go. Reggie had appraised that very question. "No, George," Reggie said, "you shouldn't do that."

He then told the stunned Steinbrenner that he'd leave the team if Martin were fired. Frank Robinson, Reggie's old ally, was lobbying for the Yankees job from afar. But Reggie backed Martin, a man he detested and believed to be a racist. It was a crass bit of realpolitik on Reggie's part—he knew that if Martin were fired, teammates and fans would blame him. It seemed inconceivable that those two groups could loathe him any more than they did, but they'd surely summon up more hatred if Martin were ousted. Aware of his own psychological frailties, Reggie knew he couldn't cope with that. His threat forced Steinbrenner to spare Martin.

Steinbrenner, still angry over the indiscretions in Boston, forced Reggie and Martin to endure another sit-down. "Goddammit," Steinbrenner thundered at Reggie, "I don't want any more bullshit about race—black, white, or purple."

Steinbrenner then demanded that Martin, to keep his job, be more "flexible" in how he deployed Reggie. Reggie was Steinbrenner's indulgence, and the Boss knew that Reggie's success or failure would reflect upon his ownership. He forced them to share a silent and awkward cab ride to Tiger Stadium. To add to the portraiture, Reggie and Martin burst through the clubhouse doors with arms around each other's shoulders and forced smiles for all. "We are allies," Reggie declared just before he took batting practice. Then he quoted scripture extolling the virtues of obedience and submission. They were the same verses that Alvin Dark had invoked to defend his bowing before Charlie Finley. The very man who, two days prior, didn't "know how to be subservient" now presented himself as the most abiding of servants. He then blew the game when he misplayed an easy fly ball. Afterward, Reggie moaned that he "ought to quit. Just give up."

They returned to New York, and on June 24 they faced the Red Sox once again. The Sox came in having won thirteen of fourteen, and they'd hit thirty home runs in their previous nine games. Before the game, Reggie had his eyes examined. The drops left his eyes still dilated near game time, but he expected to play. Martin sent the trainer to him. "I can play," Reggie said.

Martin, though, saw enough cover to keep Reggie out of the lineup, Steinbrenner's orders be damned. He scratched out Reggie's name mere moments before first pitch and inserted Roy White in his place. Reggie fumed on the bench. It was a Friday night in the Bronx, and in attendance was the largest regular-season Yankee Stadium crowd since 1961. In the first inning, Munson singled home a run. Boston countered in the second with home runs by Yastrzemski and Butch Hobson. Paul Blair homered in the home half. About that time, Reggie returned to the clubhouse to be examined by the team physician, who cleared Reggie to play. Gabe Paul sent a message to Martin: get Reggie into the game.

George Scott hit a blast in the fourth to put the Sox up 5–3. From there, Bill Lee and then the Boston bull pen smothered the Yankees' lineup. With one out in the ninth, Martin summoned Reggie to pinch-hit for Bucky Dent. He did so in glum silence and grounded out to first. Willie Randolph came up next and hit one to the gap in left center. Yastrzemski darted toward the ball and, to all eyes, had a bead on it, but the ball just escaped his grasp and rolled. Randolph made it to third standing up. Boston's Bill Campbell, frustrated and working his third inning of relief, hung the next pitch to Roy White, who hit it for a game-tying home run.

In the eleventh, Ramon Hernandez replaced Campbell for Boston. He walked Nettles and then balked him to second. Manager Don Zimmer then ordered Rivers intentionally walked to set up the double play. That brought up Reggie for the second time. The first pitch crossed the plate, so Reggie swung. He thought he missed his spot and popped it up. Instead, he lined the pitch to right field. Nettles, who read the ball off the bat, scored well ahead of Rick Miller's throw. The Yankees won, 6–5.

In the clubhouse afterward, Reggie, still angry over his treatment, deadpanned his answers to the press. Finally, one reporter asked him whether he was happy. "Oh, yes," Reggie said. "I'm happy. Real happy."

The self-satisfied Martin, meanwhile, reflected on his decisions—starting White, who had hit the crucial home run in the ninth, and pinch-hitting Reggie, who had driven in the winning run. "Managing is really a lot of fun," he said. "I've really enjoyed the last week."

Had the Yankees failed to come back, they would've fallen to six games behind Boston. Martin almost certainly would've been fired. He had defied Steinbrenner's orders to play Reggie, and, in part, it had been Reggie who had saved him. The Red Sox went on to lose their next eight games.

By early July, Reggie's numbers were customarily strong, and he led the league in doubles. The Yankees rose to first place. It remained a back-and-forth affair with Boston, and Martin continued to play occasional mind games with Reggie, batting him everywhere save cleanup and trotting out defensive replacements in the late innings.

That same month, an anonymous Yankee said that Steinbrenner, in the manner of Charlie Finley, was dictating the lineups to Martin. Normally, this wouldn't have bothered Reggie, who aligned himself squarely with Steinbrenner. If true, though, it meant that not even Steinbrenner wanted him to bat cleanup. Another anonymous source also whispered that Reggie played soft and had missed time with a strained groin while Munson suited up every day with seven stitches in his hand. For all his outward hubris and self-regard, these tiny affronts battered Reggie's confidence. He still sulked, and on occasion he still sobbed as he drove home from the stadium after games.

By the All-Star break, the Yankees had slipped to third place but were just three games off the division lead. The fans made Reggie an All-Star after leaving him out in 1976. This time the All-Star Game would be played, fittingly enough, in Yankee Stadium. After the 7–5 AL loss, Reggie, who went 1 for 2 on the night, signed autographs outside the players' parking lot. After a few minutes, he said he had to leave, which he did, for a meeting with the Standard Brands team to discuss the Reggie! bar. One spurned youngster eyeballed Reggie. "You motherfucker," he said.

Reggie chased him across the parking lot, and the boy fell down. Days later, Reggie learned that the boy had pressed charges and claimed that Reggie had pushed him down and stomped on his wrist. However, a witness refuted the boy's version, and the district attorney declined to press charges. The story nonetheless had plenty of traction with the city's tabloids, and Reggie's image in the eyes of New York fans cratered further. "I don't want to be in New York anymore," he told the *Daily News*.

Struggles in late July brought fresh rumors that Martin would be fired. Reggie knew that he needed Martin, and once again he pleaded for restraint from Steinbrenner. "The manager, he's a fine man," Reggie lied. "We don't have to like the guy . . . but we should stand by him for a few innings a day."

Around that time, rumors had it that Dick Williams, then the manager of the Montreal Expos, was in Steinbrenner's sights. Reggie had been forced to take up Martin's cause to the detriment of Frank Robinson, and now it was Williams, his favorite manager. Soon after, Reggie was fired as the host of the television series *Greatest Sports Legends*. The producer of the show, Berl Rotfeld, said Reggie was "arrogant, egotistical, and extremely hard to work with."

It all conspired to make Reggie nostalgic for what had been, in his mind, better times. The tempests in Oakland had been similar to the ones in New York, but in New York Reggie had no one to share his troubles with. There was no Joe Rudi, no Dave Duncan, no Rollie Fingers, no guys with whom he had spent time in minor-league backwaters. There was no one who knew him, how complicated he was, how he at once pined for recognition and acceptance but needed, at a moment's notice, solitude. You didn't befriend a man like Reggie; you acclimated to him. No one in New York understood that.

A trip to Oakland, the place he now longed for, came just in time. After the second game of the series, a 9–3 Yankees victory, an Oakland radio reporter asked Reggie to compare his new home to his old one. Reggie seized upon the differences in media coverage and said that back in Oakland they'd had only one writer, who regularly traveled with the team, whereas in New York the reporters on the beat could fill a major-league roster. But that wasn't the only difference. "Ninety percent of what the New York press has written about this team has not been true."

Reggie didn't know that his interview was being piped back into the clubhouse, for all the New York press to hear. When he returned, the writers confronted him. "You weren't supposed to hear that," he said.

Then came revived talk of an "escape provision" in Reggie's contract—one that would allow him to break his contract with the Yankees should he want out. Gabe Paul insisted that no such clause existed. Reggie and Steinbrenner had discussed it, but whether it had made it into the final contract, he didn't know. Yet as Reggie mourned what was likely an airtight contract, Martin batted him in the cleanup spot—on Steinbrenner's orders—and the fans warmed to him. After his performance in an August 12 doubleheader against the Angels, they couldn't help but. In the first game, he doubled, tripled, and drove in three runs. In the second game, Reggie blasted two home runs and gunned down a runner at the plate. The Yankees had won five in a row.

Other than some ill-timed comments made upon the death of Elvis Presley (Reggie reminded the writers that Presley had once said he needed just two things from black people: to shine his shoes and to buy his records), Reggie practiced measured discretion and hit. On August 23, Reggie, playing despite a sore knee, went 1 for 3 with two walks and a run scored in an 8–3 win over the White Sox. The victory lifted the Yankees into the division lead for the first time since July 9.

On August 26, they won for the seventeenth time in nineteen games.

A few days later, Reggie, challenged by more negative comments from Martin, rose up again. It was a crucial tilt against the Red Sox, one that provided an afternoon of connoisseur's baseball—pressure pitching and arresting defense. For the National Anthem, the Yankee Stadium speakers blared a recording by the Boston Pops Orchestra. The crowd booed throughout.

In the third, Carl Yastrzemski flung himself into the gap and hauled in a Munson liner. In the fourth, Jim Rice led off the inning with a single. Then Carlton Fisk drove a ball to the warning track in center, but Mickey Rivers ran it down. George Scott followed with a blast to right. Reggie, battling the sun and a ball that seemed to rise as it approached him, made a leaping stab, crashed into the right-field fence, and came down with the out. Rice stole second, but Butch Hobson popped out to end the inning.

The next inning, Boston loaded the bases with no outs. Martin ordered the infield at double-play depth. On cue, Fred Lynn grounded lamely to Ed Figueroa on the mound. Figueroa came home for one, and then Munson whipped the ball to first for the second out. Next was Yastrzemski, who crushed Figueroa's first pitch up the middle. What should have been a two-out, two-RBI single instead struck Figueroa flush on the leg. He gathered the ball and retired Yastrzemski at first. Meanwhile, Figueroa's counterpart, Reggie Cleveland, retired thirteen Yankees hitters in a row.

Boston threatened again in the seventh. Denny Doyle led off with a single in front of Reggie. Rick Burleson bunted him to second, and Bernie Carbo came up next. Carbo sank a line drive into right center. Reggie broke quickly on it. He dived at the last instant and plucked the ball inches before it hit the grass and rolled to the wall. Lynn dribbled one to second for the third out.

In the ninth, with the game still scoreless, Rivers snared a sinking liner off the bat of Scott, and then, on the next pitch, he ranged 420 feet to one of the yawning gaps and stole a home run from Hobson. "I think Mickey Rivers is going to need an oil change," Yastrzemski said later.

Munson led off the home half. In the dugout, Martin approached Reggie. "If Munson gets on . . . what kind of bunter are you?" he said.

"I'll get it down," Reggie assured him.

"Make sure you do."

Munson hit a humpback single to center. The third-base coach, Dick Howser, stopped Reggie as he strode toward the box. "You'll be bunting," Howser told him. Reggie nodded. Then Reggie stepped in. He jabbed the bat at the first pitch but missed. Bunt sign again. Ball one. Strike two. Bunt sign off. Ball two. Bunt sign back on. Ball three. Bunt sign off for good. In the dugout, Martin huffed at Reggie's inability to get Munson to second. Behind the plate, Fisk dropped one finger and patted the inside of his left shin. Cleveland nodded and on the payoff pitch tried to tease Reggie low and away. It was ball four, but Reggie lunged at it. When Cleveland heard ball on bat, he thought for an instant that it *had* to be a double play—it was too far outside to pull and too low to drive. He expected that Reggie would nub it to second, where Doyle would field it cleanly and flip it to Burleson, who would make the easy throw to first long before the lumbering Munson could bear down on him. As quickly as Cleveland could imagine it, though, Reggie somehow lifted the pitch and yanked the ball deep to right field, over Carbo's head, and into the bleachers in right center. He shouldn't have been able to touch the pitch, let alone hit it 430 feet.

His teammates—Munson, Nettles, Rivers, Randolph, all of them—waited for him at home. He stomped on the plate, and the Yankees had won, 2–0. The Red Sox dropped to third place with seventeen games to play. In the clubhouse, Reggie said his clutch home run had been "like a fairy tale" and that "you could feel everybody loving you."

In New York, rarely was there a sober middle for him—it was

either desperation or ebullience. On this night, it was finally the latter. He thanked Steinbrenner for taking a chance on him. "Tonight," Reggie declared, "they got something back from me."

In late September, the Yankees surpassed 2 million in home attendance for the first time since 1949. On October 1, they clinched the AL East title, and the next day they earned their one hundredth win of the season. The Yankees won forty of fifty to end the season, and Reggie tallied the most RBIs by a Yankee since Mickey Mantle in 1964. All the while, Steinbrenner whispered to the media that Reggie's agent was pressing him to fire Martin.

THE YANKEES' OPPONENT in the ALCS was Kansas City. In game one, Reggie and the Yankees faced a tough lefty in Paul Splittorff. Splittorff beat them with eight strong innings, and Reggie endured an 0 for 4 day at the plate. The Yankees rebounded to win game two, but back in the Bronx the Royals took the third contest, which put them one win away from their first pennant in franchise history.

As the Yankees readied for a must-win affair in game four, rumors swirled that Martin would be fired if the team lost. Reggie went 0 for 3 at the plate and played poorly in the field. Despite him, the Yankees held on to win, 6–4, and forced a deciding fifth game. Reggie was hitting just .071 for the series, but the promise of another big game invigorated him. "This is the fifth time I've been in a do-or-die game," he told the writers at his Kansas City hotel. "All the other four, we didn't lose."

After he arrived at Royals Stadium the next afternoon, Reggie found that his name wasn't on the lineup card. When Martin had bad news to impart to one of his players, he'd send Yogi Berra to talk to the whites and Elston Howard to talk to the blacks and Latinos. So it fell to Howard to tell Reggie he wouldn't start the deciding game. He was struggling, and Splittorff, who'd schooled Reggie in game one, was on the mound again. On some level, Martin's decision made tactical sense, but you simply didn't bench Reggie Jackson for this kind of game. In doing so, Martin had imperiled his job. If the Yankees lost with Steinbrenner's prized investment on the bench, Martin would surely be gone. The manager called it "probably the toughest decision I had to make in my life."

Reggie's ego drove him. It made him by turns alluring and revolting. It made him something more than even the players who were better than he was. But on that night, he needed to submerge it. He sat near Martin on the bench. Rather than brood, he cheered and congratulated returning heroes. In the eighth, Martin turned to him. "Get a bat," he said.

With the Yankees trailing 3–1, runners on the corners, and one out, Reggie, angered but determined, stepped in against reliever Doug Baird.

The first pitch from Baird dropped for a ball. Reggie swung and missed violently on a fastball up and in and then fouled off a pitch away to run the count to 1–2. Baird then hung a breaking ball. Reggie swung less ferociously than usual and dumped a single in front of center fielder Amos Otis, who had played him deep even with two strikes. Randolph scored easily from third, and Piniella advanced to second. The Royals controlled the damage, but in the ninth the Yankees pushed across three more runs and won the game 5–3. For the fourth time in his career, Reggie was headed to the World Series.

"All season I had to hold it in here," he gushed after the game. "I had to eat it in here. Thank God. I can't explain it because I don't understand the magnitude of Reggie Jackson and the magnitude of the event. I am the situation."

After the clubhouse had mostly emptied, a writer from *Time* magazine said to Martin, "I think Reggie hates you." Martin sneered. "Reggie doesn't know how to hate," he said. "*I* know how to hate."

FOR NEW YORKERS, 1977 had been a tumult beyond anyone's reckoning.

David Berkowitz, the "Son of Sam" killer, had terrorized the city for months. Berkowitz, with his .44-caliber handgun, murdered six people and wounded eight others between 1976 and August of 1977, when police finally captured him outside his Yonkers apartment. In the middle of a July heat wave, a massive blackout descended upon New York, and for two days looters, rioters, and arsonists used the darkness to despoil the city's poorest neighborhoods. Two years before, President Gerald Ford had refused to extend the city a $1 billion line of credit, and by 1977 New York remained under threat of bankruptcy. All the while, a bitter race for the mayoralty divided the city. These divided, beleaguered New Yorkers yearned for a consoling distraction, and they tasked Reggie and the Yankees with providing one.

The Los Angeles Dodgers, who boasted the best pitching staff in the league, represented the NL. They seemed a stiff challenge for Reggie and the Yankees' offense. In game one, Reggie reached base three times, and the Yankees prevailed 4–3 in twelve innings. Game two brought ugliness. Before the game, a fire broke out in Public School 3, just west of the stadium. "There it is, ladies and gentlemen," Howard Cosell told the millions of viewers at home, "the Bronx is burning." For Reggie, it called to mind the fires he'd seen from the field in Baltimore, days after the assassination of MLK in 1968. While those had been fires of outrage, this one—a fire that would rise to five alarms before the end of the game—was one of cruel randomness.

At times during 1977, Yankee Stadium was as tough as the neighborhood that cradled it. Drunken brawls were common; from the upper deck, fans would throw bottles, rocks, even darts and lit firecrackers onto the fans and sometimes the players below. Game two saw it all. The Dodgers won 6–1, but not before frustrated Yankees fans littered the field with everything they could find. Reggie went 0 for 4 with a pair of strikeouts. Worse, the Dodgers roughed up

Catfish Hunter, who was pitching for the first time in more than a month. Reggie thought it an injustice that Martin had forced his old friend to start under such circumstances. "How could the son of a bitch pitch him?" Reggie asked of Martin and his decision to start the aching and rusty Hunter.

The next night, the press dutifully read back Reggie's words to Martin. "A true Yankee wouldn't say that," Martin quipped. "He's got enough trouble playing right field without second-guessing the manager."

Just as dutifully, the writers tracked down Reggie and relayed Martin's comments to him. "I don't need to take that from nobody," Reggie said. "Especially from him. I know what I can do. If he did, we might be a lot better off."

Back to Martin: "He can kiss my dago ass."

Back to Reggie: "If I had an ethnic origin, I'd tell him what he could kiss."

The captain, Munson, attempted to restore calm. "It's just an overheated controversy," Munson said. "Reggie's struggling and would like to be doing better. Billy probably just doesn't realize that Reggie is Mr. October."

Munson coined the nickname—Mr. October—with irony and derision. Reggie, for all his noisemaking, was batting just .167 at that point in the Series and .136 in the 1977 postseason. The name would stick.

ON THE OFF day, Gabe Paul ordered both Reggie and Martin to his hotel suite for forced accords. "Everything's perfect," Martin sniffed afterward. Reggie nodded in heartless agreement.

The Series shifted to Los Angeles. During the cross-country flight, the Yankees players learned that their friends and families had been given less-than-choice seats, and Reggie threatened not to suit up until Bowie Kuhn himself delivered better tickets. Steinbrenner agreed to abandon his luxury box and sit with the players' families, and the controversy died. In game three, Reggie scored a pair of runs, including a long home run to left center in the sixth. The Yankees won, 5–3.

After the win, he and Martin smiled together for the cameras, and Reggie announced, to the astonishment of many, that he would be back in New York in 1978. With terribly perfect timing, a *Time* magazine story quoted Reggie as having said he wouldn't be back if Martin returned. Reggie denied the comments and cryptically blamed them on "someone who's never betrayed me before."

Reggie's dilemma wasn't whether he wanted to see Martin fired—he did, fervently. Rather, it was whether seeing Martin fired was worth being blamed for it. Was it worth it to suffer the ridicule that cascaded down from Martin if it kept the city from turning on him? He answered that question a thousand different ways depending upon his mood and the moment.

In game four, Reggie provided another two runs scored and an RBI, and the Yankees took a 3–1 series lead. The Dodgers rebounded to take game five 10–4. In the eighth, Reggie hit a first-pitch home run down the right-field line off of Don Sutton. Sutton, who objected to Reggie's leisurely jaunt around the bases, shouted at him. But the arrogance, even in defeat, was warranted. For the Series, Reggie was batting .353 and slugging an obscene 1.215.

The two teams flew back to New York.

SIXTEEN

"Reg-gie!"

October 18, 1977, World Series, Game Six

The Yankees trailed 3–2. Thurman Munson led off the bottom of the fourth with a sharp single to left. Then Reggie stepped to the plate, leaned in, and cocked his bat. Burt Hooton's first pitch was a fastball low, but not inside where he aimed it. Reggie ripped at it. The ball climbed lazily across the outfield and just cleared the short fence in right. It was a home run—325 feet—without his usual shattering authority, but after Munson and Reggie touched the plate the Yankees led 4–3. In the dugout, Martin put a hand on Reggie's neck and embraced him for a moment.

Elias Sosa got up for the second time in the Dodger bull pen as Hooton worked uneasily to Chris Chambliss. With the count 2–1, Tommy Lasorda visited the mound to give Sosa more time. The camera cut to Reggie in the dugout. "Hi, Mom," he mouthed. "That's one of the few times I've seen him smile in the last seven days," said Tom Seaver in the broadcast booth.

Sosa trotted in while the grounds crew cleared trash from the out-field. Chambliss lifted a pitch from Sosa to shallow left. Bill Russell went back, Dusty Baker broke in, but the ball fell in between them. Chambliss wound up on second. Graig Nettles then grounded out to the right side, and Chambliss scurried to third. Lou Piniella pushed him across with a sac fly.

In the top of the fifth inning, Mike Torrez walked Bill Russell with one out to bring up the dangerous Reggie Smith. This time, Smith, who had powered a deep homer off Torrez in the third, swung over the top of a sinker and hit into an easy double play.

In the bottom half, Mickey Rivers led off with a single past Davey Lopes. Sosa, as in the prior inning, had little command. Lefty Doug Rau loosened in the Dodger bull pen. Willie Randolph dropped a bunt in front of home plate, but Steve Yeager pounced and threw to second just ahead of Rivers. Next was Munson, who lined out to Rick Monday in center for the second out.

Reggie asked coach Gene Michael what Sosa threw. Fastballs, Michael told him, all fastballs. Reggie stalked toward the plate. The scoreboard flashed: "REG-GIE!" Sosa threw to first to force Randolph back to the bag. Then he checked the runner again and brought the pitch. Michael was right: first-pitch fastball and on the outer third of the plate, exactly where it shouldn't have been. Reggie's swing was instinctive—almost involuntary. The ball was low and hard and fast off the bat.

In right field, Reggie Smith scarcely had time to turn around. As Reggie rounded first, he glanced into the Dodger dugout and tapped his chest with his right hand. The "Reg-gie!" chants started again. In the booth, Howard Cosell, no friend of Reggie, called his second home run of the night "something I'll always remember." Back in the dugout, Reggie waved at the camera and held up a pair of fingers. "Two," he mouthed. The Yankees led 7–3.

Lasorda, one batter too late, summoned Rau from the bull pen, and Chambliss grounded out to Steve Garvey at first. As Reggie took his spot in right field to start the sixth, the fans chanted his name, threw offerings at him, and brayed for his acknowledgment. He doffed his cap. "You might call it the aggrandizement of an athlete," said play-by-play man Keith Jackson.

Even as Sparky Lyle warmed up, Torrez cruised through the top of the inning. Rau did the same to Nettles, Piniella, and Bucky Dent in the bottom half. The seventh was no different. The Dodgers failed to threaten Torrez, and Charlie Hough, the new Dodgers pitcher, worked around a single by Rivers to pitch a scoreless frame. In the top of the eighth, Torrez allowed a leadoff single to Lopes and a hard-hit lineout by Russell. Then Smith hit into an inning-ending double play.

In the bottom of the eighth, Reggie led off against the knuckleballer Hough. Any other night, Martin would've already replaced Reggie with Paul Blair, his defensive caddy. But not tonight. "Reggie Jackson has seen two pitches in the strike zone tonight," announced Keith Jackson. "And he's hit them both in the seats." The crowd's roar picked up as Reggie strutted to the plate.

The knuckleball was always an inviting pitch for a hitter like Reggie. Back in Puerto Rico in the winter of 1970, Frank Robinson had taught him to hit it, and Reggie hadn't forgotten. But Hough threw a tough one. The pitch fluttered to the outside corner, and Reggie cut the bat at it. Later, Dodgers manager Tommy Lasorda would call it "a perfect pitch."

At second base, umpire Ed Sudol doubted his own ears. Hough's tumbling pitch looked unhittable from hand to plate. But then Sudol heard the crack of the bat. He whipped around.

The ball sailed 475 feet to the blacked-out seats in distant center field. By the time Reggie reached second base, he realized the dimensions of what he'd done—three home runs on three swings, four on four swings going back to game five. Babe Ruth had twice hit three home runs in a World Series game, but nothing Ruth had ever done was so impossible, so hypnotic.

Reggie touched home plate to the loudest ovation he'd ever heard. In the dugout, he greeted them all—friends, enemies, and the once indifferent. But on this night Reggie allowed no indifference. Ray Negron pushed him out of the dugout and forced him to acknowledge the desperate cries of "Reg-gie! Reg-gie! Reg-gie!"

He emerged from the dugout, hands raised in triumph. "Thank you, thank you!" he shouted back at them. He thanked them, yet he chided them—chided them for taking so long to recognize his magnitude. "Fulfillment is written in his face," warbled Cosell. Reggie, with a smile that hid nothing, held up three fingers.

He took the field for the ninth heralded by desperate cheers. Keith Jackson announced that the decision was predictably unanimous: Reggie had won World Series MVP for the second time in his career. Again he raised three fingers for the fans in the right-field bleachers. Between outs and as Lyle warmed up yet again, the Dodgers pieced together three singles and scored a run, but history was already written. Monday drove a labored Torrez pitch to the wall in right, but Reggie steadied under it and caught the second out. Cops kneeled along the sidewalls, ready for what would happen next.

Martin considered a pitching change at the mound while fans perched themselves on the outfield walls. They threw firecrackers at Reggie. He jogged off the field. Then he stopped, retrieved a batting helmet, and returned to right field. Cosell called the fans' display "intolerable, unthinkable, disgraceful, and not worthy of this great city." With two outs, pinch hitter Lee Lacy popped up a bunt attempt to Torrez on the mound. Torrez clung to it.

Like sinners to a tent revival, fans—thousands of them—spilled onto the field. Reggie summoned his football skills, dodged most, ran over a few, and made it back to the dugout. The cops, overwhelmed at the perimeters, cracked heads with their nightsticks. Even the five police officers on horseback, even the helmeted members of the Tactical Patrol Force couldn't hold them back. Near third base, three cops gave a fifteen-year-old boy a concussion. "Jews for

Jesus" leaflets swirled about the field. The fans tore up turf, bases, plastic seats—anything to help them remember what they didn't yet believe.

The celebration—the release—bled out into the neighborhoods. The police chased fans up 161st Street. Drivers around Yankee Stadium ran red lights and went the wrong way down one-way streets, all to avoid stopping, even for a moment, in the widening chaos. On 149th, the injured and already dead turned up at Lincoln Hospital. At the nearest precinct on 167th, the police began a long night of booking. At 125th and Seventh in Harlem, young black boys blocked traffic and held up newsprint photos and glossies of their new hero, Reggie Jackson. Over at the *New York Post*'s offices on South Street, they crafted an editorial on the miracles of the night. They wrote, "Who dares to call New York a lost cause?"

REGGIE WAS BURDENED by a deep sense of occasion.

In the glow following moments when things went well for him— impossibly well on this night—he forgave too easily, was too heedless of the past. It was both a merit and a flaw.

In the Yankees clubhouse following a win that went beyond the extremities of the imagination, he was lost in the magnitude of it all. Eyes stinging from champagne, he took from around his neck the gold medallion of Jackie Robinson. He showed it to the press. "What do you think this man would think of me tonight?"

He rhapsodized to the writers at one turn and embraced his for-mer—and future—enemies at another. "Anyone fights you, skip," he told Martin, his arm around the man who had terrorized him for months, "he's got to fight both of us."

Then someone told him his father, who had traveled from Philadelphia to see Reggie win the World Series for the fourth time, was asking for him at the door. "Bring my dad over," Reggie said. "Dad? Dad?"

Martinez, plumper and moving more slowly than he ever had, appeared. Reggie embraced him. "Get a picture of me and my dad for television, for the newspapers, and for the magazines," he said. "I must have a picture with my dad. I can't say too much for this man. He has been behind me all the way, even in my darkest moments."

After a moment, it was on to Steinbrenner. "Get my bat, Nick, please," Reggie said to a clubhouse attendant. He returned with Reggie's "dues collector," and the monologue began. "I started using this bat Saturday after I broke one in Friday's game. Look at the wide grain. The older the tree, the wider the grain, the harder the wood," he said, pretending to be unaware of the scribbling writers in his audience. "I think I'll give this bat to George Steinbrenner."

On the other side of the clubhouse, others talked. "Reggie didn't do it," said Mickey Rivers to a nearby writer. "*We* did it."

"Stirs the drink, eh?" said Paul Blair. "Reggie doesn't do that. Rivers does that."

"Look," Munson said, "this was a team victory. It was the right fielder who hit the homers, not Reggie Jackson."

LATER, REGGIE PREPARED to celebrate his night with the blond fashion models who frequented one of his haunts on Seventy-ninth and Third. Munson, the only other player still in the clubhouse, poked his head in. "Hey, coon," he said. "Nice going, coon." Reggie laughed and embraced him for a few seconds. "I'm going down to the party here in the ballpark," Munson said, smiling broadly. "Just white people, but they'll let you in. Come on down."

"I'll be there," Reggie said. "Just wait for me."

Reggie dressed—it was a night in the city, so he took his time with his tailored shirt, camel-hair jacket, leather boots, and gold medallions. Munson reappeared. "Hey, nigger," he said. "You're too slow. That party's over, but I'll see you next year." Munson extended his hand. "I'll see you next year wherever I might be."

"You'll be back," Reggie said.

"Not me," Munson said. "But you know who stuck up for you, nigger, you know who stuck up for you when you needed it."

MOMENTS EARLIER, REGGIE had spoken to the writers of his new place in the Yankees pantheon. "Babe Ruth, Lou Gehrig, Joe DiMaggio, Mickey Mantle, and Reggie Jackson." He considered for a moment. "Somehow I don't fit."

It was the truest thing Reggie Jackson said all night.

SEVENTEEN

"But I Know the Score Now"

HE LEFT THE CLUBHOUSE after 2 A.M. At McMullen's, he ran into the governor of New York, Hugh Carey. They greeted each other and drank together until almost five in the morning. By 6:30 A.M., Reggie was on the set of the *Today* show and, hours later, at a ticker-tape parade up the Canyon of Heroes. Everyone wanted to glimpse his face.

Then he went to Cartier jewelers, where adoring friends and associates received him. Then it was back to the stadium to retrieve his Rolls and then on to the newsstands, where he bought every copy of every newspaper he could find—so long as the headlines blared what he'd done the night before. And they all did.

After some much-needed sleep, he dropped in at the Plaza Hotel to pick up his World Series MVP trophy. "I'd like to be thought of as a hell of a person," he said upon being presented with the award for the second time in his career. "A great person, more than a ballplayer. And maybe my accomplishments could be interpreted humanistically. What they mean for people, for mankind, for poor people, for black people, for white people. About togetherness."

A regiment of police escorted him back to his car and protected him from adoring New Yorkers. After he made it back to his apartment on Fifth Avenue, he made his visitors—the Reverend Jesse Jackson chief among them—wait in the parlor while he talked about game six to a writer from *Sports Illustrated*. Later, the Reverend Jackson would add his own rhapsodies. "Because of his intelligence and his gifts," he said, "Reggie's domain is bigger than baseball."

In the eyes of New Yorkers, the events of October 18, 1977, reconstructed Reggie like nothing else could have. Even the *Amsterdam News*, the powerful black paper that had blistered him earlier in the year, now counted him as an ally. The *News* likened his performance in game six to Jackie Robinson's breaking of the color barrier. "Black residents of New York City reacted with a special jubilation and sense of triumph to the sensational performance by Reggie Jackson," they noted.

The brilliance of that night did more than make Reggie a legend. He had justified the money ballplayers made under the new economics. "Reggie's performance clearly upped the price of the free agents," said Marvin Miller, the man who'd won baseball players their freedom, of Reggie's game six.

Some within the game feared that long-term contracts, a concept mostly foreign to the game in the pre–free agency era, would sap players of their incentive. They'd become lazy and self-satisfied, no longer driven to excellence by a ruthless system. Reggie, in one game, had proved them wrong.

PERCEPTIONS MAY HAVE changed, but the Yankees had not. Roy White, angry over the way Martin had treated him during the season, didn't show up for the victory parade. Neither did Munson, who soon demanded a trade to Cleveland. Steinbrenner allowed Mike Torrez, who'd been so vital to the Yankees' success in 1977, to leave via free agency. Torrez signed with the Red Sox. Upon doing so, he said Boston had the better team. He also said he wouldn't miss the fabled Yankees infighting. "Graig Nettles hates Jackson. Thurman Munson hates Jackson," Torrez said. "Jackson is not well liked by many members of his team."

Even though ace reliever Sparky Lyle had won the Cy Young Award in 1977, Steinbrenner signed Goose Gossage, another elite closer, to a contract worth more than $2.7 million. Lyle fumed.

Gabe Paul, weary of Steinbrenner's heavy hand, returned to the Cleveland Indians as a limited partner. Al Rosen, another of Steinbrenner's Cleveland connections and a former American League MVP, replaced him. Since Rosen, unlike Paul, was a fellow old ballplayer, Martin assumed he'd be a steady ally. But Rosen, a reserved and dignified man, had a history with Martin. During their playing days, Martin had once tried to sucker punch Rosen and on several occasions had hurled anti-Semitic slurs at him. Martin had forgotten. Rosen had not.

REGGIE SHOWED UP late to spring training in 1978. He didn't bother to warn Martin. Reggie had business at his antique automobile dealership in California, and he'd cleared his absence with Steinbrenner. "I guess some guys don't need spring training," Martin said after Reggie finally arrived.

"George understands me," Reggie said. "He's a businessman. I had business to take care of. Billy doesn't understand that. He's only a baseball manager."

There were countless ways to anger Martin. One of the surest was to lord status and money over him. Martin, despite being paid handsomely as a manager, never lived comfortably—too many women with liens on his paycheck, too many expensive habits. Reggie had made far more of his life than Martin had of his, and the older man resented him for it.

Martin also resented the presence of Gossage. He was loyal to Sparky Lyle, and when Steinbrenner signed Gossage, Martin took it as an affront on Lyle's behalf. He decided to test his new reliever. In a spring training game against Texas, Martin visited Gossage on the mound in the middle of an inning. "Drill that little nigger in the head," Martin said. The "little nigger" was Billy Sample, one of Martin's former players. Gossage stammered. "I told you," Martin said. "Drill that little nigger, Billy Sample, in the fucking head."

Gossage said he had no quarrel with Sample and that his 98-mile-per-hour fastball might well kill the man. "I don't care if you do kill him," Martin said. Gossage again refused. "You pussy," Martin hissed at him. "You cock-eating pussy. You're a fucking pussy, big fucking cunt."

Word of the exchange made it back to Reggie. Martin's bare bigotry worried him at first. But then the worry turned into a familiar anger. "They look at the money I make, and they say, 'That nigger don't deserve it. . . .'" Reggie said of Martin and his fellow travelers. "They see me working hard on my defense, and they say, 'The nigger's a showboat.' They see me sign autographs for two or three hours, and they say, 'The nigger just wants his name in the papers.' . . . Do they look at what I withstood and say, 'That nigger has fiber'? Just once I'd like to hear that."

The Yankees finished the spring schedule with a record of 10–13, and Steinbrenner, even though the games didn't yet count, leaned on Martin for better results. The glow of the World Series seemed dimmer than it should have.

THE SEASON BEGAN with more of the surreality that defined the team. After they dropped four of their first five—and after the newly acquired Gossage struggled—the Yankees returned to New York for the home opener on April 13. Mickey Mantle and Roger Maris presented the World Series trophy to the team, and Mayor Ed Koch told the crowd, "Happiness is a world championship."

As well, Standard Brands had hired female models to distribute to each ticket holder, all 44,667 of them, the long-anticipated Reggie! bar. It was a small, square block of chocolate, peanuts, and corn syrup, wrapped in orange wax paper and adorned by the image of Reggie at the crest of his power stroke, admiring what was surely another home run.

In the bottom of the first inning, Reggie took two balls from Wilbur Wood and then punished a knuckleball deep into the seats beyond right center. From somewhere in the upper deck, a lone Reggie! bar fluttered to the field as he rounded the bases. Dozens more followed. The fans in the mezzanine joined in, and then those in the field boxes did the same. Soon enough, roughly 15,000 of the candies littered the playing surface. Some fans scurried over the outfield walls and onto the field to retrieve them. The familiar chants of "Reg-gie! Reg-gie!" rose once again. The candies kept coming. It took five minutes for the grounds crew to clean the field.

After the game, one newsman theorized that Standard Brands had planted someone to start the barrage of Reggie! bars. Reggie denied it and said that the gesture had been "an honest appreciation" of him.

"When you unwrap a Reggie! bar," quipped Catfish Hunter, "it tells you how good it is."

"People starving all over the world," said Bob Lemon, the manager of the opposing White Sox, "and thirty billion calories are laying on the field."

On the field, the Yankees tried to keep pace with Boston. Off the field, things unraveled. Munson was in pain, Gossage still struggled, White was angry over his playing time, and Randolph was angry over his contract. Martin and Munson, two old allies, almost came to blows on the team's chartered plane. And Martin drank heavily—on planes, in airport bars, at his apartment, in his office, in the backs of taxis on the way to the park. During a game against Chicago in May, he almost passed out drunk in the dugout.

At the heart of Martin's anxieties was Heather Ervolino. Martin had left his longtime girlfriend for Ervolino, and the two were now living together. The rub—and there was always a rub with Martin: he was fifty and Ervolino was a sixteen-year-old neighborhood girl from the Bronx.

He had a weakness. When he'd managed the Twins, he had a relationship with the college-aged granddaughter of team owner Calvin Griffith. In Detroit, he had at least one night with the seventeen-year-old daughter of a local minister. Before, Martin had been reasonably discreet. Now, though, his drinking, his passion for the physically stunning Ervolino, and the stresses of the job made him careless. Word of the affair made it back to Steinbrenner. It didn't take much to imagine his manager's name splashed across the tabloid headlines. Worse, he imagined Martin arrested for statutory rape.

Steinbrenner confronted him. Martin denied the relationship and all the while wondered how Steinbrenner had learned of it. Perhaps one of his coaches had betrayed him, or maybe one of his trusted friends outside of baseball had gone to Steinbrenner. Steinbrenner might have even bugged his phone. Martin tore apart his office phone. He found nothing, but he began making his calls from a nearby pay phone.

As the days ticked by, the Red Sox began to pull away (despite their 41–29 record, the Yankees lagged Boston by eight and a half games on June 26). Steinbrenner wondered aloud whether Martin was the right manager for this team. The tacit threat—that he could be fired even though he had won the pennant in 1976 and the World Series in 1977—drove Martin to the brink of madness. He raided the writers' liquor cabinet before games. Doctors found an ominous spot on his liver.

Reggie, meanwhile, was struggling. At the end of June, the Brewers swept the Yankees and sank them to nine and a half games off the pace in the AL East. "The veterans let us down," Steinbrenner said afterward. "Jackson, the cleanup hitter, 0 for 7?" He went on to recite more of Reggie's underwhelming recent statistics. "How can we win when a guy like Reggie, who means so much to the team, is failing us like that?"

Steinbrenner had reproached him publicly, at a time when the alcoholic manager could barely function. "George said he was my friend," Reggie said. "If you're my friend, stay my friend. You don't get mad at me for one off day. But I know the score now."

The fans booed Reggie at home. In Detroit, a fan lobbed a lit cherry bomb at him. "Go out there someday, put on number 44, paint your face black," he said. "See what it's like."

The next day in Detroit, Reggie hit a grand slam and plated five runs. One writer ventured that Steinbrenner's comments had motivated him. "That stuff," Reggie began, "is as weak as a five-cent pack of Kool-Aid in the ocean with two teaspoons of sugar."

Steinbrenner's tactics weren't as weak as the Yankees' chances. The All-Star break found them in third place and eleven and a half games behind Boston. On July 20, the deficit stretched to fourteen games. The sports pages hummed with rumors of Martin's firing, but Steinbrenner showed uncharacteristic patience. He told the press that he'd received threatening phone calls. "They may be Mafia," Steinbrenner said of the callers. "They say I better keep the Italian guy managing my club or I'll end up wishing I had."

Martin once claimed that a man who had tormented his daughter had wound up with both legs broken. And he'd once attempted to arrange a Mob hit on umpire Dale Scott. Whatever the truth, Steinbrenner ordered changes, and those changes didn't involve Martin. He ordered Roy White benched. He ordered Thurman Munson, whose knees were ailing to new extremes, moved to right field. And he ordered Reggie and Lou Piniella platooned at DH. Reggie would never take the field, and he'd never start against left-handers.

Coming from Martin, these changes would've been hard enough

to take, but coming from Steinbrenner they were worse. Steinbrenner made other changes, too, and as he announced them in the clubhouse, he sensed the rising frustrations. "If you don't want to do things my way, then I'll accommodate you by sending you somewhere else," Steinbrenner said. "This is my team. I pay the bills. I'll do what I want."

Not long after Steinbrenner's lecture, Reggie was about to take in a movie with his girlfriend when a black woman approached him for an autograph. Reggie politely declined and said that if he gave her an autograph, everyone else in the theater lobby would want one. The woman screamed at Reggie. Reggie tried to calm her, but she turned on his white girlfriend. Reggie stepped between them, and the woman fell backward. She shrieked that Reggie had slapped her. After security intervened, the woman went to the nearest precinct and pressed charges.

Reggie's fondness for white women often hurt him. In his Oakland years, he dated a married white woman back in Arizona, and her cuckolded husband sued Reggie for alienation of affections. During a photo shoot for *Sport* magazine, he hit on the photographer, the white wife of the film director Michael Ritchie. He dated Finley's white ball girls, and at one point in 1974 he had three white girlfriends at the same time—one a UCLA coed and the other two both local girls in Oakland. He took his white girlfriend to his opening press conference as a Yankee, and he soon courted New York's abundance of white models.

People noticed. After Reggie signed with the Yankees, a black woman approached Graig Nettles in an airport and asked for an introduction to Reggie. "Maybe if you had a blond wig," Nettles told her. On another occasion, a female fan asked Reggie whether he signed autographs for black girls.

In earlier days, whites had objected, but gradually it became blacks who most resented Reggie's sexual appetites. It seemed to Reggie that no matter where he went, some faction of people refused to let him be himself. New York turned out to be no different. "Sometimes," he said after the incident at the movie theater, "I wonder whether any of this is all worthwhile."

Steinbrenner had diminished his role, and now he couldn't even take in a movie. He thought of Steinbrenner's clubhouse promise—that he would accommodate any player who wanted out. He went to Steinbrenner and asked him to live up to his word. Steinbrenner refused. He told him to earn his paycheck instead of trying to get out of New York. "You better get your head on straight, boy," Steinbrenner said.

Reggie had often fawned over Steinbrenner in the press, and those had been honest evaluations: Reggie thought much of the man and regarded him as a genuine friend. But he wasn't. He was the owner—a man, like Finley, motivated by the expedient. To Steinbrenner, Reggie was an employee, a means to an end, someone to fetch him things like championships and headlines and glory. He was a boy. "Who the hell do you think you're talking to?" Reggie said.

"I'm talking to you," Steinbrenner shot back.

Reggie leaned in. "Don't you ever talk to me like that as long as you live," he told Steinbrenner.

"Jackson," Steinbrenner said, "get the hell out of my office."

Reggie didn't move. "I don't feel like leaving," he said. "I kind of like it here. I'm staying." He hoped Steinbrenner would be foolish enough to try to remove him. Instead, Steinbrenner huffed at Reggie's refusal and walked out of his own office.

Word of the meeting leaked to the press, and one writer asked Reggie what he thought of Steinbrenner's choice of words. "When you're racially slurred by the owner, have had problems with the manager, and aren't appreciated by the fans, it's time to look elsewhere."

Steinbrenner insisted to the press that he "didn't mean it as a racial slur, and Reggie knows it." The Urban League even vouched for Steinbrenner's sincerity and insisted that he'd been a valuable patron of black college sports.

That night against the Royals, Reggie came up to bat in the

tenth, tie game, no outs, Munson on first. Betrayed by Steinbrenner, he saw a chance to distinguish himself in the eyes of his manager and perhaps charm his way back into right field. It had already been an eventful evening. Earlier in the game, Sparky Lyle, still angry over the signing of Goose Gossage, had refused Martin's orders to work the sixth after he'd already logged an inning and a third. "Fuck it," Lyle had said to Martin when summoned. "I'm no long reliever. I'm going home." He'd left the dugout and driven home to New Jersey.

But Reggie wasn't thinking about Lyle's insubordination. He was thinking about making a statement of his own. As Munson approached the plate, Reggie told him, "If you get on, I'm going to bunt you over." Doing so of his own accord, Reggie thought, would cast him as a team player. Going against type and sacrificing himself would curry favor with Martin.

Reggie glanced over at Dick Howser, the third-base coach, and for one of the few times in his career he received the bunt sign. Miffed—and stunned by the coincidence—Reggie squared away, but the pitch from Al Hrabosky was unreachable. George Brett crept in at third. Martin removed the bunt sign. Reggie looked in at Howser again and received his "swing away" orders. To hell with it, he thought. He attempted another bunt and missed for strike one. Howser approached. "Billy wants you to swing the bat."

"I'm gonna bunt," Reggie said.

"Yeah, but Billy wants you to hit."

"Listen, Dick, nothing against you, but I'm bunting."

"I hope you know what you're doing."

He squared around again and fouled off the pitch for strike two. In the dugout, Martin screamed, "What the fuck does he think he's doing?" Again Howser gave the swing sign, and again Reggie ignored him. He fouled the bunt attempt into the catcher's mitt for a strike-out. "Okay," Martin said to Elston Howard, his emissary to black players, "tell him that's his hit for the fucking day."

Howard didn't say anything when Reggie returned to the dugout.

After the inning, Martin told Gene Michael, his first-base coach, to tell Reggie to leave the dugout. Michael relayed the message. "If Billy wants me to go inside," Reggie said, "let him come over and tell me himself."

Reggie was angry that his lone weapon at that moment—ingratiation—had been taken from him. He reacted with the immaturity that typified his worst moments. Back on the bench, he removed his glasses, ready for a fight if Martin wanted one. But Martin, against his strongest impulses, said nothing. At that moment, he wanted the job more than he wanted to fight Reggie.

After the game—a 9–7 Yankees loss in eleven innings and one that dropped them to fourteen games behind the Red Sox—the consequences unfolded quickly. Martin hissed, "Goddamn you," as he passed Reggie in the clubhouse and then threw a tantrum in his office. He consulted with Steinbrenner and implored the owner to suspend Reggie for the balance of the season. Steinbrenner refused. "I've never been angrier in my life!" Martin screamed into the phone. "I'm the manager, and if he comes back he does exactly what I say! Period!"

Reggie, in somber tones, talked to the press. They asked whether he had missed the sign. "I don't miss signs," he said. "My job was to advance the runner. I tried to do that. How can they say I'm a threat if I swing the bat? I'm not even an everyday player. I'm a part-time player."

In the end, Steinbrenner agreed to suspend him for five games, which would cost Reggie almost $10,000 in salary. Steinbrenner and Martin never discussed Lyle's actions in the same game.

Reggie was about to leave the clubhouse when Ray Negron, who had heard the team's statement on the radio, told him about the suspension. He was dumbfounded. Minutes earlier, he had told Negron that "everything will be all right," and he believed his own words. Now the team had suspended him, but Martin hadn't meted out any punishment to Lyle. Reggie and a few voices in the press would conclude that Martin had a different set of standards for Reggie than he had for his white players. But the more popular narrative was that Reggie's misbehavior hurt the team and justified the suspension. "No matter what I do, I come off as the big, greedy moneymaker, and he's the tough little street fighter," Reggie said of Martin.

In the eyes of the Yankees partisans—many of whom were white, Archie Bunker types from deep in the outer boroughs—Martin and Reggie were incompatible archetypes. Martin was the volcanic, embattled, hardscrabble "paisan" who, in defiance of his slight build, took a supernatural delight in brawling. He was, in his own words, "the people's manager."

Reggie, meanwhile, was the chiseled, pensive, lushly compensated, acquisitive black who dated white models, sipped Pinot Grigio, spent his Saturday nights at Studio 54 or Xenon, lived across the street from the Metropolitan Museum of Art, tended to his balcony flower garden, owned cats, and tooled around Manhattan in a burgundy-and-silver Rolls-Royce Corniche. No surprise that Martin accrued believers faster than Reggie did. Martin's struggles, joys, and long-ago attainments on the field seemed, to the fans, nearer at hand than the impossible home runs and whipsaw strikeouts of Reggie. Martin, they believed, was like them. So Reggie they booed, and Martin they cheered with full throats. It all made Martin believe that when he terrorized Reggie, he did so with the fans' sanction.

Reggie left Kennedy Airport for California. At the San Francisco airport, the American Airlines plane stopped before it reached the gate so Reggie could avoid the media. He spent the next few days at one of his girlfriends' apartments. Then he went to see friends in San Diego.

Reggie's lawyer asked him to read an apology for the media, but he refused. The president of Standard Brands, the makers of the Reggie! bar, flew to California to discuss his behavior. It would be bad for their relationship, he cautioned, if Reggie agitated his way to the bench or out of New York.

On his first day back, Reggie missed the team bus and wound up taking a taxi to Comiskey Park. After he arrived, more than thirty reporters and multiple television crews mobbed him. "The magnitude of me, it's uncomfortable," he said, invoking his old refrain. "I'm not the story. What have I done? The magnitude of me is overemphasized."

He wouldn't apologize to Martin, he said, and he didn't know whether they could ever get along. Reggie learned secondhand that he wouldn't be in the lineup that day. The Yankees won their fifth straight game in his absence and whittled Boston's lead down to ten games.

Off the field, though, things were no better. When told of Reggie's comments, Martin, who'd been drinking at Chicago's O'Hare International Airport and awaiting the team's charter flight, said Reggie wouldn't play unless he kept his mouth shut. He said that if Steinbrenner had other ideas, then he could fire him as manager. Murray Chass of the *Times* reminded Martin that Reggie, shortly after the fated bunt attempt, claimed that his manager "hasn't talked to me in a year and a half."

Martin, as he made his way to the plane for Kansas City, harrumphed. "The two of them deserve each other," he said of Reggie and Steinbrenner. "One's a born liar, and the other's convicted."

It was a reference—not especially veiled—to Steinbrenner's illegal campaign contributions to Nixon. Not long after the plane landed in Kansas City, Martin's comments got back to Steinbrenner. After Steinbrenner conferred with Al Rosen, he offered Martin a choice: be fired for breach of contract or resign and receive the money remaining on his contract. Martin, denying the comments all the while, agreed to step down.

The next morning, Martin held a tearful press conference at the Crown Center Hotel. He wore dark glasses and cut a cadaverous figure. He held his head down as he read a prepared statement. His hands shook. He was leaving, and that's all he would say about it. Days before, Henry Hecht of the *Post* had written that Martin had connived to push Reggie over the emotional edge. In the end, though, Reggie got the better of Martin.

Martin thanked the fans and then collapsed into sobs. The next day, Roger Kahn wrote in the *Times*, "Babe Ruth and Lou Gehrig went out of the arena more quietly to face their deaths."

To REPLACE MARTIN, Steinbrenner and Rosen turned to Bob Lemon, the former White Sox manager. Lemon, who had been inducted into the Hall of Fame just two years prior on the strength of his pitching career, was a welcome departure from the fire-breathing Martin. Lemon was a drunk, but unlike Martin he was a happy and uncomplicated one. Even his physical appearance put players at ease. He had a shock of white hair, a large belly, and a thick nose that lit up after enough scotch. His managerial style—hands-off, tailored to personalities and moods—could easily be mistaken for indifference. "You guys were world champions last year," Lemon said in his first address to the team. "Just go out, relax, play like you can, and everything will take care of itself."

Lemon, whether he realized it or not, was ministering to the fallen. And no one had fallen harder than Reggie. Lemon told him that he was back in right field and in the cleanup spot. Reggie would still behave outrageously at times, but Lemon would let him do so.

Once, Bill Madden of the *Daily News* looked on as Lemon autographed a baseball for a young fan. Madden noticed that Lemon, contrary to tradition, signed the side of the ball and not the center. Madden asked him why. Lemon held up the ball and showed Madden the sweet spot where the manager's name was supposed to go. Reggie had already claimed it with his autograph. Lemon laughed.

When the team returned to New York on July 26, the fans made Reggie pay for Martin's dominating absence. He wasn't in the lineup, but the Yankee Stadium crowd assailed him anyway with handmade signs. BILLY'S THE ONE WHO'S SANE, REGGIE'S THE ONE TO BLAME read one. ARE YOU HAPPY NOW, REGGIE? said another. Others were profane enough to be confiscated by ushers and police.

Yet Lemon's assurances carried him through it. The next night, Reggie played for the first time since his suspension. He went 3 for 3 with a home run in an 11–0 win over Cleveland. The boos weren't quite so loud this time. "All the fans in those sections are black, under ten, and don't read the papers," Reggie said of those who cheered him.

During Lemon's early days as Yankees manager, Reggie lifted his batting average by almost thirty points and played with a vigor not seen in months. Steinbrenner, though, was less immune to the Martin fallout.

After the team returned to New York, the Boss began to grasp the loyalty the fans had toward Martin—a *Post* poll found that 99 percent of respondents believed Martin had been wronged. Ingrates, he thought. It had, after all, been his dollars that had brought them a championship. But he still wondered whether he'd made a mistake.

All the while, the Yankees slowly, improbably surmounted Boston's lead.

IT WAS OLD Timers' Day at Yankee Stadium. The Yankees, a team tethered to its history as no other, staged many such affairs, and like all the others this one packed the stadium to the rafters. Reggie was in the dugout when public address announcer Bob Sheppard intoned the names of the Yankee legends in attendance. Then he came to his final introduction: "Managing the Yankees in the 1980 season, and hopefully for many seasons after that, will be number one . . ."

The raucous cheers drowned out Sheppard's voice. But Reggie had heard enough. Number 1 was Martin. He was back. Martin emerged beaming, doffing his cap to the fans and then to Steinbrenner in the owner's box. Every cheer for Martin—the ovation lasted a full seven minutes—felt like a voice against Reggie.

Martin's return surprised almost everyone, but it had been in the works since soon after he resigned. The reaction back in New York had troubled Steinbrenner, and he feared that, as rumors suggested, Martin might wind up with the Mets. So he had made quiet overtures to Martin. The overtures worked, as did Steinbrenner's efforts to keep it all a secret. On the day of the announcement, the fans, the players, Bob Lemon, and even the best-sourced and most resourceful reporters were shocked.

For many of the writers and others not invested in Martin's return, there was an absurdity to it—something like Caligula's making his horse a senator. For Reggie, it seemed that his "win" over Martin had turned out to be nothing of the sort. He was hurt—hurt by the thought of playing for Martin again and hurt that Steinbrenner would make such a move without consulting him or at least warning him. "That fucking guy should've told me something," he muttered from the dugout.

Reggie stumbled through the game. "I'll definitely be in Anaheim after this," he said afterward in the clubhouse. "No question about this, I'm going to be in Anaheim next year. Can you believe this?"

It was his way of again asking Steinbrenner to trade him. And again Steinbrenner refused. A few days later, one reporter asked Martin whether he could manage Reggie again. "I've always said I could manage Adolf Hitler, Benito Mussolini, and Hirohito," Martin said. "That doesn't mean I'd like them, but I'd manage them."

Martin then met with a group of handpicked writers at Alex & Harry's restaurant in the Bronx to discuss his return. Naturally, they asked Martin about the comments that had led to his firing. "I didn't mean what I said about George," Martin explained. "But I did mean it about the other guy."

The other guy, of course, was Reggie. "I never looked at Reggie as a superstar," continued the man who had managed him for game six of the 1977 World Series. "He never showed me he was a superstar."

Steinbrenner, who hadn't known about Martin's press luncheon, was, in the words of one Yankee official, "mad as hell about the whole thing." Elston Howard suggested that Reggie call his own retaliatory press conference. Al Rosen, whom Martin had assumed was on his side, was also pressed for a reaction. "I'm for number forty-four," he said, referring to Reggie. "That's the point I want to make."

THE YANKEES' QUIET gains early in August were gone by the thirteenth, when Boston's lead grew to nine. Reggie slumped. At one point, he endured a 3-for-28 stretch, and, in a game against the Orioles, Lemon dropped him to eighth in the batting order. Not even Martin at his most vengeful had deigned to bat Reggie eighth. Reggie arrived at the park, saw the lineup card, and went straight to the first member of Lemon's staff he saw. "I don't feel so good today," Reggie told pitching coach Clyde King. "Tell the man I'm sick and can't play."

King told Lemon, and Lemon, with no dramatics, removed Reggie's name from the lineup card. After the game, the press asked Reggie why he hadn't started. "I'm sick," he said.

"Sick from batting eighth?" one writer asked.

"Just plain sick. Sick of here."

The next day, Lemon put Reggie seventh hole. He played, and the controversy died. Under Martin, Reggie would have raged and the team would have panicked. But the tides common to any pennant race—even a pennant race in the Bronx—didn't faze Lemon. Martin had managed like a vise in times like these, but Lemon filled out the lineup card and watched the game unfold.

A newspaper strike in New York City also eased the pressure. Members of the New York Newspaper Printing Pressmen's Union walked off the job in early August and didn't return for eighty-eight days. That meant no city dailies for almost three months. That also meant, for the Yankees, no city beat writers. With no Martin and only a small suburban press contingent following them, the Yankees played outside the crucible when it mattered most. They surged.

By the end of August, the Yankees had clipped the margin to six and a half games. When they arrived in Boston on September 7 for a four-game series, the deficit was just that: four games. Over the next thirty-six innings, the Yankees outscored the Red Sox 42–9 and outhit them 67–21. Reggie tallied six RBIs, half of which came on a clutch three-run homer in the only close game of the series. Not since the 1940s had the Yankees swept a four-game set in Fenway. The Hub tabloids called it "The Boston Massacre." It seemed to banish any doubt that the Yankees would prevail.

In the middle of September, they took two of three from Boston to pull in front by three and a half games, but then the Red Sox won eight straight to end the season. The two teams wound up tied in the standings. For the first time in the American League since 1948, the full schedule failed to yield a winner.

On October 2, the day after the regular season was supposed to end, the Yankees and Red Sox met in Boston to play one final game, one that would decide the division title. "If there is anything else going on in this world today, I don't know what it is," said Red Sox broadcaster Ned Martin.

In the top of the first, Reggie laced a high, outside fastball to deep left field. It wouldn't clear the Green Monster, but it looked like a certain double off the bat. Carl Yastrzemski, patrolling Fenway's left field in his eighteenth season, charged toward the line and snagged it at the last moment.

In the fourth, Reggie hit the ball sharply again, but Jim Rice made a deft play in right to rob him of a hit. Going into the seventh, the Yankees trailed 2–0, and Mike Torrez, the former Yankee, was in full control. With two men on and two out, the light-hitting Bucky Dent used Mickey Rivers's bat to lift a fly ball to left. In any other park, it would have been a routine fly out. But in Fenway, on that one windy day, it sneaked over the Green Monster for a go-ahead home run. Dent had hit his first home run in two months.

Reggie led off the eighth with another home run, and Goose Gossage, after surrendering two runs in the eighth and putting two men on in the ninth, closed it out. The Yankees won the game, 5–4. It was their one hundredth win of the season.

After the stunning victory in Boston, the writers asked Reggie about his home run, one that history would overlook in favor of Dent's unlikely blast. "It was an insurance run," he said, a grin cutting his face. "So I hit it to the Prudential Building."

Moments later, he said, "We never would have won it with Billy."

IN THE ALCS, Reggie hit .462 and paced the Yankees in their three-games-to-one triumph over the Royals. That set up a World Series rematch against the Dodgers. Game one provided little drama. The Dodgers jumped to an early lead off Ed Figueroa and never relinquished it. They won the game easily, 11–5. Game two was much closer. Reggie had a two-run double in the third to put the Yankees up 2–0, but the Dodgers came back. With L.A. up 4–3 in the ninth, Reggie came up to bat again.

Two were on and one was out when he stepped in against Bob Welch, the Dodgers' touted young flamethrower. Their encounter reduced the game to its most primitive elements: pitcher versus hitter, power versus power.

For seven agonizing minutes, Welch pumped fastballs at the plate, and Reggie fouled them off with home-run cut after home-run cut. Reggie worked ball three. He fouled off the first two full-count offerings. Then, focused on timing Welch's fastball, Reggie momentarily forgot the count. The runners again took off with the pitch, and Reggie, for an instant, lost his focus and struck out swinging.

He cursed as he stomped back to the dugout, hurled his bat narrowly past Dick Howser's head, and shoved Lemon out of the way.

Lemon, in a rare moment of emotion, went after Reggie and drove him into the wall, fists raised. Reggie began to cry, and Lemon let him go. After the game, Reggie blamed Bucky Dent for upsetting his concentration when he ran on the 3–2 count. Later, though, he apologized to his manager and to Howser and Dent.

Back in New York, the Yankees won game three on the strength of Ron Guidry's pitching. In game four, the Yankees trailed 3–1 in the sixth inning. With Munson on second and Reggie on first, Piniella smacked a line drive to short. Bill Russell, the Dodgers shortstop, dropped the ball but recovered in time to start what should've been a routine double play. After Russell recorded the force-out at second, Reggie, in a canny bit of gamesmanship, thrust out his hip and deflected the throw to first. The ball bounded behind the bag at first, and Munson scored. The Dodgers protested that Reggie had interfered, but the umpires let the play stand. The Yankees won the game in the tenth. The next day, one New York paper called Reggie's maneuver a "subtle illegality." Licit or not, the "Sacrifice Thigh," as it came to be known, made the difference. The Yankees took game five easily, 12–2.

In game six, Reggie got another shot at Bob Welch. Welch relieved Don Sutton to start the seventh, and Reggie came up with one out and one on and the Yankees leading 5–2. The Dodgers had been pitching Reggie inside. To counter, Reggie reverted to an old habit—he backed up in the batter's box about four inches and leaned out over the plate to give the illusion of standing in his normal position. Doing so allowed him to get around on the inside fastball, which he struggled to do throughout his career, especially against someone like Welch. This time Welch teased him inside, and Reggie dipped back into position and yanked a fastball to deep right field for a clinching home run. The Yankees won the game and the World Series.

For the series, Reggie batted .391 and slugged .696. The writers gave Bucky Dent World Series MVP honors, but by any sensible standard Reggie deserved to win it for the third time in his career. For the *fifth* time in his career, he was a champion.

EIGHTEEN

"That Makes Me Angry, and It Hurts"

TEN DAYS AFTER the last out of the 1978 World Series, Bob Lemon's son, Jerry, overturned his Jeep in California. He was dead at age twenty-six. In spring training, Lemon hid his pain, but his passion for managing—which had always been muted—was gone. "It isn't as important whether we win or lose," he admitted.

Soon after, Martin, the manager in waiting, punched out a sportswriter in Reno, thereupon humiliating Steinbrenner and worrying the Yankee front office that he would never change. Then, according to Reggie in his 1984 autobiography, Nettles called the *Post*'s Henry Hecht a "back-stabbing Jew cocksucker."

"It was the way he thought," Reggie went on to write of Nettles and his comments. Lost on him, though, were his own similar failings. He wasn't in the same class as Martin, who had been hostile toward Jews for much of his life. And he'd never said anything as offensive as what Nettles had. But Reggie did stereotype Jews in unfortunate ways.

His father had long counseled him to go out and get a Jewish lawyer the second he had any money. And when that Jewish lawyer, Steven Kay, sold a Mercedes that Reggie had given him as a gift, Reggie told him he had betrayed a "typically Jewish attitude." Some thirty years later, Reggie was filmed haggling with a New York street artist over a painting. "Are you Jewish?" Reggie said to the man as the bargaining intensified. Reggie suspected as much, he said, because "he's always working me."

Once the 1979 season began, though, the furor over Nettles's comments gave way to other distractions. Reggie opened the season on the disabled list with a torn leg muscle. After just eleven games, Gossage hurt his thumb in a clubhouse brawl with Cliff Johnson—a brawl helped along by Reggie's needling—and was lost for the year. With Sparky Lyle already traded to Texas, the Yankees bull pen was in tatters.

The Yankees responded in uncharacteristic fashion—like strangers to turmoil. Upon his return, Reggie hit, but early May found the team two games below .500 and in fourth place. Then Reggie strained his calf again and wound up on the disabled list for almost a month. Meantime, the Orioles ran away with the division.

Steinbrenner joined the team in Texas and invited the injured Reggie to watch the game with him from the stands. They sat through another tough Yankees loss. "Do you think I should fire Lemon?" Steinbrenner asked him.

"Hell, no," said Reggie. "You can't do that to the man after what he did for you last year."

Reggie knew that if Steinbrenner fired Lemon, it would likely mean an early return for Martin. He couldn't contemplate it. But Steinbrenner felt that the team no longer responded to their diminished manager. Despite Martin's recent brawl and Reggie's wishes, Steinbrenner put him back on the job ahead of schedule. He gave the grieving Lemon a scouting sinecure and sent him home to California. "What am I going to do?" Reggie said after he learned of

Martin's early return. "I can't play for that man. He hates me." He then learned that Steinbrenner had met with Munson and Piniella in the hours before he decided to bring Martin back. Steinbrenner had marginalized him.

When the team returned to New York, he called Steinbrenner at three in the morning. "You had to know what this news would do to me, and you couldn't even give me the courtesy to tell me yourself?"

"I don't need any advice from you on how I run my ball club," Steinbrenner said, mere days after he'd asked Reggie for just that.

"Well, let me tell you something," Reggie said. "You better make another move right now. You better trade me. Because if you don't, I plan to be hurt all year long. I've played for that man for the last time."

"When I want your advice on how to run my team," Steinbrenner told him, "I'll ask for it." Steinbrenner hung up. Reggie packed his things, phoned his advisers, and told them he would go home to California and not play another game until he'd been traded. Gary Walker and Steven Kay talked him out of it.

Steinbrenner had abandoned him, and Martin was coming back. Even Ray Negron, Reggie believed, had moved against him. Negron, at Martin's urging, had gone to Reggie to arrange a sit-down with the prodigal manager. When he learned that Negron had spoken to Martin, Reggie flew into a jealous rage. "How can you be my friend and his friend at the same time?" he screamed at Negron. "Don't you know what the man has against me? He hates me because I'm the wrong color. He's fucked me, and he's going to fuck you. Because you're the wrong color, too."

"You're so goddamn wrong it's pitiful," Negron said.

Even in his thirties, Reggie didn't know how to feel about race. "People see me today," he'd said earlier in the year, "and I'm talking about my own people—black people—and they see me dating white women or associating with white businessmen, and they tell me I don't understand what it's like for blacks who don't make the kind of money I do. That makes me angry, and it hurts."

Reggie hated being reminded of his skin color. When his fellow blacks questioned his loyalty, it reminded him of his obligations. When he collided against or even contemplated a man like Martin, it reminded him of his burdens. If he had to, he would use his race as a cudgel, but mostly he was like his father—he preferred not to think about it.

Reggie and Martin never talked. The day Martin returned to the job, Reggie's name showed up on the American League waiver list. General manager Cedric Tallis dismissed the move as "just a formality," but Reggie knew they were trying to trade him.

The trade didn't happen. Once Reggie returned from the disabled list, Martin played him in right field, batted him cleanup, and left him alone. Martin's accommodations meant that Reggie could redirect his anger back to Steinbrenner. Al Rosen's sudden resignation allowed him to do just that. Reggie told the press that Rosen, whom he'd come to admire, had left because he was "tired of taking bullshit from Steinbrenner."

One writer asked whether he feared the Boss might do the same to him. Reggie said that Steinbrenner could do nothing to hurt him. "Because I can hit the motherfucking baseball over the wall," he said. "When I can't hit, they'll get me. I know he'll get me one day."

Steinbrenner blew up. He wouldn't permit Reggie to shoot a television commercial in Yankee Stadium, and he refused Reggie's request to present a gift to Catfish Hunter—a trophy that commemorated their five championships together—in a pregame ceremony. Then he schemed a way to damage Reggie in the eyes of the fans. Steinbrenner ordered Martin to tell the press that Reggie had filed a grievance with the union over a scheduled exhibition in Columbus, Ohio. According to Steinbrenner, Reggie was protesting Martin's return. Reggie had not filed any grievance, but Steinbrenner hoped the lie would tar him as a privileged superstar—one who was undermining the fans' beloved manager. "I don't think any player should be big enough to dictate who the manager should be," Martin, on orders, said of Reggie.

When that didn't work, Steinbrenner leaked to the press that Reggie had failed to make payments on the $250,000 loan that was part of his contract. He also told them that Reggie owed money to all sorts of businesses all over town. None of it was true.

Reggie and Steinbrenner shared haunts in Manhattan, and Reggie had seen things—things that would blemish Steinbrenner's reputation as a family man and civic steward. Through back channels, Reggie let Steinbrenner know that he would talk if the lies persisted.

But their squabbles were about to lose all meaning.

THURMAN MUNSON WAS older, and the pull of home was stronger. He looked forward to retirement, when he would go back to Ohio, have a few knee surgeries, and open a business. The son of a long-haul trucker, later estranged from his father, Munson worried that his three children didn't see enough of him. That fear—that yearning—had led him to become a pilot.

He loved to fly, but more than that he loved being able to zip home to Canton on a whim to be with his family. Eventually, he upgraded to a twin-engine Cessna so he could get home to Diana and the kids with even greater ease. In mid-July, Reggie and Nettles had flown with Munson from Seattle to Anaheim. As he landed, Munson descended too quickly, which depressurized the cabin, and then came in too low and buzzed the airfield. The flight attendant Reggie was dating was at the airport to pick him up. After Reggie landed, she told him how dangerous Munson's approach had been.

Munson knew he needed more training now that he was flying a more complicated aircraft. So after a Yankees win on August 1, he flew home to Canton to meet with more experienced pilots. The next day, an off day for the team, he practiced landing maneuvers at the Akron-Canton Airport. He had more than five hundred hours of flight time, but barely thirty hours in the Cessna. On his final approach, he came in too low and began to lose control. He tried to pull up. The plane clipped through some trees and lost its wings. It hopped a ditch, bounced off a tree stump, and finally came to a battered rest almost a thousand feet off the runway.

The call came through to Steinbrenner. "Your player, Thurman Munson," said an official with the FAA. "He's been killed."

Munson had snapped his neck, and the crash had trapped him under the steering column. His two instructors had struggled to dislodge him, but the flames had grown too hot, and they had abandoned him in the wreckage. Munson was thirty-two years old.

Reggie heard the news on the radio. In the early days of Reggie's Yankee tenure, his insecurities had bruised against Munson's. But Reggie knew that Munson, more than Nettles, Lyle, Martin, and even Steinbrenner, had judged him on performance. Reggie had come to respect the captain, and he appreciated that Munson, in his quiet, gruff way, had forgiven him for attacking him in the press.

He sent a consoling telegram to Munson's family, and Munson's wife requested that it be read during the funeral service. At the team meeting, Reggie stood up and spoke. He talked to his teammates about soldiering on. He quoted some of his favorite Bible verses and reminded them that tragedy can strengthen the survivors. He hauled an oversized Bible onto the charter flight that took the team to the funeral. Reggie's theatrics in the days following Munson's death angered some teammates. They permitted Reggie his grief. But they would not let him make those awful hours about himself.

THE YANKEES WON eighty-nine games in 1979, but they finished in fourth place, a distant thirteen and a half games behind Baltimore. Despite the turmoil, Reggie batted a career-best .297 and ranked seventh in the league with twenty-nine home runs.

Not long after the season ended, Martin sucker punched a marsh-mallow salesman in a Minnesota bar, and Steinbrenner once again fired him. Then, Martin would allege, Steinbrenner tried to wiggle out of Martin's contract by planting whiskey and marijuana in his Yankee Stadium office. Reggie sent Martin a note of support. Inside, though, he rejoiced that someone else would manage the Yankees.

That someone else was Dick Howser, the longtime Yankee coach. At his press conference at Tavern on the Green, a reporter asked Howser about Reggie's role. "He's my right fielder," Howser said.

The winter brought other changes. Gone were Chris Chambliss and Mickey Rivers, and replacing them were Bob Watson and Ruppert Jones. Catfish Hunter and Roy White had retired. Steinbrenner added left-hander Rudy May to the rotation and brought in Rick Cerone to replace Munson behind the plate. The changes pleased Reggie—no more Martin and fewer of the unsympathetic holdovers from the 1976 team. But those welcome departures didn't make him any more gracious or temper his vainglory.

First, he waited until camp had started to close on a new $500,000 home in Carmel, California—one that would make him neighbors with Clint Eastwood, Paul Anka, and Kim Novak. Then, at one point early in the season, a clubhouse attendant handed Reggie a business card and told him a man was asking to see him. Reggie recognized the name on the card, and he saw that the man had scribbled "Cheltenham High, 1964" on the back. "Tell him I knew him then," said Reggie. "But I don't know him now." The attendant told the man to go away.

THE FANS WERE finally on his side. Munson and Martin were gone, and with them went the divided loyalties. Reggie was free to seduce New York once again. One night early in the season, a long home run earned him a lengthy ovation. "I think I finally won them over," he said after the game. "I think they love me. I really think they do."

They didn't. But he was the last one standing, and that earned him respect, if not genuine love.

On May 31, at Yankee Stadium, Reggie dug in against Toronto right-hander Joey McLaughlin. It was a tie game in the bottom of the eleventh, one out and Lou Piniella on first after a sharp single. McLaughlin nibbled carefully and ran the count to 3–0. Reggie stepped out of the box and looked for the sign. After he received it, he shook his head. He glowered at the third-base coach and then at his manager, Dick Howser, in the dugout. Reggie had been given the take sign, and he didn't like it.

He slouched back into the box. McLaughlin, lured by the promise of a free strike, grooved his next pitch over the heart of the plate. In an instant, Reggie shape-shifted from the posture of frustrated indifference to coiled readiness. In another instant he uncoiled. Reggie, who had merely *pretended* to receive the take sign, crushed McLaughlin's lazy pitch to deep right field for a game-winning home run.

He left the park late to celebrate at Oren & Aretsky. On the way, a car cut him off, words were exchanged, and the driver called Reggie a "stupid nigger." The man then brandished a handgun and fired three shots, perhaps directly at Reggie. Reggie was unhurt, but police collared the twenty-five-year-old East Village man and charged him with attempted murder. A media storm surrounded Reggie for days. "If they keep kicking me around," Reggie said of the press, "I might let the guy go. Let him shoot somebody else. I don't want to be on the front page."

Soon enough the attention was on Reggie for his hitting. At the break, he had twenty home runs and a slugging percentage of .591. He started in right field and batted cleanup for the AL All-Star team. On August 11, in the fourth inning of a game against the White Sox and with his father in attendance, Reggie went deep off of Britt Burns and became the nineteenth player in major-league history to reach 400 home runs. He rounded the bases, embraced teammate Eric Soderholm at home plate, detoured to the box alongside the dugout to share a moment with his father, and then the rest of his teammates engulfed him. The Yankee Stadium crowd demanded two curtain calls. New York won the game and pushed their lead over the Orioles to two and a half games.

Reggie celebrated his night of history at McMullen's on Third Avenue. He liked McMullen's because there he could hobnob with New York bigwigs like John McEnroe, Donald Trump, Cheryl Tiegs, and, in better times, Steinbrenner. Reggie always got the same table—number 40, close enough to scope out the Eileen Ford models but removed enough to discourage autograph seekers. On that night, Reggie had drinks and ordered the swordfish. He left late. Just after he stepped into his Rolls, a black teen poked a .45 into Reggie's temple and told him to hand over everything. Reggie turned to him. The kid recognized him and, in shock, dropped the gun. Reggie abandoned the car, ran, and escaped.

In late August, he slumped just as the Orioles surged. Baltimore reduced the Yankees' lead to half a game, and Steinbrenner blamed Reggie. "Reggie isn't doing the job," he said. "I don't know what's wrong with him."

Reggie resisted the urge to strike back. Instead, he and the Yankees rebuilt their lead and won 103 games and the division title. He hit in thirteen straight games to end the season, and for the first time he hit .300. He also tallied forty-one home runs and ranked second in the league in slugging percentage and sixth in on-base percentage. Reggie finished second in the AL MVP voting for 1980, losing out to George Brett.

Brett's Royals awaited Reggie and the Yankees in the postseason. Improbably, the Royals swept the two-time defending champions. After a hitless game one, Reggie went 3 for 7 in the final two games, including a clutch, go-ahead double in the finale. In the end, though, his efforts meant nothing.

NINETEEN

"I Don't Know If I'm Secure Enough and Mature Enough Not to Be the Top Banana"

THE 1980 SEASON had been a failure in Steinbrenner's eyes. He fired Howser, Reggie's favorite manager since he had arrived in New York, and replaced him with the longtime functionary Gene Michael. Then Steinbrenner reached out to Reggie, who was in Florida broadcasting for ABC. He wanted to talk. Reggie flew back to New York.

Steinbrenner was thinking of going after that winter's marquee free agent, outfielder Dave Winfield. Reggie said it was a good idea, but he also wanted his own contract situation addressed. He'd be taken care of, Steinbrenner assured him.

Reggie was in the final season of his five-year pact with the Yankees. The uncertainty didn't sit well with Reggie, and neither did the feeling that his Yankee contract, fulsome when he had signed it, had become somewhat ordinary in the intervening years. By 1981, he was making $750,000 per year for television appearances, and since 1975, he'd made more money off the field than on it. He'd earned a fortune before the age of thirty-five, but a number of players were paid as much as or more than he was.

When the Yankees announced Dave Winfield's seemingly dimensionless ten-year, $23 million deal, Reggie's envy consumed him. On an annual basis, Winfield would make almost five times as much as Reggie. "I don't know if I'm secure enough not to have the largest numbers next to my name," he spilled. "I don't know if I'm secure enough and mature enough not to be the top banana."

Steinbrenner summoned him to Winfield's introductory press conference at Jimmy Weston's in New York. Hours before, he learned that Winfield would wear a conservative blue suit. Reggie showed up in a fur.

A WEEK BEFORE spring training, Reggie traveled to Fort Lauderdale to meet with Steinbrenner once again. Reggie wanted a five-year deal, but Steinbrenner wouldn't go beyond three. Instead, Steinbrenner pitched him a business relationship that would extend beyond his playing days, one that would make him a part of the Yankees' brain trust for years to come. Reggie would be a part of the "whole corporate structure," Steinbrenner assured him. It would be a "long-term association." It wasn't team ownership, which Reggie still craved, but it *was* the promise of power. They shook hands on it.

Afterward, Reggie called a hasty press conference to talk about his future. "He talked to me as a business associate," he said of Steinbrenner. "He really thinks something of my name, my drawing ability, what I mean to the sport. . . . I always thought I'd like for someone to say, 'We want you to be a part of us.'"

Steinbrenner's offer soothed Reggie for a time, but the size of Winfield's contract remained an obsession. He showed up late to spring training and made himself, rather than Winfield's contract, the story of first resort. Even in his absence, though, Reggie phoned writers in Florida and asked them how Winfield was hitting.

When Reggie finally arrived at camp, he couldn't find his batting helmet. He grabbed the notebook of a nearby *Times* reporter and scribbled, "Jax shows up in camp, has no helmet, wants to know if he's been forgotten already." The reporter then asked why he'd reported late. "Because," Reggie lied airily, "I knew there would be a disproportionate magnitude to any contract negotiations with Reggie Jackson."

Steinbrenner was furious. After he'd made such a generous offer to Reggie, the player—the employee—didn't have the decency to report on time. "If I wanted to build a lasting relationship, the last thing I would do is show up late," the Boss said. "That's common sense. You kind of hope that a guy who is known as Mr. October, who wasn't Mr. October in 1980 and didn't drive in a run in the play-offs, would want to make amends and come in early, wouldn't you?"

Then: "There has been no invitation to my business."

The slightest of rebukes could overcome a Steinbrenner promise. He now had no intention of making a partner of Reggie. That much Reggie had squandered. Steinbrenner even fined him $5,000 for his tardiness and revoked permission for him to shoot a Jeep commercial on the Yankees' grounds.

Steinbrenner's denial of the business offer first stunned Reggie. Then it fertilized his paranoia. He talked to the writers in strictly off-the-record terms, something he rarely did. He told them Steinbrenner was avoiding him. When he struggled early in spring training, he blamed Steinbrenner for leaving his contract situation unresolved. "It's just killing me," he said, nearly sobbing. "When you don't have Mom and Dad saying 'How are you?' you can't deal with it. I so much want to have a confrontation with him, and I can't wait for it to happen. I want to tear this fucking building down, but I know he won't come in here."

He talked for a full hour. He talked about feeling rejected by Steinbrenner and about not knowing whether he even wanted to

return to New York. He talked about getting older. When he finished, he felt better.

Talking was medicine to Reggie, albeit one that merely treated
symptoms. And the writers, compelled by their profession to listen, offered him the appearance of friendship. Sometimes it was all
Reggie had. Among the many words used to describe Reggie over
the years—powerful, colorful, bombastic, intelligent, complicated,
accomplished—one was lastingly true: lonely.

In Wyncote, he had been lonely among the whites in town and in
his own broken home. At Arizona State, he had been lonely among
the black athletes whom he contrived and failed to be like. He had
been lonely in segregated Birmingham, in his marriage, and in
Oakland because of Charlie Finley's terminal neglect. He was lonely
in New York because of stoked envies and in his sexual encounters,
as vacant as they were numerous. He was a lonely child grown into a
lonely man.

"One of these years," Steinbrenner said after Reggie's outburst,
"you won't pay much attention to him."

Reggie feared he was right.

LATE IN SPRING training, Reggie pulled his Achilles tendon, which
cost even more preparation time. He stayed behind when the team
went north, and in the solitude he readied himself. Initially, it paid
off. Upon joining the team, Reggie hit, tallying seven hits and two
home runs in his first six games. But then he struggled again.

Steinbrenner summoned him for a meeting. Reggie assumed it
was to talk contract. Instead, Steinbrenner told him that they would
soon talk contract. Steinbrenner saw it as a gesture that would put
Reggie into the proper state of mind. Reggie thought he was being
strung along. Days later, Reggie hit into a double play during a 12–5
loss to Cleveland. "Reggie is killing us," Steinbrenner griped.

He then praised what Winfield had done for the team and said he might order Gene Michael to drop Reggie in the batting order. As he had been with Martin, Steinbrenner was a master at teasing out Reggie's insecurities. Reggie, jokingly it was assumed, mentioned suicide: "I hope I get a low-floor room in Baltimore."

On June 4, the struggling Reggie came to bat in a key situation in the eleventh inning, and he struck out for the third time in the game. The Yankees went on to win, but Reggie's average dropped to .204. He stamped his way back to the clubhouse in a rage. "What the fuck is happening to me?" he screamed and flipped a table.

He asked Gene Michael to give him a night off. It didn't help: upon his return, he endured a 1-for-14 stretch that left him hitting .193. At age thirty-five, he feared his skills were slipping. He faced free agency, and he was putting up the worst numbers of his career. Before a game in Chicago, he asked Jimmy Piersall of the White Sox whether he thought he was done. Piersall said he had no way of knowing. "Well, I'm not," said Reggie, in a conspiratorial whisper. "God told me when I woke up this morning that everything was going to be all right, starting today."

His religious faith was intermittent—called upon when he needed it and discarded when he didn't. He'd needed it at times in Oakland, he'd needed it during his 1977 meltdown in Boston, and he needed it now that he was showing mere trace elements of his former abilities. Only Reggie knows whether he heard a divine voice, but that day he went 0 for 3, struck out twice, and once was tagged out on the bases after he forgot how many outs there were. Michael told him he would pinch-hit for him in the ninth. Reggie was relieved.

He mourned aloud to teammates and writers that perhaps he'd lost it. After his attainments of the previous year, it seemed unlikely, but Reggie looked like a very old ballplayer. A possible strike diverted his attention—he was the Yankees' players representative and one of the union's most vocal and important members—but in the past distractions had nourished him. This time it was different.

Days later in Chicago, after he rode the bench in a loss to the White Sox, Reggie learned from Marvin Miller that the strike had begun. It was after midnight, and the Yankees were scheduled to go to their downtown hotel and then travel to Minnesota the next day. They weren't going, Reggie decided. He told the team's traveling secretary as much, and the traveling secretary, after conferring with Steinbrenner, said the players would now be responsible for their own bags, hotel arrangements, and transportation. Fine, Reggie said. He left with two friends who waited to drive him, while his Yankee teammates foraged for cabs.

The strike, over the issue of free-agent compensation, lasted almost two months. By the time it ended, almost 40 percent of the season had been snuffed out. As a consequence, Major League Baseball adopted a play-off format that would declare prestrike and poststrike winners in each division. The Yankees had won the AL East first-half crown and thus secured their spot in the makeshift postseason.

During the layoff, Reggie dwelt on his future. He admitted to himself that Steinbrenner wouldn't offer him a new contract. Reggie didn't want to leave New York—familiarity had a power—but he had no control over it. His ego, though, wouldn't allow him to be the spurned one. After the strike, he returned to New York with a new refrain: "Sixty days, and I'm a free man!"

The next day Reggie cursed at and gave the finger to some fans who heckled him during a workout. Their taunts reminded him that he'd gone into the layoff hitting worse than .200. He started the revived season slowly and distractedly. "Why doesn't he at least make it look good?" one anonymous teammate asked.

By the middle of August, Michael returned him to right field. He hadn't played the field since late May, but Reggie—by design or accident—hit better when he wore the glove. His average steadily climbed, but that didn't stop his countdown: "Thirty-five more days!" he said on August 17.

The next day, Winfield, who had opened the second half in a funk, left the dugout in the seventh inning to watch video of his most recent at bat. After a few moments, Reggie followed him.

Ray Negron set up the Betamax machine, which had been installed in the clubhouse for Reggie. Reggie appeared and saw Winfield as he loomed over the television. "What are you doing?" Reggie shouted at Negron. "Put the game on."

Negron explained that Winfield wanted to see what he was doing wrong at the plate. "It's my machine," Reggie said. "Put the game on."

Negron did as Reggie told him. "I'm sorry," he said to Winfield.

"Sorry?" Reggie shrieked. "It's. My. Machine. Furthermore, I'm taking it home in October."

Then he turned to Winfield. "Let George buy you a fucking video machine."

ON AUGUST 25, Gene Michael pinch-hit for Reggie in the eighth inning of a game against the Twins, a game the Yankees went on to lose. After being removed, Reggie stormed into the clubhouse and screamed, "They're not going to get the best of me out of this one! Those motherfuckers!"

Yankees fans booed him. He hadn't hit a home run in thirty-five games, and he was batting .212. The next morning, he arrived at the park early for extra batting practice under hitting coach Charlie Lau. He'd done so for weeks, to little avail. In the clubhouse, he found a memo from upstairs: Steinbrenner was invoking his right to force Reggie to undergo a physical examination.

He was slumping, even scripting the worst numbers of his career, and the new kid, Winfield, was besting him. But to take this step, to force a player to undergo a full battery of tests when he wasn't injured or ill, was unheard of.

Reggie marched upstairs to Cedric Tallis's office. Tallis explained to Reggie that, following the physical, he was to fly to Tampa and have dinner with Steinbrenner at his home. For what purpose, Tallis didn't know, but the implication was clear: Steinbrenner might offer Reggie a new contract, provided his medicals turned up clean. Reggie refused on principle, but he walked out of Tallis's office and thought about what he'd just been told. He had hope.

Then he ran into one of the Yankee attorneys. Moved to truth for reasons unknown, the lawyer told Reggie about a private conversation among Steinbrenner, Michael, and Lau. Michael and Lau had counseled Steinbrenner not to re-sign him because, in Lau's words, "Reggie's through."

A faithless Lau was particularly hard for Reggie to take. During the emotionally taxing 1981 season, he'd leaned upon Lau for reassurance and promises that things would get better. They hadn't, but Lau had maintained that they would with time.

The next day, Reggie went to NYU Medical Center for the physical, passed easily, and even registered 20/16 vision. After the exam, he visited the young son of his teammate Tommy John, who was being treated at the same hospital after nearly dying in a fall. Reggie and the young boy talked, laughed, and joked for more than two hours. After they both felt better, Reggie left.

Back at the stadium, he found Tallis waiting for him. The frantic Tallis confessed to him that he'd already promised Steinbrenner that Reggie would fly to Tampa to talk. Reggie called Tallis a liar and told him again that he wouldn't go to Tampa. Tallis said it would mean his job. "I don't owe you anything, Cedric," Reggie said.

He left to rejoin the team in Chicago. En route to LaGuardia, a familiar and angry pride overtook Reggie. He told his driver to pull over, turn around, and go back to the stadium. "I'm scared of George," Reggie confided to the driver. "I don't know why I'm afraid of George, but I'm scared of George."

When he got there, he barged into Tallis's office. "You've been lying long enough!" Reggie screamed at him. "Now let's call George right here and now."

"I'm going to be honest," Reggie told Steinbrenner once Tallis had him on the line. "I'd given up on the season. . . . But now with this thing on the physical, I'm not going to give you the satisfaction. This thing makes me look like shit. Makes me look weak. There's five weeks left to the season, and I'm going to get out of this fucking town in glory. I don't need the glory; I just want to show you guys. I'm going to show you guys and I'm going to show everybody else what I'm made of. And after that you can take that contract and wipe your ass with it."

Steinbrenner allowed Reggie to vent. Then he asked him about the results of the physical. Reggie told him he was fine, perfect even. "Then what's wrong with you?" Steinbrenner barked.

"The only thing I'm doing wrong," Reggie said, "is I'm going out and getting a little pussy."

After the media learned of the exam, Steinbrenner affected loyalty. "The man has performed for me," he said. "He's come through for me. Reggie hasn't quit on me this year. Anybody who says he's quit will have to fight me. When things aren't right for him, I'm there. He's not going to be alone."

Reggie caught up with the team in the midst of their road trip. Before his first game back, he took extra batting practice from one of his coaches, Jeff Torborg. Reliever George Frazier trotted out to shag his flies. "Go sit in the upper deck," Reggie told him. Torborg threw him twenty-five-odd pitches, and Reggie hit all but two out of the park. "Go tell the man what you think of my eyesight," he said as he left the field. Steinbrenner ordered Reggie back into the lineup and back into the cleanup spot.

In a game in Minnesota on September 1, Twins reliever John Verhoeven brushed back Reggie in the seventh inning of a Yankees romp. In the ninth, Reggie homered off the gangly right-hander and strolled most of the way to first base. The Yankees won 11–6. "The next time Reggie Jackson does that," Verhoeven was quoted as saying in the next morning's papers, "I'm going to hit him in the head."

That night's game was a 7:35 P.M. start. Reggie showed up at Metropolitan Stadium almost six hours before game time. He made his way to the Twins' clubhouse, found Verhoeven's locker, and sat in his chair. Then he waited for him. Finally the Twins summoned Gene Michael to persuade Reggie to leave before Verhoeven showed up.

In the span of a week, Reggie hit safely in eight straight games, mashed three home runs—including the one off Verhoeven—and raised his batting average by fifteen points. That, he figured, would move Steinbrenner to talk contract.

Instead, Steinbrenner fired Gene Michael and replaced him with Bob Lemon. The timing was absurd. The Yankees had scuttled since play resumed, but they'd already clinched a play-off berth. Reggie was puzzled, and then, when Michael's firing forced his contract woes from the sports pages, he was angered.

In Lemon's first game back, Milwaukee pitchers brushed back Reggie three times. He smoldered as opposing hitter after opposing hitter came to the plate without any retaliation from Ron Guidry. "I can't see why my guys won't protect me!" Reggie shouted in the dugout. "I thought we had more guts on this team than this!" In the seventh, he stood in right field with his feet planted and his arms crossed. He barely moved the entire half inning. Back in the dugout he told Lemon, loud enough for all to hear, "If we're not going to knock somebody down, I'm leaving." The inning ended without a knockdown. Reggie undressed in the clubhouse and went home.

IN THE FIRST round of baseball's first-ever three-tiered play-off, the Yankees faced the Brewers. The Yankees took the first two on the road, but then they dropped the third and fourth games at home and set up a decisive fifth game. After an uninspired performance by the Yanks in game four, Steinbrenner scalded the team in a closed-door meeting. Steinbrenner didn't mentioned Reggie by name. He sat quietly in a distant corner of the clubhouse, and Steinbrenner probably never even laid eyes upon him. Steinbrenner's scorn had been directed mostly at Rick Cerone, who in turn told the Boss "Fuck you" to his face.

Reggie envied his boldness. Cerone, the Yankee catcher, had been tasked with replacing Munson in the lineup and in the hearts and minds of Yankee fans. He'd also had the reckless courage to tell Steinbrenner what Reggie himself wanted to say. In his veteran years, though, Reggie had become more calculating in his outbursts.

After the meeting broke up, Reggie emerged to meet with more than one hundred anxious reporters. He wasn't the story on this night—the Brewers and Steinbrenner and Cerone were—but Reggie did something about that. "What I got out of it," Reggie said of Steinbrenner's lecture, "was that if we lost tomorrow, I was gone."

The next day, Tommy John's son, the young boy had Reggie visited in the hospital, was introduced to the Yankee Stadium crowd. Just as he and his mother were about to emerge from the dugout to receive their ovation, Reggie lunged from his spot on the bench, swooped the boy up in his arms, and walked onto the field with both of them. The crowd began the familiar chant of "Reg-gie! Reg-gie! Reg-gie!"

Back in the dugout, his teammates looked on in anger. Was he really so insecure, so thirsting for validation, that he would steal the spotlight from a young boy who days before had been near death? "Jesus Christ," one Yankee said from the bench, "the man is sick."

If his self-centeredness was depressingly predictable, his majesty in the big moment was brilliantly typical. Against the Brewers in the deciding game five, he hit a breathtaking upper-deck home run to tie the game in the fourth inning. The Yankees won, 5–3.

Next up were the Oakland A's, managed by none other than Billy Martin. The story line was as obvious as it was compelling. From afar, from across the country instead of across the clubhouse, Martin's loathing of Reggie reached new depths. The year before in Oakland, Martin had begun dating a baseball groupie named Jill Guiver. She was as tempestuous as Martin—a fact that made their relationship at once absorbing and dangerous. At times Martin adored her—he called her the sexiest woman he'd ever seen—and at times he hated her. The knowledge that she had once dated Reggie fueled that hatred. When Reggie had played in Oakland, Guiver had hung around the ballpark and snapped pictures of players, most often in an effort to meet them. Her time with Reggie had been brief and uncomplicated, but that didn't matter to Martin.

The old foes this time had different loyalties, and the series promised to be a hotly fought affair. It wasn't. The Yankees swept the A's in three games and outscored them 20–4 in the series. The encounter was, for many, disappointingly free of hostilities. The hostilities were confined to the Yankees.

Following the sweep of the A's, the Yankees held a team party at Vince's restaurant in Oakland. The evening was uneventful until Graig Nettles's wife lost her purse. She had set the purse in her chair, but when she and their twelve-year-old son returned from the buffet line the purse was gone and one of Reggie's many Oakland friends was sitting in the chair. Unaware that the purse had fallen to the ground, Nettles's wife believed Reggie's friend had stolen it. Reggie, who'd gone hitless in the series and injured his calf in the second game, was already in a sour mood. He'd failed to make an impact against his old team and against Martin, and now he worried that he'd miss the World Series.

"I ain't liked the dude for ten years," he told his friends of Nettles. "I don't care if I play in the World Series. I don't have a contract. I can go anywhere. I ain't drunk. I ain't gonna take this stuff anymore."

He found Nettles at the bar. A few sharp words later, Reggie slapped a beer out of Nettles's hand, and Nettles slugged Reggie on the side of the head and knocked him to the ground. Steinbrenner heard the commotion. "Goddammit, Jackson!" he shrieked as he got between the two men. "What the hell are you doing? You're disgracing me again! You're degrading the Yankees!" He ordered Reggie and his friends to leave the party.

"You'll regret this," Reggie told him.

THE UPCOMING WORLD Series against, once more, the Dodgers would be played according to National League rules. That meant no DH, and that meant that Reggie, despite his hobbled leg, would have to play the field. Reggie, after an aggressive treatment regimen, would do just that—play right field and be in the lineup. Before game one, he put himself through a battery of running drills and declared himself ready to play. But Lemon told him he was on the bench. He was certain Lemon was acting on Steinbrenner's orders. Surely the Boss wanted to prove his team could win without Reggie Jackson. Reggie had passed his forced physical, and that left Steinbrenner still in need of a tidy rationale. A championship without any contributions from Reggie would put an end to talk of a new contract.

Reggie didn't play in the first two games of the series, and the Yankees won both at home. Game three would be in Dodger Stadium, and since Nettles was injured, Reggie assumed he'd be in the lineup. Once again, he wasn't. "Those motherfuckers want to win it without me," he said. He'd badly wanted to face Fernando Valenzuela, the young Mexican left-hander whose screwball had dominated the National League in 1981. He didn't get that chance. Although Lemon said before the game that Reggie was available to hit, he never called on him, not even when they had the chance to strike in the fifth inning. The Dodgers won, though, and Steinbrenner's plans changed.

In game three, the Yankees had left too many runners on base— they needed vintage Reggie, particularly with Nettles hurt. So he played in game four. The Yankees lost again, but Reggie went 3 for 3 with two walks and a home run. In the ninth, though, he botched a fly ball and put the eventual tying run on base.

Before game five began, the story broke that Steinbrenner had signed Jerry Mumphrey to a six-year, $4.5 million contract extension. Mumphrey was a switch-hitting, slick-fielding outfielder, and he was six years younger than Reggie. Reggie knew then that he would not play another season with the Yankees.

Game five turned out to be the third straight one-run loss for the Yankees. The disconsolate Reggie went 1 for 4. In the eighth inning Mumphrey replaced him in the field.

Game six was back in the Bronx. It was a 9–2 Yankee loss, and it sealed the first Dodgers championship since the days of Sandy Koufax and Don Drysdale. The Yankees set a Series record for most runners left on base through six games. In the finale, Reggie went 0 for 5 with two strikeouts. With two outs in the ninth, Reggie hit a hard ground ball to Davey Lopes. Lopes bobbled it, and Reggie beat the throw to first. The next batter, Bob Watson, flew out to center. In front of a morbidly silent crowd, the Dodgers mobbed Steve Howe on the mound. Reggie jogged off the Yankee Stadium field.

THE NEXT DAY, Reggie went to the ballpark to pack up his things and say his good-byes. He dropped in on Steinbrenner in his office. Just after the Series, Steinbrenner had apologized to the city of New York for the team's performance, but Reggie saw no point in striking back. It was over.

Together they walked to Steinbrenner's limo. Steinbrenner said he'd talk to Reggie's agent about a new contract. "I'll be in touch," he said as he climbed into his waiting car.

The two men wouldn't speak again for twelve years.

TWENTY

"Steinbrenner Sucks!"

FOR THE SECOND time in his career, Reggie was a free agent. He was thirty-five years old and coming off one of the worst seasons of his career. He feared that no team would select him in the free-agent draft leading up to the 1982 season. In baseball, though, reputation overpowered reality, and Reggie Jackson—because he was Reggie Jackson—would have suitors. He had eight of them, in fact: the Orioles, Angels, Braves, White Sox, Pirates, Rangers, Blue Jays, and Yankees all drafted Reggie. Gary Walker encouraged Reggie to go back to New York. He needed "continuity" in his personal life, Walker told him.

Reggie couldn't hear it, though. Going back to the Yankees—back to Steinbrenner, Winfield, Lau, everyone who'd undermined him—was too much. He'd go back to Baltimore, contenders and Yankees rivals, or to the California Angels, who had plenty of veterans and were a five-hour drive from his Oakland home.

Steinbrenner, though, told his fellow owners that Reggie would return to New York. Reggie, he said, was using everyone else to drive up the price. Angels GM Buzzie Bavasi believed him. Finally, in December, when Reggie was in Hawaii to broadcast the Hula Bowl for ABC, he called Bavasi. Bavasi offered him $400,000 for one year. Reggie told Bavasi that if the Angels wanted him, they'd need to make a legitimate offer and set up a meeting with team owner Gene Autry.

Autry, the "Singing Cowboy," preached—and lived—the "Cowboy Code," which, among other commandments, said that a true cowboy "must never go back on his word or a trust confided in him." Autry wondered whether he could trust the complicated slugger.

Reggie flew to Palm Springs and met Autry at his house. The Angels' owner was caring and earnest, different from Finley and Steinbrenner in a way that charmed him. Reggie told Autry he didn't need to be the highest-paid Angel. Autry told him that was "as fair as I've ever heard an athlete be."

In the end, they agreed on a four-year contract, with options for two more seasons. The contract would pay Reggie $900,000 and a bonus should the Angels' home attendance exceed 2.4 million in any season. Contrary to team policy, the Angels would table $1.9 million of Reggie's salary and pay him double-digit interest on the deferred money. As well, Reggie's father, Martinez, would be paid to scout American Legion games in the Philadelphia area. "The only thing he scouts," Reggie later said of his father's new job, "is the mailbox when his check shows up each month."

For the first time since 1978, Reggie showed up early to spring training. He was in the clubhouse by 9 A.M. each morning, and he didn't leave until after three in the afternoon. Even in meaningless exhibition games, the team set attendance records, and Angel fans showered their new star with cries of "Reg-gie! Reg-gie!"

Expectations were high. The 1981 team had finished eight games below .500, but the 1982 roster was larded with veteran stars like Reggie, Rod Carew, Bob Boone, Fred Lynn, Bobby Grich, Don

Baylor, Brian Downing, and Ken Forsch. Reggie, Boone, and third baseman Doug DeCinces were new to the team, and Gene Mauch was in his first full season as manager.

Mauch, who'd managed Dick Allen and the rest of the 1964 Phillies and had later gone on to the Expos and Twins, was a tactically involved sort who demanded that his teams bunt, make contact at the plate, and play sound defense. The aging Reggie didn't play the game Mauch's way. Yet much to Reggie's relief, Mauch assured him that he was the regular right fielder and that all he asked of him was to "play for me like you played against me."

ON APRIL 27, Reggie, batting .173 on the season without a single home run and hindered by an injured calf, returned to Yankee Stadium for the first time as an Angel. He had let down his new team, and he didn't know how the fans in New York would welcome him.

On the day of the game, Reggie held one press conference to launch his new Pony baseball cleat and then another for the New York writers. Afterward, he took almost an hour of batting practice. In most situations, Mauch would have benched Reggie—struggling, aging, wringing his hands—against a bedeviling left-hander like Ron Guidry. But this was different. "I know you have to be in there tonight," Mauch told Reggie in the clubhouse.

"I don't have any business being in there tonight against Guidry," Reggie said. "But, yeah, I got to be there."

His first time up, Reggie heard the chants of his name. He popped up to second base on a tough Guidry slider. In the fifth, Reggie singled up the middle and later scored on a Bob Boone squeeze bunt. In the seventh, Reggie led off the inning to growing applause. The "Reg-gie!" chants started up again. In the light rain, Guidry lost his grip and hung a slider. Reggie kept his hands back just long enough and then uncoiled on the rare Guidry mistake. He hit it off the facing of the upper deck.

Reggie rounded the bases to deafening cheers. After he touched home plate and the Angel dugout emptied to greet him, the fans in front of the club suites turned to Steinbrenner, who was looking down disgustedly from the owner's box. A cry started up among the fans just below him. Soon it spread to every corner of the park— "Steinbrenner sucks! Steinbrenner sucks!" Over and over again. In awful, piercing unison, every voice in Yankee Stadium, it seemed, had taken Reggie's side. He didn't urge them on or visibly delight in what he heard, but inside his heart leaped.

Reggie left the clubhouse late. Fans behind police barricades chanted his name in the rain and screamed for his autograph. As Reggie surveyed them, the elevator behind him opened. It was Steinbrenner. The two men locked eyes. Steinbrenner let the door close. He must have forgotten something, Reggie thought. He waited for him to return. After a few minutes, the elevator doors parted again. Again, Steinbrenner and Reggie stared at each other. Again, Steinbrenner let the door close without stepping out. Reggie left.

IN LESS THAN a month, Reggie lifted his batting average by almost a hundred points. However, Mauch began platooning him with Juan Beniquez, and Reggie's role frustrated him. He screamed at his teammates to be "nastier" on the field, he started fights with the opposition, and he accused an umpire of holding a fifteen-year grudge against him.

In time, though, he rediscovered the peace that had drawn him to California. On off days, he'd take his Vespa scooter over to Balboa Island. He would browse the fruit stands and occasionally stop in a doughnut shop or go to Mione's to have a meatball sandwich and a beer and play Pac-Man. In his idle hours, he'd fulfill his duties as muscle car editor for *Super Chevy* magazine and automotive editor for *Penthouse*. He also savored the women of southern California. "The ladies here are like home runs," he said. "Outstanding. Better than

New York? If they're not better, they're certainly giving New York a run for the money."

In July, the Yankees—absent the New York women—came to California. Before the series, Steinbrenner criticized Dave Winfield, comparing him unfavorably to Reggie. "Yes," Reggie said when told of Steinbrenner's latest comments. "And in the meantime he made the mistake of letting me go."

In 1982, Winfield had been the better player. Reggie had outhomered Winfield eighteen to fourteen, but Winfield had the higher batting average and the higher slugging percentage. But it was Reggie's series. The Angels swept, and Reggie in three games went 5 for 11 with two home runs. Winfield was 1 for 12.

Less than two weeks later, Reggie and the Angels, by then up three games in the West, were back in New York. Reggie batted .400 for the series and hit another home run. The Yankees took two of three, but the Angels left New York still in first place.

Reggie made the All-Star team, and the second half of the season would be even kinder to him. After the break, he hit .295 and slugged close to .600. As the homers mounted for Reggie and the wins mounted for California, Steinbrenner looked on in anger. In a televised interview with Howard Cosell, Steinbrenner said that Reggie and several other Angel hitters illegally corked their bats. "I take anything George says with a grain of salt," Reggie replied. "He's trying to make people in New York forget about all the mistakes he made."

Then Reggie accused Steinbrenner of not making league-mandated payments to other teams. "If anyone has financial problems," Steinbrenner responded, "it might well be Reggie because several New York restaurant owners have told me that Reggie has an awful lot of unpaid checks at their restaurants."

On September 7 against the White Sox, California's home attendance surpassed 2.4 million, which meant that Reggie's bonus kicked in. The Angels would soon set an AL record for attendance. In each of Reggie's five seasons in New York, the Yankees had drawn more than 2 million at home and on the road. His ability to "put meat in the seats," as he had phrased it in the spring of 1977, had never been in doubt.

In doubt was California's claim on the AL West. On September 19, the Angels lost in Toronto and slipped into a tie with the Royals—the eleventh time since early August that Kansas City had caught them in the standings. They flew back to Anaheim for a defining three-game series against those same Royals. Reggie went 0 for 10 in the series, and twice Mauch lifted him for pinch hitters. The Angels still managed a sweep.

In the 161st game of the regular season, the Angels beat Texas to clinch the division title. In the first inning, Reggie hit his thirty-eighth home run of 1982 to set the franchise record. He homered again the next day to tie Milwaukee's Gorman Thomas for the AL home-run title. On the opposite coast, the Yankees finished the season with a losing record, in fifth place, and sixteen games off the lead.

The Angels would face the Brewers in the ALCS. The Angels took the first two games and then traveled to Milwaukee to close out the series. The Brewers, however, won game three thanks to Don Sutton's solid outing. Reggie managed just his second hit of the series, and he struck out three times. In game four, he went hitless in another Angels loss and dropped his average for the series to .133. The two teams would play a deciding game five.

In the seventh inning of that game five, Reggie hit into an inning-ending double play. In the home half, the Brewers scored twice to take a 3–2 lead. The Milwaukee bull pen made it hold up. The Angels had blown a 2–0 lead, and Reggie had hit .111 for the series.

In spite of the team's success in 1982, the Angels fired Mauch. John McNamara replaced him. The last time he and Reggie had been together, during the emotionally punishing 1970 season, McNamara had obeyed Charlie Finley's orders to make him a part-time player.

Later that same year, McNamara had stood by as Finley tried to force Reggie to sign a statement of apology. McNamara's uncommon loyalty in Birmingham wasn't forgotten, but neither were his offenses.

REGGIE SAT ON 464 career home runs. Based on his performance in 1982, he might reach 500 late during the 1983 season. That milestone drove him. He spent the winter back in Oakland. He lifted weights, ran on a treadmill in his basement, and reported to camp in exceptional shape. Soon, though, his aging body undermined his hopes. A sore left calf slowed him early on, and eventually it sidelined him. "What's it mean to look as good as I do," Reggie asked, "and still not be able to play?"

His injuries, however, did allow another milestone. On May 13 in a loss to the Twins, Reggie went 0 for 5 and became the first batter in baseball history to strike out 2,000 times. The Anaheim Stadium crowd booed him as they watched the highly paid slugger's average drop to .213. "These people couldn't boo me as badly as I've been booed," he said after the game.

He caught a fever that stayed with him for a month. Then McNamara made Ellis Valentine the regular right fielder and confined Reggie to the DH role. McNamara made the proper decision—Reggie by then had little range in the outfield—but Reggie resented any reminder of his diminishing abilities.

He continued to struggle until a rib injury in late June forced him to the bench. Even so, fans voted him into the All-Star Game as the AL's starting right fielder. He didn't deserve it and was no longer a true right fielder, but he healed in time to play.

The Angels were in the race at the break. However, a 9–20 record in July buried them in the standings for good. Reggie, desperate and flailing, experimented with his batting stance. He spread his feet farther apart, stood flat-footed, and shortened his swing. He changed bats, tried different grips, and stood at different depths in the batter's box. In his own words, he was "trying to learn to hit again."

Nothing helped. He didn't hit another home run after July 31. "It's all I think about," Reggie said. "I don't even enjoy sex anymore."

He ended the season with a .194 batting average and just fourteen home runs. The Angels, thanks to a 28–56 record after the break, tumbled to fifth place. Speculation followed. The thirty-seven-year-old Reggie would retire, or the Angels would cut him loose and swallow the rest of his contract. "If the party's over for Jax," Reggie said, "no apologies, no regrets. It was super."

He sought out advice from his fellow veterans. Gaylord Perry told him to relax. Carl Yastrzemski told him to make adjustments. Hal McRae told him not to swing as hard. He would not retire. He wanted 500 home runs—he needed just twenty-two more—and he didn't want the Reggie of 1983 to be the one people remembered.

Despite the struggles of the previous season, McNamara returned to the dugout in 1984. That meant Reggie would again be the DH. In April he hit five homers and slugged better than .500. But the distractions soon set in.

Reggie's self-titled autobiography, coauthored with New York *Daily News* sportswriter Mike Lupica, would be released later in the summer, and in April *Playboy* ran a series of excerpts. In those excerpts, Reggie claimed that the Yankees had a segregated clubhouse, that a number of players were anti-Semitic, and that the team had employed a "subtle form of racism" in its treatment of Mickey Rivers. Back in New York, a *Daily News* headline blared "Reggie Blasts Racist Yankees."

"There's prejudice all over America," Reggie responded. "I didn't say the Yankees were any different."

In the book, Reggie also repeated the myths of his early life: his father's playing days in the Negro Leagues, his benching during the Dixie Series, and the Mets' objections to his white girlfriend. He also took shots at Martin, Lyle, Nettles, and, of course, Steinbrenner.

Steinbrenner warned that the book "might be more damaging to Reggie in the end."

On the field, the Angels climbed to first place in May, and they led the division for most of the first half. Reggie's old excellence eluded him, but he fared much better than he had in 1983. Again the fans voted him onto the AL All-Star Team, again as the starter in right field. The break found him just eight home runs shy of 500.

On August 12, the Angels came from behind to beat the A's in extra innings and stay within a game and a half of the Twins. After Juan Beniquez's second homer of the day, Reggie emerged from the dugout, waved his arms, and begged the fans to show more appreciation. "These people are dead ass here," Reggie said after the game. "We draw twenty-two thousand in a pennant race, and the fans are as dead ass as we are."

Shortly thereafter, the Angels fell out of contention for good, and that meant the focus was squarely on Reggie's chase for 500. Aware of the pressure, he sat on 497 for more than a month. Then, in mid-September, he hit one off of Floyd Bannister of the White Sox, and the next day he hit another off of Tom Seaver. The day after, he failed to hit one out against Chicago's Rich Dotson. The team had distributed T-shirts that read I WAS HERE FOR REGGIE'S 500TH, it had made plans to stop the game for a brief ceremony, extra press credentials had been authorized, and Gene Autry was attending. But the pomp failed to satisfy Reggie, who craved the glory and attention that came with the number 500 as much as he craved the home run itself. "I won't lie about it," he said of the Angels' promotional efforts. "I think some of it has been chickenshit. They haven't shown much interest in Reggie and 500, but this is the wrong time to talk about it."

The next afternoon, September 17, they hosted Kansas City and its tough lefty Bud Black. The Royals won the game 10–1, but in the seventh inning Reggie saw an inviting first-pitch fastball from Black. He swung powerfully, connected just as powerfully, and sent the ball deep into the right-field terrace. He rounded the bases slowly.

He shook Bobby Grich's hand at home plate, accepted a few words of congratulations from home plate umpire Durwood Merrill, and then walked back to the dugout with his arm around Bob Boone. On the way, he pointed at Gene Autry's box. Reggie had become the thirteenth player ever to reach 500 home runs. His historic blast had come seventeen years to the day after his first major-league home run, and it had come in the same stadium.

The crowd chanted his name for several minutes. Reggie thanked his father, Buzzie Bavasi, John McNamara, and his "second father," Autry. He gave the ball to his dad, the bat to Autry.

The Angels ended the 1984 season with a record of 81–81, but they finished just three games back of the division-winning Royals. Despite the improvement, McNamara didn't survive the winter. Autry brought back Gene Mauch.

Reggie could've retired. He was wealthy beyond his dreams. He'd gone into the oil business, added a few more names to his endorsement portfolio, and even purchased a Cessna aircraft. Autry had promised him a broadcasting job upon his retirement. But he wasn't done. He'd played enough for his option year to vest, which meant he had two years left on his Angels contract. He wanted to honor that contract, and he wanted to redeem himself in the postseason.

Spring training 1985 was mostly uneventful until Reggie and Brian Downing brawled with a heckler in a Palm Springs parking lot. Ten days later, Reggie got into another fight with a man who attacked him with a tire iron. Once the season opened, Reggie struggled, but the Angels barged to the division lead. The Yankees-like dramatics continued when Reggie, after a loss in Toronto, cursed out two reporters.

At the same time, unwelcome light was thrown upon baseball's drug problems. In what came to be known as the Pittsburgh Drug Trials—at the time the darkest stain upon baseball since the Black Sox scandal of 1919—eleven players were conditionally suspended, Willie Mays and Willie Stargell were accused of providing amphetamines to John Milner of the Pirates, Keith Hernandez testified that as many as 40 percent of major-league players used cocaine, and even the Pirates' mascot confessed to having acquired the drug for a number of players.

Reggie, in his disgust, saw it as more of a racial tragedy than a baseball tragedy. "I'm very hurt that most of the people I read about involved with drugs are black," he said as the scandal in Pittsburgh unfolded. "I'm no angel. I'm not asking anyone to be a saint. But I am hurt by the black guys."

Of the eleven players suspended by Commissioner Peter Ueberroth, seven were black. Reggie was "hurt" because those seven black players hurt him—and other black players—by association. Spared from his outrage were those who would tar all black athletes because of the actions of a few.

The older he grew and the more his fortune swelled, the more he made a virtue of self-reliance. Once, during the early years of his career, he received a phone call from a young black woman who asked him to pay her college tuition. She told him he owed something to his race. Reggie refused and said he worked hard for his money. From time to time, others would call with similar requests. The bitterness toward hangers-on stayed with him. "I'm a strong Reagan supporter," he said in his Angels days. "People who don't work shouldn't be given a free ride."

It was a common sentiment during the 1980s. Reggie, though, worked to forget that back in Wyncote he and his family had lived off government cheese and "welfare bags of food," as Reggie called them. To hear him tell it, his success had had little to do with luck or favor and everything to do with his own resolve.

AMID IT ALL, Reggie enjoyed a fine season. He chipped in twenty-seven homers and seventy-eight walks, and the Angels surged to ninety wins under Mauch and held the division lead as late as October 1. However, they lost three of their last four and once again ceded the flag to the Royals.

Reggie had the right to invoke his option and play the 1986 season at the same salary, but the Angels wanted him to do otherwise. GM Mike Port called Reggie not long after the World Series and told him the Angels no longer had room for him. He advised him to opt for free agency. Later in November, Gene Autry's wife, Jackie, told Reggie that he should retire. "If that's the way you feel," Reggie told Autry, "then you should move me elsewhere."

The Giants, then run by Al Rosen, and the Brewers both wanted to sign Reggie, but, in part to frustrate the Angels and in part not to uproot his life, he exercised his option for 1986. Soon after, Jackie Autry denied having pressed Reggie to retire, and Gary Walker angled for a contract extension through 1987. Reggie wanted 1987 to be his final season, and he wanted to announce it beforehand. By doing so, he'd assure that ceremonies and days in his honor would await him at every stop. But the Angels refused to extend his deal.

Fronted by a strong rotation—which included the veterans Don Sutton and John Candelaria and a pair of twenty-five-year-old right-handers, Mike Witt and Kirk McCaskill—the Angels would be serious contenders in 1986. Reggie, still the regular DH, started off magma hot. At the start of play on April 26, he was hitting a muscular .429. By night's end, though, no one would be talking about his batting average.

The Angels were in Minnesota to play the Twins. However, high, damaging winds battered the Metrodome and interrupted the game in the eighth inning. During the delay, several writers flocked to ask Reggie about the shaking speakers suspended high overhead, the swaying lights, and the billowing roof. "But the dome's not the story here," Reggie corrected them. "The real story is why there's not any colored boys over there." He pointed toward the Twins' clubhouse.

"There's only one black player here," he continued, referring to Kirby Puckett, the Twins' star center fielder. "There's [Alex] Sanchez, too, but he don't count. He's a foreigner."

Then he turned on the writers. "You'll make me sound like a racist and a pop off," he said, "when you're the ones who should be writing about it on your own, exposing it. It's a shame, a damn disgrace, an embarrassment to have one colored boy on that team. . . . It has to be the organization's fault."

Puckett, indeed the only American-born black on the roster, was asked about Reggie's comments. "If I was a veteran, maybe I'd say something," Puckett offered. Andy MacPhail, the Twins' director of player personnel, promised things would change in Minnesota.

By the end of April, Reggie was batting .407. But in May he went 2 for his first 22. Early that same month, Reggie choked a fan at Major Goolsby's bar in Milwaukee, and the fan pressed charges. Days later he tied Mickey Mantle on the all-time home-run list when he hit number 536.

On July 7, the Angels beat Milwaukee 3–1 in sixteen innings and snared first place for good. Reggie, though, rarely played the field, and Mauch platooned him. Reggie believed the role he occupied was beneath him, and he regretted not having lashed out more over the winter, when the team had tried to get rid of him. "I'm disappointed in myself," he said. "I allowed them to play me." He said his teammates sympathized with him, but speaking out made you "a marked man" on the Angels. After he signed with the Angels, he called it "utopia." But what happened there happened everywhere he went: Reggie was left spoiling for respect.

The Angels won the division by five games over Texas and faced Boston in the ALCS. California charged to a 3–1 lead in the series, and in game five it was one pitch away from Gene Mauch's—and the franchise's—first pennant. Then Dave Henderson hit an impossible home run off of Angel closer Donnie Moore, and the Red Sox went on to win in eleven innings. They won the next two games to take the series. Reggie, once again, had failed the Angels in the postseason. He batted .192 for the series, and in the crushing game five loss, he went 1 for 5 with three strikeouts.

"I might have gone out on that," he later said of his appearance in the 1986 postseason. But the Angels' collapse and Reggie's own failures left him wanting one more season.

Not long after the Angels' loss, GM Mike Port told the press, "We will not be inviting Reggie back for 1987." He'd hit eighteen home runs in the regular season, but he'd batted just .241 and, in typical fashion, had turned nasty as the end drew near.

TWENTY-ONE

"Number 44, Reggie Jackson. Number 44."

OVER THE WINTER, rumors had it that he would go to the A's, Royals, Orioles, or even Yankees for the 1987 season. But it was Oakland, where it had all begun, that captured Reggie's imagination. The A's pursued him out of a devotion to history and because they wanted a "slugger emeritus" to nourish their two young power hitters, Mark McGwire and Jose Canseco. "I want you to be full of care for these guys," manager Tony La Russa told him not long after he signed.

La Russa had faith in him as someone who could nurture and instruct. So Reggie thought about one day managing—not as an end but as a bridge to ownership, his dream for years. In early April, not long after the season had begun, Reggie called Dodgers executive and longtime acquaintance Al Campanis. He asked Campanis to help him become a major-league manager. Campanis told Reggie that, despite his status and money, he'd start out in the lowest rungs of the minor leagues. Reggie would have to prove himself all over again, prove that he could impart the wisdom and skills that had made him a certain

Hall of Famer, and, most challenging for someone of Reggie's gifts, have patience with the players who would never be as great as he was.

Reggie didn't like Campanis's answer. He imagined riding buses and frittering away season after season in minor-league backwaters. Then he imagined never getting his chance. He told Campanis that that was unacceptable. Campanis, an old-school sort who saw toil and suffering as saintly distinctions, couldn't believe what he was hearing. That was how things were—you apprenticed, bided your time, and survived. Then perhaps came the reward.

A few nights later, ABC News devoted *Nightline* to the fortieth anniversary of Jackie Robinson's major-league debut. Don Newcombe was to be interviewed, but because Newcombe's flight was canceled, Campanis, who had been Robinson's roommate in the minors, appeared instead. Host Ted Koppel asked Campanis why so few blacks had become managers or general managers in baseball. The seventy-year-old Campanis, tired after a night game in Houston, blinked into the television lights and lurched for an answer. He thought of Reggie. He thought of how the black star felt a managing job at the highest level should be his by right. He wasn't willing to work or pay the dues. Reggie, Campanis reflected, didn't have what it took.

"They [blacks] may not have some of the necessities to be, let's say, a field manager or perhaps a general manager," Campanis told Koppel and a national television audience.

His comments, noxious and ignorant as they were, traced back to his conversation with Reggie. The blowback was swift and furious. Protests and boycotts followed, and two days later Campanis resigned from the Dodgers in shame. The media sought out Reggie, baseball's most decorated black star and a friend of Campanis, for comment. He said Campanis was "not a racist . . . not a prejudiced man. I do believe he meant what he said, but this is not a man with malice, this is not a bad man."

Soon after, Reggie dictated his thoughts on race and baseball to

Peter Gammons of *Sports Illustrated*. His ruminations became the cover story of the May 11 issue. In a piece titled "We Have a Serious Problem That Isn't Going Away," he took on the Campanis affair at the outset. "Al Campanis's statement about blacks lacking the 'necessities' to be major league managers and general managers is the best thing to happen to minorities in baseball since Jackie Robinson," Reggie said. "Campanis is not a bad man or a racist, but he made a stupid, irrational statement that brought the problem into a sharper focus than we could have ever asked for."

After baseball began coping with the Campanis fallout, Reggie returned to his role with the A's. He advised the younger players on hitting and the rigors of the baseball life. And he counseled them on the cruel, exacting business that baseball had always been. On one occasion, he overheard Tony Phillips, a young black player, bragging about the "great" contract for which he was bound.

"Great?" Reggie said. "How great?" Phillips told him he was sure it would pay him more than $400,000. Reggie asked him whether he would go to arbitration. Phillips said yes. Reggie asked him whether he'd memorized his most important statistics from the previous season. Phillips said no. "You gotta know," Reggie told him. "How can you not know?"

They talked about Phillips's agent and whether he could be trusted. Reggie lectured him on finances and retirement planning. Phillips walked away. "I don't give a shit if he listens or not, to be honest," Reggie said. "I just don't care."

On the field, he contributed little. For much of the first half of 1987, his average fluttered around the .200 mark. He went through the same suite of adjustments he'd tried in 1983, but nothing helped. At the plate and on those rare occasions on which he reached base, Reggie felt pathetic and awkward, like someone dancing after the music had stopped. He feared that someone was watching him and feeling sorry for him, just as he had felt watching Willie Mays blunder his way through the 1973 World Series. Mays had been forty-two then. Reggie was forty-one.

IN LATE JULY, he made his last trip to Boston. "Ladies and gentlemen," said Sherm Feller over the Fenway public address system, "number 44, Mr. October, for possibly the last time in Fenway Park." Reggie then doubled to right center. Less than a month later came his last trip to Anaheim Stadium. Before his first at bat, the Angels played a video montage of Reggie's career, and in the Angels dugout Gene Mauch saluted. Later in the game, Reggie homered.

Toward the end of August, Reggie and all of New York looked forward to his final trip to Yankee Stadium. He still hadn't spoken directly to Steinbrenner since he had left the Yankees, and no one, least of all Reggie, could guess what kind of tribute the Boss would allow.

Hours before the A's left for New York, Reggie legged out a double in Toronto and strained his hamstring. He wouldn't be in the lineup. "I'll be able to [pinch-] hit if it has meaning," Reggie said before the third and final game of his last series in the Bronx. "But I'm not going to do it if there is a chance of reinjuring the leg. . . . This team is in a pennant race. There is October to consider."

In the first game, Guidry pitched the Yankees to a 4–1 victory, but Reggie's absence was the story. Several times during the game, the fans chanted his name and begged for one last appearance. Whether too hobbled or too uninspired, he didn't oblige them. But moments before the final game of the series began, Yankee Stadium public address announcer Bob Sheppard, whom Reggie had once called the "voice of God," spoke to the crowd. "We direct your attention to the home-plate area, where the umpires are awaiting the lineup cards," Sheppard recited. "And here to present the Oakland Athletics lineup card is a player who while a Yankee gave New York Yankee fans many memorable memories. Number 44, Reggie Jackson. Number 44."

The crowd and their voices rose. Reggie savored it. Then he limped to home plate in Yankee Stadium for the last time.

ON SEPTEMBER 26, the A's held Reggie Jackson Day. Reggie's father was too ill to attend, but Reggie's mother threw out the first pitch. Before the game, team owner Walter Haas gave Reggie a framed collage of his career, and a statement from President Ronald Reagan was read to the crowd. Reggie stepped to the microphone. "I was afraid to have a day because I didn't know if anyone would come," he told the crowd of almost 30,000. "Today, I know I have friends.

"Damn," he said. "It's been great. Thank you."

October 1 was the final home game of the season for Oakland. In the eighth inning of an eventual loss to Cleveland, Reggie pinch-hit for Luis Polonia. With an 0–2 count, he singled up the middle off Ed Vande Berg. As Stan Javier came out to pinch-run for him, the Oakland Coliseum crowd gave Reggie a minute-long standing ovation. He waved his helmet and blew kisses to them, and he jogged back to the dugout.

"This was my last at bat," Reggie said after the game.

It wasn't. The A's moved on to Chicago for the final series of the season. Charlie Finley flew back early from a European vacation so he could see Reggie play for the final time. The morning of October 4, Finley took Reggie to breakfast at the Westin Hotel. They reminisced, they laughed, and they talked about buying a football team together. Finley told him he'd forgotten his wallet.

That afternoon, in the city where Finley had signed him to his first professional contract, Reggie played one last game. In the first inning, he doubled Canseco home. In the fourth he walked, and in the sixth he thrilled the Comiskey Park crowd with a drive to the warning track. His last at bat came with two out in the eighth and Chicago in front. The fans stood and shouted "Reg-gie!" over and over again. He broke his bat on the pitch from Bobby Thigpen, but he managed to rap a single up the middle. He made it to second on a Carney Lansford bunt hit. He was stranded there when Terry Steinbach struck out. The A's went quietly in the ninth, and Chicago won 5–2. The losing pitcher was Dave Stewart, once the boy Reggie had found hiding in the bleachers of the Oakland Coliseum.

And then—after 563 home runs, 1,702 RBIs, fourteen All-Star Games, eleven division titles, six pennants, and five World Series rings—it was over.

TWENTY-TWO

"What Should I Do? Leave? Go Away? Come Back?"

HE SPENT TIME in his house on Valenzuela Road in Carmel. He wandered through the five bedrooms and among the Monterey pines that dotted his six acres. He took in his arresting view of the Pacific, played with his golden retrievers, and tooled around Carmel in his 1955 Chevrolet Bel Air. Like so many retired athletes, Reggie felt almost disembodied without the game he'd played for most of his life.

In August 1988, Reggie met with Bill Goodstein, one of his attorneys, and discussed a return to the Yankees for the September stretch drive. Lou Piniella was managing the team, and Reggie, despite the loss of his skills, longed to join him in New York. Goodstein relayed Reggie's wishes to Steinbrenner. Although Steinbrenner hadn't spoken with Reggie for years, he was receptive. Goodstein went public.

Surprised by the furor that followed, Reggie denied the story. Ultimately, he talked to Piniella, confessed that Goodstein's words were true, and decided against a comeback. He pined for the game, but, out of shape, out of practice, and forty-two years old, he feared embarrassment. He then received a $1 million offer to play the following season in Japan. For the same reasons he wouldn't go back to New York, he declined.

Reggie wanted more from baseball than playing again or even managing could ever give him. He wanted power. He wanted to hire and fire, buy and sell—just like Finley and Steinbrenner and Autry. He wanted ownership.

Reggie trudged through an unfulfilling stint as an Angels broadcaster. He asked his girlfriend, a California beauty named Inger, to marry him, but she said no. Reggie couldn't be faithful, she reasoned. Then an Oakland fire spread to the warehouse that housed many of his classic cars. The blaze destroyed more than thirty automobiles, and Reggie's losses exceeded $4 million. Arson, he was sure.

On Christmas Day 1989, Billy Martin's truck ran off an icy road in Binghamton, New York, and crashed into a culvert. He died from massive internal injuries. When Ray Negron learned of his friend's death, his first urge was to phone Reggie for consoling words. But Negron feared that Reggie would say something awful, and he never called.

Months after Martin's death, Reggie and Gary Walker tried to lure a National League expansion franchise to the Phoenix area, but their bid failed. Five years later, MLB awarded a Phoenix-based club to a group led by the basketball mogul Jerry Colangelo. Reggie forgot the dream of ownership for a time in early 1991, when a girlfriend gave birth to his daughter. They named her Kimberly. She lived with her mother in southern California, but Reggie remained a constant presence in her life.

Reggie's broadcasting career eventually took him back to Oakland and the A's. In addition to his announcing duties, he made an additional $65,000 as a part-time hitting coach. However, later that year A's GM Sandy Alderson trimmed the budget and ordered manager Tony La Russa to fire Reggie. Already frustrated by the path of his postbaseball life, Reggie took it as a direct attack. For years, the two would feud from a distance. Alderson ordered his security team to check Reggie's identification whenever he tried to enter the park, and Reggie vowed he wouldn't go into the Hall of Fame as an Athletic because of his distaste for Alderson. He also wouldn't allow Oakland to retire his number. "When Sandy Alderson is gone," Reggie said, "I will put it up there."

The same year, another fire destroyed his home in the Hiller Highlands neighborhood of Oakland—the very site on which his condominium burned to the ground in 1976. He had the sprawling residence in Carmel and another in Newport Beach, but the Oakland property had housed his baseball memorabilia, his art, and his gun collection. Better days were to come.

On January 5, 1993, Reggie became just the twenty-ninth player in history to be voted into the Baseball Hall of Fame in his first year of eligibility. He shared the ballot with such stars as Phil Niekro, Steve Garvey, Orlando Cepeda, and Tony Perez, but, fittingly, Reggie was the only one to make it. Voters named him on 396 of 423 ballots, the tenth highest percentage of all time. Having his greatness recognized gratified him. But he remained frustrated by his inability to climb through the ranks, particularly as a black man. Asked whether he'd use his induction speech to agitate for change, he said no. "I could do that when I had a bat in my hands, but not now."

Because Alderson still ran the A's, Reggie went into the Hall of Fame as a Yankee. He was the thirty-sixth Yankee to make it to Cooperstown, but he was the first black Yankee. Some in the press speculated that Steinbrenner, after twelve years of not speaking to Reggie, had reached out and promised him a high-level job if he agreed to be enshrined as a Yankee.

Steinbrenner had again been excommunicated from baseball. Dave Winfield had sued Steinbrenner for failing to pay $300,000 to his charitable foundation, as his contract stipulated. In response, Steinbrenner gave $40,000 to a gambler named Howard Spira. Spira was to dig up compromising information on Winfield—information that Steinbrenner could use against the highly paid outfielder. But the plot came to light, and in July 1990 Commissioner Fay Vincent suspended Steinbrenner for life. The owners soon forced Vincent out, and Bud Selig took over as de facto commissioner. In March 1993, he reinstated Steinbrenner.

Steinbrenner's return came at a time when baseball and the Yankees were being criticized for a lack of minority executives. Earlier that year, Reggie's old friend, the Reverend Jesse Jackson, had threatened a boycott of major-league stadiums unless baseball launched a hiring initiative to address the problem. The Yankees, besides having no minority coaches and just five minorities in the front office, were charged with culling black players from the roster. Over the winter, the club had traded Roberto Kelly, left Charlie Hayes unprotected in the expansion draft, and failed to re-sign Jesse Barfield and Mel Hall.

So Steinbrenner's first act after he returned to power was to hire Reggie. Reggie would remain in California so he could fulfill his four-year contract with the Upper Deck trading card company, but he would also serve the Yankees as a special assistant to the general partners. Steinbrenner had yet to lay out his duties, but he assured Reggie and the press that he'd be "a vital cog in the decision-making process."

Some in the media suspected that Steinbrenner had made the move to pacify Yankee critics. "Oh, yes, I happen to be black," Reggie said at the time. "I'm proud of the fact that I'm a black man who has a job with the Yankees, which I feel is extremely important."

By May, though, there was tension. On the night of a home game against the Orioles, Reggie attended a Knicks-Bulls play-off game at Madison Square Garden. Steinbrenner scolded him in a memo. Then, in June, he forbade Reggie to play in a Mets-A's exhibition at Shea Stadium, a game featuring retired players who had appeared in the 1973 World Series. Reggie did as he was told, but then he told the press about Steinbrenner's orders. Steinbrenner denied even knowing that Reggie had been invited to the game.

Later in the summer, Steinbrenner forgot those characteristic squabbles: Reggie was about to become a Hall of Famer. Days before his August 1 induction, Reggie spoke with a writer from *Sports Illustrated* about his legacy: "When I started talking, I was really one of the first guys who had the skills to articulate what I was saying," he said. "Jackie, Mays, Newcombe, Campanella, Gibson, those guys who set a precedent of greatness, those fellas could've stood up to it too, but they were taught 'You're a colored boy, and you're lucky just to be here.' That wasn't good enough for me, as an educated young Negro."

Reggie chartered two private planes to fly in family and friends, and he invited more than a hundred of his baseball acquaintances. Steinbrenner was there, but Willie Mays, Joe DiMaggio, Mickey Mantle, Hank Aaron, and the Autrys, to Reggie's disappointment, didn't show up.

He strode to the podium in a navy suit. The "Reg-gie!" chants started up from the Cooperstown meadow. He nodded at his fans, and then he gave a twenty-four-minute speech, much of which admonished players and owners to remember their obligations to the game. He recognized his father in the audience. He thanked John McNamara for teaching him, Frank Kush for making him tough, and Steinbrenner "for the pinstripes."

New York governor Mario Cuomo declared it Reggie Jackson Day. Representative Sherwood Boehlert did the same in the U.S. Congress. A Pittsburgh candy company reintroduced the Reggie! bar to commemorate his induction. So measured and forward-looking was his speech that afterward there was talk that he might be nominated for commissioner. The rumors reminded Reggie that he deserved greater things. He left Cooperstown with ownership once again in his thoughts.

The Yankees retired Reggie's number 44 on August 14. According to tradition, Bob Sheppard recited the names of the honored Yankees over the public address system. He called all the names—Reggie, Babe Ruth, Lou Gehrig, Joe DiMaggio, Mickey Mantle, Yogi Berra,

Whitey Ford, Phil Rizzuto, Bill Dickey, Casey Stengel, Roger Maris, Elston Howard, Thurman Munson—save for one: the deceased Billy Martin. Those who watched at home saw a slow pan across the all the retired numbers, but before the camera reached Martin's number, the telecast faded to a commercial.

THE FOLLOWING APRIL, Reggie's father died in Philadelphia weeks after suffering a stroke. He was eighty-nine years old. In his pocket were the business cards he always carried. They read, "Marty the Tailor, Father of Famous Reggie Jackson."

Reggie had mentioned his dream often to Martinez. He'd told his father that when he owned a team, he would make him a scout. He'd assumed that ownership would come as easily to him as the home runs had.

AFTER GAME TWO of an opening-round play-off series against the Rangers in 1996, a twelve-inning victory for New York, Reggie boarded the team bus. They were bound for Newark and a charter flight that would take them to Texas. Reggie assumed he'd been cleared to travel with the team and sat next to manager Joe Torre. Steinbrenner and one of his sons sat behind them. They crossed the George Washington Bridge and merged onto the Jersey Turnpike. Steinbrenner tapped Reggie on the shoulder. "The next time you want to go where you're not invited," the Boss said, "check with me."

Reggie was stunned. He stood up. "I'm fifty years old," he screamed. "Why do you treat me like you do?" Torre separated the two men. Later, one Yankee said that Steinbrenner had been "trying to break Reggie all year."

Steinbrenner had grown resentful in the days since Reggie had made the Hall of Fame. He hated the "Reg-gie!" chants. He hated seeing Reggie fawned over by the press and by other members of the organization—during spring training, Steinbrenner had angrily refused one executive's suggestion to create the position of team president just for Reggie. He wanted the attention and adulation that Reggie enjoyed, but at the same time Reggie craved Steinbrenner's power. Envy was all they had in common.

Humiliated and angry, Reggie went home to California. "I'm thinking of doing what Yogi did," he said, referring to Berra's long-standing boycott. "Not going back to Yankee Stadium as long as Steinbrenner owns the club. Not going to Old-Timers' Day. Nothing."

Two months later, Charlie Finley, age seventy-eight, passed away. Reggie and Catfish Hunter attended his funeral service, but none of his other players did. Reggie called it "shocking" and a "poor display of loyalty."

IN THE LATE 1990s, Reggie and coinvestor Andy Dolich offered $120 million for Finley's old team, the A's. Dolich had run the A's marketing department for almost fifteen years, and Reggie of course had a deep history with the franchise. Initially, the Dolich group had recruited Joe Morgan, but they soon cut Morgan loose in favor of Reggie, who, they assumed, could propel their group to the top. Soon, though, all such negotiations were frozen so that Major League Baseball could probe its economic straits. Reggie assumed his bid for the A's was dead, so he pooled investors from Orange County and tried to purchase the Angels from Disney. Nothing came of it.

REGGIE'S MOTHER, HER health waning from decades of smoking, moved to Carmel so Reggie could look after her. In January 2000, she died from, according to her death certificate, cardiac arrest, pneumonia, and dementia.

By 2003, Reggie was making more than $1 million per year. He owned a gym, and he occasionally sold one of his vintage cars for tens of thousands of dollars. He'd been paid $1 million by a memorabilia dealer to sign 30,000 autographs and make a handful of personal appearances. He worked in customer relations for four different companies, and he'd launched a sports memorabilia Web site. For a while, he even peddled his canceled checks, which fetched as much as $500 apiece. His job as a special adviser to Steinbrenner paid him $150,000 a year. But he was unsatisfied.

Yogi Berra, Whitey Ford, Don Mattingly, and Clyde King had held the same position within the Yankees. To Reggie, the job carried no meaningful responsibilities. He was not, as Steinbrenner had promised, a "vital cog." He showed up at spring training. He occasionally comforted Derek Jeter or Alex Rodriguez with platitudes. He charmed free agents the Yankees targeted. He helped Paul O'Neill learn to hit lefties, and he counseled two black players, Gerald Williams and Hensley Meulens, after the club demoted them to the minors. Occasionally, he turned in scouting reports. But he had no power. The job didn't propel him toward anything, didn't require him to think or strategize or sift through his wisdoms. He wasn't asked questions. It was a sinecure, and there was something pitiful about it. "I'd like to have a meaningful title that would be of value to me and the minority community," Reggie told the *Times*. Yankee GM Brian Cashman responded, "We like him in the limited role he's in."

Reggie resented that limited role, and he pushed harder than ever to buy a team. In 2003, the Nederlander family, who had run the Yankees during Steinbrenner's second banishment, recruited Reggie as the minority face of their effort to buy the Angels. Reggie's stake would have been small, but it was something. However, the Angels were sold to Arte Moreno, who became the first Hispanic to own a major sports franchise in the United States. Reggie looked to Oakland once more.

The A's were for sale. According to Reggie, Selig's top adviser, a

Milwaukee attorney named Bob DuPuy, counseled him not to contact the team directly. Wait, he told Reggie, and they'd inquire on his behalf. In those conversations with DuPuy, Reggie said he would like to move the A's to Las Vegas. He was also interested in the Montreal Expos, should they be moved to Las Vegas or Washington, D.C.

In June 2004—almost eleven years after he had gone into the Hall of Fame and long after Sandy Alderson had moved on—the A's finally retired his number. Reggie's daughter was there, as were Dick Williams and several former teammates. His reception by the fans was warm and lasting, but Reggie was thinking about the owner, Steve Schott. He wanted to feel him out, talk numbers, and perhaps even make an informal offer. But he didn't. Reggie followed orders. Selig and DuPuy would lobby for him, he believed.

In December, Reggie spoke to DuPuy once again. Call the A's, he told Reggie. He did. He hoped—knew on some level—that he was about to realize the dream that had held him in thrall for more than thirty years. He would move the franchise to Las Vegas, and he would become the first black managing partner in baseball history. "Reggie," Schott told him, "I'm sorry. We've been engaged in an option to purchase since July."

A man named Lewis Wolff held the option. Wolff had made his money in Los Angeles real estate, but, more important, he was a friend and former fraternity brother of Selig. Wolff offered $180 million. Reggie and his group were willing—and had enough capital— to pay more than $200 million. Selig's commitment to diversifying baseball's ranks was an honest one, but just as strong was his desire to fill the owner's boxes with fellow travelers—those who would extort public subsidies and stanch the power of the Players Association. Perhaps what hurt Reggie's chances was his history as a vocal union rep, or perhaps it was that, as he'd said in a Boston hotel room in 1977, he didn't "know how to be subservient." Selig valued lockstep.

Days after he talked to Schott, Reggie visited Selig, who was at Memorial Sloan-Kettering in New York recovering from cancer surgery. "The A's are about to be sold to your friend Lew Wolff," Reggie said. "What is that?"

"What are you doing here so early?" Selig asked him. It was before 7 A.M.

"What should I do?" Reggie asked. "Leave? Go away? Come back?"

"Well, there's a lot going on," Selig said. "You don't understand. You need to know the whole story."

It may have been Reggie's ties to Las Vegas and, in the words of Mayor Oscar Goodman, his "drive to bring baseball to Las Vegas." By that point in his life, Reggie maintained a part-time residence in nearby Enterprise, Nevada, and within his investment group were Brian Greenspun, the editor of the *Las Vegas Sun*, and Stephen Ross, a powerful Vegas developer. Vegas, of course, was a town of gamblers, and ever since the Black Sox scandal of 1919, gambling had been baseball's bête noir. Reggie's coinvestors insisted on moving the team to Vegas, but baseball feared such proximity to the sports-book industry.

If it was Las Vegas that kept Reggie from buying the A's, it was the expanding steroids scandal that ensured he'd never own a team, at least as long as Selig lorded over the game. In March, Reggie, speaking as a Yankee official, flouted a Selig gag order when he questioned the accomplishments of his distant cousin and reputed steroid user, Barry Bonds. He also said the commissioner "doesn't know what's happening here." Selig told the Yankees to keep Reggie quiet.

But Reggie had watched as the offensive records and benchmarks of his day lost their shine. Worse, he imagined his legacy diminished. That fear, and not a childlike nostalgia for the game, had stoked his outrage. He saw feats at the plate that he knew had been beyond him. He saw bodies muscled to the point of being obscene and numbers that surpassed old notions of the possible. In reality, what happened in baseball in the 1990s and beyond wasn't reducible to steroids alone. Performance-enhancing drugs likely played a less vital role than the construction of smaller ballparks, pitching staffs thinned out by expansion, and perhaps even the hopped-up baseball itself. But to Reggie, steroids needed to be the tidy foil. "Why isn't anyone doing anything about this?" he begged a group of reporters in 2002. " . . . Ten years from now, I'll be fifty-sixth on the home run list, because of the juice." At the time, Reggie was unaware of his role in bringing about the era that so raised his anger. But he would soon learn of it.

After he retired from the game in 1987, Reggie longed for some kind of physical challenge. His search took him to a power lifter named Curtis Wenzlaff. Wenzlaff was renowned in the Bay Area for his unthinkable strength and bizarre training methods—he shocked himself with a cattle prod and slept in a sensory deprivation tank. One day at an Oakland gym, Reggie approached Wenzlaff. They talked about lifting weights and Wenzlaff's grueling regimen, and soon they began working out together. They became fast friends. Wenzlaff stayed at Reggie's home on Yankee Hill and worked part-time at one of his Chevrolet dealerships.

Soon, Reggie introduced him to his old Oakland teammates. Wenzlaff spent time in the clubhouse, watched games from the luxury boxes, and even traveled with the team on occasion. Despite their close associations, Reggie didn't know Wenzlaff's secret: he was one of the Bay Area's most prominent steroid dealers.

Jose Canseco would later earn infamy as the man who introduced baseball to steroids, and indeed he'd juiced since he was a minor leaguer in the mid-1980s. But Wenzlaff taught Canseco about the more complicated—and more effective—mixtures and how to administer them and properly cycle on and off. Wenzlaff, according to the testimony of informants, also introduced Mark McGwire to the drugs that may have helped him to the single-season home-run record. After Wenzlaff made repeated sales to an undercover agent, the FBI arrested him in 1992 at a Santa Monica motel. By then, though, the scourge had spread through the sport.

Not until July 2004, when Wenzlaff testified at a Senate hearing, did Reggie learn what he'd done. Soon afterward, the New York *Daily News* revealed the breadth of Reggie's involvement and traced his and Wenzlaff's relationship back to the late 1980s. The day the story broke, Reggie called Wenzlaff and asked him what he'd told the press. "What do you want me to say?" Wenzlaff pleaded.

Despite the whiff of scandal, Reggie regrouped and later in 2005 pursued the Twins, the same organization he had once decried as racist. The Twins were not for sale at that time, but he reached out to the owner, Carl Pohlad, anyway. Pohlad rebuffed him. Some in the Minnesota legislature, which was sparring with Pohlad over the issue of a taxpayer-funded stadium, thought it a ruse. The threat of relocation to Las Vegas would rouse Minnesotans to save the team, and lawmakers would have the political cover they needed to buy the Twins a ballpark. Whatever the reasons or urgings from on high, Reggie was never a serious bidder. In 2006, he talked to Florida Marlins owner Jeff Loria about purchasing a stake in his team, but nothing came of it.

He'd pursued ownership with a dogged tenacity, the same tenacity that had allowed him to play football with a broken spine and survive the psychic wounds of Birmingham in 1967 and New York City ten years later. But tenacity meant nothing in a game of back channels, one in which connectedness trumped drive or force of will or even money. In Reggie's mind it had been a clarifying struggle, and he had failed.

A reporter asked him about his job with the Yankees, the one that hadn't quenched him for so many years. "I'll be here," he said, "until the family throws me out."

Epilogue

July 15, 2008, was a New York night: Yankee Stadium, in its final season, was set to host the All-Star Game. Earlier in the day, the All-Stars and forty-nine Hall of Famers had paraded up Sixth Avenue to the cheers of millions. The NYPD band traveled with them and played "Take Me Out to the Ball Game." When paradegoers saw Reggie, the chants of his name rose up. When the chants weren't loud enough, he held one hand to his ear and begged for more. Reggie was not—as he had long strived to be—powerful by his own estimations. But in the eyes of those people—some of them witnesses to his long-ago miracles—he had magnitude.

Before the game, the Hall of Famers were announced one by one as they took their old positions. In right field, Reggie was introduced after Hank Aaron and to louder cheers. Then George Steinbrenner, seventy-eight years old, his mind and body failing, rode out in a golf cart. He delivered four balls to the four surviving Yankee Hall of Famers, Yogi Berra, Whitey Ford, Goose Gossage, and Reggie. Steinbrenner wept. Reggie bent down and embraced him.

Those four Hall of Famers were to throw out the ceremonial first pitches. Reggie's pitch, if he threw it true, would settle into the glove of Alex Rodriguez. The chants of "Reg-gie! Reg-gie!"—the chants he'd first heard on the Cheltenham football field almost fifty years earlier—knelled within the stadium walls. He took it in for a moment. Then Reggie gripped the ball, nodded at Rodriguez, cocked his arm, and took a long, leaning stride toward the plate. And he let go.

Acknowledgments

Without the abiding and tireless efforts of my agent, Sydelle Kramer, this book would not be in your hands. I can't imagine ever taking on a project of this scope without her. Sydelle's wisdom and professionalism are irreplaceable, and if I didn't have such a wonderful wife I would've dedicated this book to her.

David Highfill, my editor at Morrow, believed in this book and was beyond generous with his time and talents. He's a writer's editor and a good, good man. I'm privileged to have worked with him. The same goes for David's associate editor, Gabe Robinson. Also, my thanks to Beth Silfin and Esi Sogah.

The work of Robin Rainer, my research assistant and one of my best friends in the world, is everywhere in this book, and without him I would have whisked past deadline after deadline. Consider me indebted for life.

Thanks also to the many beat writers who shared their recollections with me. Without them and their toil, so much would be lost to history. Let's remember this as technology refashions journalism and shakes the lives of those writers.

Special gratitude to Andy Kelly, an old friend and a great writer, for reading parts of an early draft. His advice helped these pages. Alex Belth gave me valuable feedback, encouragement, and a New Yorker's perspective. I'm lucky to call him a colleague; I'm blessed to call him a friend.

Thanks also to the wonderful staff at the Baseball Hall of Fame: Tim Wiles, Pat Kelly, Freddy Berowski, John Horne, and Gabriel Schechter. Others: Mark Brand at the Arizona State University Athletic Department; Dan Stein, who was helpful in ways he probably doesn't realize; Noel Steere; the staff at the Harold Washington Library in Chicago; and the wonderful and learned community of baseball fans at Baseball Think Factory. I'm also grateful to my friends and editors at FOXSports.com: Ed Bunnell, Steve Miller, Todd Behrendt, Aram Tolegian, Jim McCurdie, and Kerouac Smith.

Then there are those who uplift me in ways that go far beyond the writing of this book. My thanks—but most of all my love—to the Perrys, the Bloomfields, the Langenfelds, the Licatas, the Sullivans, the Seitzers, the Billigs, and—of course—my wife, Mary, and son, Wyatt.

And above all, thanks be to God.

Chicago
November 2009

Notes on Sources

In the process of writing this book, I made two formal requests for an interview with Reggie. His business manager, Matt Merola, assured me that he had passed along my requests, but I never received a response. As a result, I wrote this book without my subject's cooperation, but thanks to my interviews with those who knew and covered Reggie and the wealth of reportage already out there, I was able to tell his story.

At certain points in the book, I enter Reggie's head and presume to communicate his thoughts. I do so in the service of the narrative, and any thoughts I relay, while ultimately assumptions of what I believe he may have felt at certain instances, are informed by the facts and by what I came to learn of Reggie's inner workings. All quotes and statements of fact within the book are sourced and verified.

Below you'll find an exhaustive bibliography and selected notes from the text. However, certain sources merit further recognition.

Helpful throughout were Reggie's autobiography, coauthored with Mike Lupica; Maury Allen's bio of Reggie, *Mr. October: The Reggie Jackson Story;* and Reggie's retelling of the 1974 season, *Reggie: A Season with a Superstar*, coauthored with Bill Libby.

A number of excellent books tell the story of the Finley-era Oakland A's. Especially vital to this project were Bruce Markusen's *A Baseball Dynasty: Charlie Finley's Swingin' A's*, Tom Clark's *Champagne and Baloney: The Rise and Fall of Finley's A's*, and Ron Bergman's *Mustache Gang: The Swaggering Saga of Oakland's A's*. And no recounting of those days would be complete without Bergman's reporting in the *Oakland Tribune*.

I'm also indebted to the many wonderful writers who covered Reggie's Yankee years. Time and again I turned to works like Steve Jacobson's *The Best Team Money Could Buy: The Turmoil and Triumph of the 1977 New York Yankees*; Bill Madden and Moss Klein's *Damned Yankees: A No-Holds Barred Account of Life with "Boss" Steinbrenner*; and *Steinbrenner's Yankees: An Inside Account* by the late, great Ed Linn. Jonathan Mahler's opus, *Ladies and Gentlemen, the Bronx Is Burning: 1977, Baseball, Politics, and the Battle for the Soul of a City*, was also helpful. For details of George Steinbrenner's and Billy Martin's lives, I leaned heavily upon Peter Golenbock's richly reported book, *Wild, High and Tight: The Life and Death of Billy Martin*.

The *Los Angeles Times* archives were particularly valuable in chronicling Reggie's time with the Angels.

Author Interviews

Maury Allen, Dave Anderson, Marty Appel, Alex Belth, Ron Bergman, Howard Bryant, Jeff Chang, Murray Chass, Alvin Dark, Glenn Dickey, Dr. Harry Edwards, Joe Fitzgerald, Steven Goldman (via email), Peter Golenbock, Fran Healy, Henry Hecht, Steve Jacobson, Pat Jordan, Roger Kahn, Tyler Kepner (via email), Moss Klein, Darold Knowles, Ted Kubiak, Frank Kush, Bill Madden, Bruce Markusen, Jim McCurdie (via email), Marvin Miller, Ray Negron, Ross Newhan, Murray Olderman, Scott Ostler, Phil Pepe, Monte Poole, Ray Robinson, Glenn Schwarz, Jim Street, Bobby Winkles

Books

Abrams, Roger I. *The Money Pitch: Baseball Free Agency and Salary Arbitration*. Philadelphia: Temple University Press, 2000.

Alexander, Charles C. *Our Game: An American Baseball History*. New York: Henry Holt, 1991.

Allen, Dick, and Tim Whitaker. *Crash: The Life and Times of Dick Allen*.
    New York: Ticknor & Fields, 1989.

Allen, Maury. *All Roads Lead to October: Boss Steinbrenner's 25-Year Reign
    over the New York Yankees*. New York: St. Martin's, 2000.

———. *Mr. October: The Reggie Jackson Story*. New York: Times Books,
    1981.

Appel, Marty. *Now Pitching for the Yankees*. Toronto: Sport Media
    Publishing, 2001.

Armour, Mark L., and Daniel R. Levitt. *Paths to Glory: How Great Baseball
    Teams Got That Way*. Washington, D.C.: Brassey's, 2003.

Bass, Amy. *Not the Triumph but the Struggle: The 1968 Olympics and the
    Making of the Black Athlete*. Minneapolis: University of Minnesota
    Press, 2002.

Bergman, Ron. *Mustache Gang: The Swaggering Saga of Oakland's A's*. New
    York: Dell, 1973.

Bryant, Howard. *Juicing the Game: Drugs, Power, and the Fight for the Soul of
    Major League Baseball*. New York: Plume, 2006.

Chadwin, Dean. *Those Damn Yankees: The Secret Life of America's Greatest
    Franchise*. New York: Verso, 1999.

Chang, Jeff. *Can't Stop Won't Stop: A History of the Hip-Hop Generation*.
    New York: Picador, 2005.

Clark, Tom. *Champagne and Baloney: The Rise and Fall of Finley's A's*. New
    York: Harper & Row, 1976.

Gibson, Bob, and Reggie Jackson with Lonnie Wheeler. *Sixty Feet, Six
    Inches: A Hall of Fame Pitcher & a Hall of Fame Hitter Talk about How the
    Game Is Played*. New York: Doubleday, 2009.

Golenbock, Peter. *George: The Poor Little Rich Boy Who Built the Yankee
    Empire*. Hoboken, N.J.: Wiley & Sons, 2009.

———. *Wild, High and Tight: The Life and Death of Billy Martin*. New
    York: St. Martin's, 1994.

Halberstam, David, ed. *The Best American Sports Writing of the Century*.
    New York: Houghton Mifflin, 1999.

Hartmann, Douglas. *Race, Culture, and the Revolt of the Black Athlete: The
    1968 Olympic Protests and Their Aftermath*. Chicago: University of
    Chicago Press, 2003.

Jackson, Reggie. *Reggie Jackson's Scrapbook*. New York: Windmill, 1978.

Jackson, Reggie, and Bill Libby. *Reggie: A Season with a Superstar*. Chicago: Playboy, 1975.

Jackson, Reggie, and Mike Lupica. *Reggie: The Autobiography*. New York: Villard, 1984.

Jacobson, Steve. *The Best Team Money Could Buy: The Turmoil and Triumph of the 1977 New York Yankees*. New York: Atheneum, 1978.

Kahn, Roger. *October Men: Reggie Jackson, George Steinbrenner, Billy Martin, and the Yankees' Miraculous Finish in 1978*. New York: Harcourt, 2003.

Kashatus, William C. *September Swoon: Richie Allen, the '64 Phillies, and Racial Integration*. University Park, Pa.: Penn State University Press: 2004.

Leventhal, Josh. *The World Series: An Illustrated Encyclopedia of the Fall Classic*. New York: Black Dog & Leventhal, 2001.

Libby, Bill. *Charlie O. and the Angry A's*. Garden City, N.Y.: Doubleday, 1975.

————. *The Reggie Jackson Story*. New York: Lothrop, Lee & Shepard, 1979.

Linn, Ed. *Inside the Yankees: The Championship Year*. New York: Ballantine, 1978.

————. *Steinbrenner's Yankees: An Inside Account*. New York: Holt, Rinehart, and Winston, 1982.

Lyle, Sparky, and Peter Golenbock. *The Bronx Zoo*. Chicago: Triumph, 1979.

Madden, Bill, and Moss Klein. *Damned Yankees: A No-holds-barred Account of Life with "Boss" Steinbrenner*. New York: Warner, 1990.

Mahler, Jonathan. *Ladies and Gentlemen, the Bronx Is Burning: 1977, Baseball, Politics, and the Battle for the Soul of a City*. New York: Picador, 2005.

Markusen, Bruce. *A Baseball Dynasty: Charlie Finley's Swingin' A's*. Haworth, N.J.: St. Johann Press, 2002.

Michelson, Herb. *Charlie O*. New York: Bobbs-Merrill, 1975.

Miller, Marvin. *A Whole Different Ball Game: The Inside Story of the Baseball Revolution*. Chicago: Ivan R. Dee, 1991.

Munson, Thurman, and Martin Appel. *Thurman Munson*. New York: Coward, McCann & Geoghegan, 1978.

Nettles, Graig, and Peter Golenbock. *Balls*. New York: Putnam, 1984.

Olderman, Murray. *Mingling with Lions: The Greats of Sports Up Close*. Santa Ana, Calif.: Seven Locks Press, 2004.

Olsen, Jack. *The Black Athlete: A Shameful Story*. New York: Time-Life, 1968.

O'Toole, Andrew. *The Best Man Plays: Major League Baseball and the Black Athlete, 1901–2002*. Jefferson, N.C.: McFarland, 2003.

Pepe, Phil. *Talkin' Baseball: An Oral History of Baseball in the 1970s*. New York: Ballantine, 1998.

Pietrusza, David; Matthew Silverman; and Michael Gershman, eds. *Baseball: The Biographical Encyclopedia*. Kingston, N.Y.: Total Sports, 2000.

Powell, Shaun. *Souled Out?: How Blacks Are Winning and Losing in Sports*. Champaign, Ill.: Human Kinetics, 2008.

Rhoden, William C. *Forty Million Dollar Slaves: The Rise, Fall, and Redemption of the Black Athlete*. New York: Three Rivers Press, 2006.

Schaap, Dick. *Steinbrenner!*. New York: Avon, 1982.

Scully, Gerald W. *The Business of Major League Baseball*. Chicago: University of Chicago Press, 1989.

Shropshire, Kenneth L. *In Black and White: Race and Sports in America*. New York: New York University Press, 1996.

Snyder, Brad. *A Well-Paid Slave: Curt Flood's Fight for Free Agency in Professional Sports*. New York: Viking, 2006.

Stout, Glenn. *Yankees Century: 100 Years of New York Yankees Baseball*. New York: Houghton Mifflin, 2002.

Sullivan, Neil J. *The Diamond in the Bronx: Yankee Stadium and the Politics of New York*. New York: Oxford University Press, 2001.

Tygiel, Jules. *Baseball's Great Experiment: Jackie Robinson and His Legacy*. New York: Oxford University Press, 1983.

Van Hyning, Thomas E. *The Santurce Crabbers: Sixty Seasons of Puerto Rican Winter League Baseball*. Jefferson, N.C.: McFarland, 1999.

Vrusho, Spike. *Benchclearing: Baseball's Greatest Fights and Riots*. Guilford, Conn.: The Lyons Press, 2008.

Wigginton, Russell T. *The Strange Career of the Black Athlete: African Americans and Sports.* Westport, Conn.: Praeger, 2006.

Williams, Dick, and Bill Plaschke. *No More Mr. Nice Guy: A Life of Hardball.* New York: Harcourt, 1990.

Newspaper and Magazine Archives

Baltimore Examiner, Baltimore Sun, Black Sports, Chicago Tribune, Detroit News, Esquire, Life, Los Angeles Times, Minneapolis Star-Tribune, New York *Daily News, New York Post, New York Times, New Yorker, Newsday, Oakland Tribune, Philadelphia Daily News, San Francisco Chronicle, San Francisco Examiner, Sport, Sporting News, USA Today, Us, Washington Post*

Other Sources

BaseballLibrary.com; Baseball-Reference.com; Bronxbanter.com; ESPN .com; Office of the Registrar, Arizona State University; Office of Vital Records, Department of Health, State of California

Notes

ABBREVIATIONS

BE	*Baltimore Examiner*	*NYDN*	New York *Daily News*
ETM	*ESPN the Magazine*	*NYP*	*New York Post*
LAT	*Los Angeles Times*	*NYT*	*New York Times*
MST	*Minneapolis Star-Tribune*	*PDN*	*Philadelphia Daily News*
ND	*Newsday*	*SI*	*Sports Illustrated*
NY	*New Yorker*	*TSN*	*Sporting News*

CHAPTER 1

8 *"Your mom and I are splitting up"*: NY, "The September Song of Mr. October," David Remnick (1987), found in ed. David Halberstam, *The Best American Sports Writing of the Century* (1999).

9 *But she couldn't—wouldn't—abide his infidelities*: Allen, *Mr. October*, 22.

9 *Reggie, Beverly, James, and Tina were hers*: Jackson, *Reggie*, 18.

9 *Soon Beverly left to join her, and James returned to Wyncote*: Libby, *The Reggie Jackson Story*, 11.

10 *Eventually, though, his gambling schemes caught up with him*: Allen, *Mr. October*, 20.

11 *Years later, when asked what he'd taken from such unlikely environs*: Steve Jacobson, interview with the author.

12 *In reality, though, Reggie played regularly throughout the series*: *SI*, "Letters," ed. Gay Flood (July 27, 1987); see also, Mahler, *Ladies and Gentlemen, the Bronx Is Burning*, 148.

15 *"This boy does everything well with exception of hitting"*: *SI*, "Scorecard," (July 28, 1969).

CHAPTER 2

19 *An assistant football coach went to one of Jennie's uncles*: Allen, *Mr. October*, 53.

19 *living and working among other blacks*: Jackson, *Reggie*, 40.

20 *"He looks whiter all the time"*: *SI*, "Red Hot Factory for the Pros," John Schullan, (August 12, 1974).

23 *According to Reggie, Winkles told him*: Jackson, *Reggie*, 48.

24 *Winkles, however, denies he told*: Bobby Winkles, interview with the author.

CHAPTER 3

26 *As a boy, Finley bought rejected eggs*: Michelson, *Charlie O*, 12–13.

26 *He tasted baseball for the first time*: Clark, *Champagne and Baloney*, 4.

26 *In high school, he finagled*: Michelson, *Charlie O*, 19.

27 *In a bit of irony that would*: Clark, *Champagne and Baloney*, 7.

27 *He snapped at his nurses*: Michelson, *Charlie O*, 27.

27 *he concocted an idea*: Clark, *Champagne and Baloney*, 7.

28 *Finally, in 1960, following the timely death*: Michelson, *Charlie O*, 90.

31 *St. Joseph's records, however, showed that they admitted Reggie*: *SI*, "Letters," ed. Gay Flood (July 27, 1987); see also, Mahler, *Ladies and Gentlemen, the Bronx Is Burning*, 148.

33 *The closest he came was when he drove the Newark Eagles' bus*: BE, "Clarifying the Negro League's History," Phil Wood (June 15, 2007).

CHAPTER 4

40 *one he would never finish*: Arizona State University Registrar's Office employee, interview with the author.

44 *In one of his first meetings with Oakland Coliseum officials*: Michelson, *Charlie O*, 148–149.

45 *and from the field Reggie*: Clark, *Champagne and Baloney*, 42.

47 *"Thanks for coming to my wedding"*: Allen, *Mr. October*, 55.

48 *"Finley will pay for this come contract time"*: Bergman, *Mustache Gang*, 50.

CHAPTER 5

54 *Finley had official Reggie's Regiment*: Clark, *Champagne and Baloney*, 50.

CHAPTER 6

62 *During the season, she discovered scribbled phone numbers*: Allen, *Mr. October*, 58.

63 *He talked to older black players like Ernie Banks*: Libby, *Charlie O and the Angry A's*, 105.

64 *So Reggie chose a furnished*: Michelson, *Charlie O*, 168.

65 *"Don't be telling me that shit"*: Clark, *Champagne and Baloney*, 59.

66 *One night after a game, he drank with Catfish Hunter and admitted*: Steve Jacobson, interview with the author.

70 *and raised his middle finger at the old man*: Markusen, *A Baseball Dynasty*, 2.

70 *He mouthed, "Fuck you"*: Michelson, *Charlie O*, 171.

71 *"What do you think of this?"*: Libby, *Charlie O and the Angry A's*, 119.

71 *He never did sign it*: Clark, *Champagne and Baloney*, 64.

71 *Finley's statement read*: Michelson, *Charlie O*, 173.

72 *"We had only two problems on our ball club"*: Michelson, *Charlie O*, 211.

72 *"One day," Finley explained*: Bergman, *Mustache Gang*, 102-103.

73 *"I've heard a lot of bad things"*: Markusen, *A Baseball Dynasty*, 7.

75 *whip his bat into the stands of Hiram Bithorn Stadium*: Van Hyning, *The Santurce Crabbers*, 114.

77 *"Get me the kind niggers drink"*: Markusen, *A Baseball Dynasty*, 39.

CHAPTER 7

81 *"Well, I know you won twenty-four games"*: Michelson, *Charlie O*, 177.

84 *Epstein asked Reggie for his allotted tickets*: Markusen, *A Baseball Dynasty*, 116–117.

84 *"You hate my guts, don't you?"*: Kahn, *October Men*, 133.

84 *In September of that year, when Palestinian terrorists*: Markusen, *A Baseball Dynasty*, 107.

87 *"I hate Martin because he plays tough"*: Clark, *Champagne and Baloney*, 104.

90 *He went on to say that the National League*: Markusen, *A Baseball Dynasty*, 143.

92 *"The worst feeling I've ever had"*: Markusen, *A Baseball Dynasty*, 169.

CHAPTER 8

96 *"You got all black guys on one end"*: Clark, *Champagne and Baloney*, 155.

98 *forbade Williams to do so*: Markusen, *A Baseball Dynasty*, 249.

98 *In September, Reggie was summoned, cryptically*: Libby, *Charlie O and the Angry A's*, 251.

100 *"I'm Reggie Jackson"*: Markusen, *A Baseball Dynasty*, 238.

102 *Dr. Harry Walker poked and prodded at Andrews . . . "disabled for the rest of the year"*: Clark, *Champagne and Baloney*, 177–178.

103 *If he didn't sign it, Finley admonished*: Clark, *Champagne and Baloney*, 179–180.

104 *"Sometimes all of us have to be men"*: Michelson, *Charlie O*, 252.

104 *"I'm going to deny this if it leaks out of this room"*: Clark, *Champagne and Baloney*, 180.

105 *"To him, all people are the same color"*: Markusen, *A Baseball Dynasty*, 250.

108 *"Please don't give Finley credit"*: Markusen, *A Baseball Dynasty*, 259.

CHAPTER 9

114 *Early on, the press floated Frank Robinson's name*: Clark, *Champagne and Baloney*, 201.

115 *he'd once tore off a finger*: Clark, *Champagne and Baloney*, 30.

115 *he'd left his wife for a comely young flight attendant*: Libby, *The Reggie Jackson Story*, 83.

116 *"Exhort servants to be obedient"*: Clark, *Champagne and Baloney*, 202.

116 *"We have trouble because we have so many Spanish-speaking and Negro players on the team"*: Libby, *Charlie O and the Angry A's*, 156.

116 *But Orlando Cepeda said Dark had banned Spanish conversation*: Markusen, *A Baseball Dynasty*, 281.

117 *Reggie told the press that the rings*: Clark, *Champagne and Baloney*, 203.

117 *Reggie said no*: Clark, *Champagne and Baloney*, 205.

118 *Finley lied that he'd decided to allow*: Clark, *Champagne and Baloney*, 208.

118 *"I don't think we're executing"*: Clark, *Champagne and Baloney*, 213.

119 *"Well, look, I can talk to you, and you understand"*: Jackson, *Reggie: A Season with a Superstar*, 73–74.

120 *on occasion a white editor from a television station in Phoenix*: Time, "The Muscle and Soul of the A's Dynasty" (June 3, 1974).

120 *He even shared his apartment and his clothes with a white teammate*: SI, "Everyone Is Helpless and in Awe," Roy Blount (June 17, 1974).

121 *North told Reggie how his black teammates really felt about him*: Jackson, *Reggie: A Season with a Superstar*, 50.

122 *"I've made a special effort to help my own kind"*: Time, "The Muscle and Soul of the A's Dynasty" (June 3, 1974).

122 *Reggie, according to most contemporary reportage*: Allen, *Mr. October*, 150–151.

122 *"She doesn't go out with niggers"*: Allen, *Mr. October*, 150.

124 *"They can't give you the job because they got the team in Orange County"*: Jackson, *Reggie: A Season with a Superstar*, 115.

124 *He was also angry at Winkles because*: Markusen, *A Baseball Dynasty*, 292.

125 *"If they ever do that again"*: Clark, *Champagne and Baloney*, 228.

125 *but one of his Oakland trainers suggested at the time*: Allen, *Mr. October*, 85.

129 *Along the way, some—like the A's team chaplain*: Jackson, *Reggie: A Season with a Superstar*, 146.

CHAPTER 10

132 *At the winter meetings in New Orleans*: Clark, *Champagne and Baloney*, 256.

133 *He shaved off his beard for fear*: Jackson, *Reggie: A Season with a Superstar*, 268.

134 *There he met with Dodgers executive*: Clark: *Champagne and Baloney*, 289.

135 *"Claudell should be taught how"*: Clark, *Champagne and Baloney*, 298.

135 *"He knows he's not articulate"*: Markusen, *A Baseball Dynasty*, 309.

136 *Since his divorce from Jennie*: Allen, *Mr. October*, 145.

137 *"Sure, I will"*: Clark, *Champagne and Baloney*, 330.

140 *"The connotation is much worse"*: Clark, *Champagne and Baloney*, 351.

140 *He assured everyone that Reggie*: Clark, *Champagne and Baloney*, 352.

CHAPTER 12

159 *An understanding grew out of Secretary Wilson's involvement*: Golenbock, *Wild, High and Tight*, 86.

160 *He humiliated her to the point of tears*: Golenbock, *Wild, High and Tight*, 129.

160 *In 1962, Joan filed for divorce*: Golenbock, *Wild, High and Tight*, 131.

161 *In the fourth quarter, he was called for a technical foul*: Jacobson, *The Best Team Money Could Buy*, 32.

161 *In reality, though, Steinbrenner inherited McLendon*: Golenbock, *George*, 72.

162 *Then he reopened old wounds*: Golenbock, *Wild, High and Tight*, 219–220.

163 *To wit, he wanted to win government contracts . . . that impeded his takeover of two rival firms*: Golenbock, *Wild, High and Tight*, 229–230.

163 *To those ends, Steinbrenner*: Golenbock, *Wild, High and Tight*, 231.

163 *He told one reporter that his wife was terminally ill*: Golenbock, *Wild, High and Tight*, 233.

163 *Only after he forced his terrified employees*: Golenbock, *Wild, High and Tight*, 236.

164 *On both counts, Steinbrenner appears to have lied*: Golenbock, *Wild, High and Tight*, 242–243.

165 *Reggie became an afterthought*: Linn, *Steinbrenner's Yankees*, 67–75.

167 *which were still fresh in the minds of many New Yorkers*: Kahn, *October Men*, 114–115.

CHAPTER 13

174 *as the "downtown nigger"*: Mahler, *Ladies and Gentlemen, the Bronx Is Burning*, 145.

175 *Less than two weeks prior, Martin's daughter*: Mahler, *Ladies and Gentlemen, the Bronx Is Burning*, 32.

176 *However, when Appel knocked*: Appel, *Now Pitching for the Yankees*, 272.

CHAPTER 14

178 *"The East Coast is not philosophically or socially as liberal"*: Jacobson, *The Best Team Money Could Buy*, 56.

182 *More than once, teammates called Healy a "nigger lover"*: Allen, *All Roads Lead to October*, 81–82.

186 *However, years after the story came out, he admitted to Ira Berkow*: *NYT*, "Mr. October Is Now a Man for All Seasons," Ira Berkow (August 1, 1993).

186 *Reggie, though, made an abrupt turn and entered*: Jacobson: *The Best Team Money Could Buy*, 119.

186 *Each time, Randolph ignored him*: Linn, *Steinbrenner's Yankees*, 126.

CHAPTER 15

190 *He lobbed a towel*: Mahler, *Ladies and Gentlemen, the Bronx Is Burning*, 141.

191 *Reggie and his friends would park their muscle cars at a nearby church*: *SI*, "Everyone Is Helpless and in Awe," Roy Blount (June 17, 1974).

193 *"The Yankees have never fucked anybody like I've been fucked"*: Linn, *Steinbrenner's Yankees*, 136.

194 *Shortly after he arrived in New York, Reggie had talked about*: *PDN*, "Rod Carew Toasted, Reggie Jackson Roasted," Chuck Stone (July 14, 1977).

194 *In the coming months and years, black Yankees such as Willie Randolph*: Jackson, *Reggie*, 193–194.

195 *"They can't accept the idea of a black man being"*: Jacobson, *The Best Team Money Could Buy*, 161.

196 *"No, George," Reggie said, "you shouldn't do that"*: Linn, *Steinbrenner's Yankees*, 138.

196 *But Reggie backed Martin*: Jacobson, *The Best Team Money Could Buy*, 163.

199 *The producer of the show, Berl Rothfeld*: Mahler, *Ladies and Gentlemen, the Bronx Is Burning*, 258.

200 *Other than some ill-timed comments made upon the death of Elvis Presley*: Jacobson, *The Best Team Money Could Buy*, 246.

203 *All the while, Steinbrenner whispered to the media*: Linn, *Steinbrenner's Yankees*, 162.

203 *When Martin had bad news to impart to one of his players*: Linn, *Steinbrenner's Yankees*, 165.

206 *"How could the son of a bitch pitch him?"*: Jacobson, *The Best Team Money Could Buy*, 338.

CHAPTER 16

214 *"But you know who stuck up for you, nigger"*: *NYT*, "The Two Seasons of Reggie Jackson," Dave Anderson (October 20, 1977); Dave Anderson and Jeff Chang, interviews with the author.

CHAPTER 17

216 *After he made it back to his apartment on Fifth Avenue, he made his visitors*: *SI*, "Reg-gie! Reg-gie!! Reg-gie!!!" Ron Fimrite (October 31, 1977).

218 *"You pussy," Martin hissed at him*: Bradley, *The Greatest Game*, 76.

220 *At the heart of Martin's anxieties was Heather Ervolino*: Golenbock, *Wild, High and Tight*, 302.

220 *When he'd managed the Twins, he had a relationship*: Golenbock, *Wild, High and Tight*: 176.

220 *In Detroit, he had at least one night*: Golenbock, *Wild, High and Tight*, 199.

221 *"If you're my friend, stay my friend"*: Kahn, *October Men*, 277.

221 *"They may be Mafia," Steinbrenner said of the callers*: Kahn, *October Men*, 281.

221 *And that he once attempted to arrange a Mob hit*: Golenbock, *Wild, High and Tight*, 434.

222 *In his Oakland years, he dated a white married woman back in Arizona*: Jackson, *Reggie: A Season with a Superstar*, 8–9.

222 *During a photo shoot for* Sport *magazine, he hit on the photographer*: Murray Olderman, interview with the author.

224 *"If you get on, I'm going to bunt you over"*: Linn, *Steinbrenner's Yankees*, 184.

228 *Days before, Henry Hecht of the* Post *had written*: Linn, *Steinbrenner's Yankees*, 192.

CHAPTER 18

235 *Nettles called the* Post's *Henry Hecht a "back-stabbing Jew cocksucker"*: Jackson, *Reggie*, 190.

236 *His father had long counseled him to go out and get a Jewish lawyer*: Jackson, *Reggie*, 134.

236 *Reggie told him he had betrayed a "typically Jewish attitude"*: Jackson, *Reggie*, 134.

236 *"Are you Jewish?" Reggie said to the man*: NYP, "Swing and a Diss by Reggie," Eric Lenkowitz and David K. Li (July 14, 2008).

237 *"How can you be my friend and his friend at the same time?"*: Linn, *Steinbrenner's Yankees*, 213.

238 *"Because I can hit the motherfucking baseball over the wall"*: Linn, *Steinbrenner's Yankees*, 215.

238 *Steinbrenner ordered Martin to tell the press*: Linn, *Steinbrenner's Yankees*, 216.

239 *When that didn't work, Steinbrenner leaked to the press*: Linn, *Steinbrenner's Yankees*, 216.

239 *Through back channels, Reggie let Steinbrenner know*: Golenbock, *Wild, High and Tight*, 329.

239 *she told him how dangerous Munson's approach had been*: Jackson, *Reggie*, 265.

241 *Then, Martin would allege, Steinbrenner tried to*: Linn, *Steinbrenner's Yankees*, 222–223.

241 "Tell him I knew him then," said Reggie: Allen, *Mr. October*, 225–226.

242 *"If they keep kicking me around"*: *NYT*, "Man Charged in Assault on Jackson," Clyde Haberman (June 2, 1980).

CHAPTER 19

245 *Even in his absence, though, Reggie phoned writers*: Linn, *Steinbrenner's Yankees*, 17.

246 *"There has been no invitation to my business"*: Jackson, *Reggie*, 289–290.

246 *"When you don't have Mom and Dad saying"*: Linn, *Steinbrenner's Yankees*, 22–23.

248 *"God told me when I woke up this morning"*: Linn, *Steinbrenner's Yankees*, 256.

249 *He left with two friends who waited to drive him*: Linn, *Steinbrenner's Yankees*, 259–260.

250 *"What are you doing?" Reggie shouted at Negron*: Linn, *Steinbrenner's Yankees*, 268.

251 *Moved to truth for reasons unknown, the lawyer told Reggie*: Linn, *Steinbrenner's Yankees*, 3.

252 *"I'm scared of George"*: Linn, *Steinbrenner's Yankees*, 1.

252 *"The only thing I'm doing wrong"*: Linn, *Steinbrenner's Yankees*, 6.

252 *"Go tell the man what you think of my eyesight"*: Madden and Klein, *Damned Yankees*, 145.

253 In *the seventh, he stood in right field with his feet planted and his arms crossed*: Linn, *Steinbrenner's Yankees*, 274.

254 *"What I got out of it," Reggie said of Steinbrenner's lecture*: Linn, *Steinbrenner's Yankees*, 283.

254 *"Jesus Christ," one Yankee said from the bench*: Linn, *Steinbrenner's Yankees*, 284.

255 *The knowledge that she had once dated Reggie*: Golenbock, *Wild, High and Tight*, 442.

255 *Nettles's wife believed Reggie's friend had stolen it*: Vrusho, *Benchclearing*, 181.

256 *"You'll regret this"*: Madden and Klein, *Damned Yankees*, 153.

CHAPTER 20

261 *Again, Steinbrenner let the door*: Jackson, *Reggie*, 11.

262 *"I take anything George says with a grain of salt"*: TSN, "Corked Bats Set Off George, Jax," Moss Klein (August 30, 1982).

265 *"It's all I think about"*: LAT, "Slump Is Driving Reggie to Altered States, Stance": Ross Newhan (August 12, 1983).

266 *"These people are dead ass here"*: LAT, "Reggie Blasts Crowd After Angel Victory," Ross Newhan (August 13, 1984).

266 *"I think some of it has been chickenshit"*: LAT, "Reggie Wonders If Angels Care About His 500th," Ross Newhan (September 17, 1984).

267 *The Yankees-like dramatics continued when Reggie*: LAT, "Angels Lose Game, Reggie Loses Temper," Ross Newhan (May 15, 1985).

268 *Reggie, in his disgust, saw it as more of a racial tragedy*: LAT, "He's Had an Overdose of Bad News About Athletes and Drugs," Scott Ostler (September 10, 1985).

269 *Later in November, Gene Autry's wife, Jackie, told Reggie*: LAT, "Reggie Says Management Suggested He Leave," Ross Newhan (March 14, 1986).

269 *"The real story is why there's not any colored boys over there"*: MST, "Some Color Commentary on Twins' 'Real Story,'" Patrick Reusse (April 27, 1986).

270 *Reggie choked a fan at Major Goolsby's bar*: LAT, "Attorney Gives Reggie's Version of Incident," Mike Penner (May 5, 1986).

CHAPTER 21

273 *He thought of how the black star felt a managing job*: LAT, "The Nightline That Rocked Baseball," Steve Springer (April 6, 1997).

CHAPTER 22

278 *Surprised by the furor that followed*: NYP, "Lou, Reggie Discussed Comeback," Michael Kay (August 30, 1988).

279 *Reggie couldn't be faithful, she reasoned.*: LAT, "Tired of Swinging, Jackson Is Ready for Settling Down," Larry Stewart (August 31, 1990).

279 *But Negron feared that Reggie would say something awful*: Ray Negron, interview with the author.

280 *"When Sandy Alderson is gone"*: NYP, "Reggie a Nowhere Man," George King (April 6, 1997).

282 *He called all the names . . . save for one*: Golenbock, *Wild, High and Tight*, 522.

286 *Days after he talked to Schott, Reggie visited Selig*: NYT, "Reggie Jackson and One Amazing Bud Selig 'Fairness' Tale," Murray Chass (March 8, 2005).

287 *his "drive to bring baseball to Las Vegas"*: "Reggie Jackson's Surprise Shakes Up Twins," Joe Christensen, *MST* (November 5, 2005).

287 *He also said the commissioner "doesn't know what's happening here"*: NYT, "Yanks Muzzle Jackson After Steroids Comments," Charlie Nobles (March 12, 2004).

288 *"Why isn't anyone doing anything about this?"*: Bryant, *Juicing the Game*, 285.

288 *His search brought him to a power lifter named Curtis Wenzlaff*: ETM, "Who Knew? Part 1: The Dealer," Shaun Assael and Peter Keating.

288 *Wenzlaff stayed at Reggie's home*: NYDN, "Hitting the Mark: FBI Informants Say McGwire Was Juiced," Michael O'Keefe, T.J. Quinn, and Christian Red (March 13, 2005).

288 *also introduced Mark McGwire to the drugs*: NYDN, "Hitting the Mark: FBI Informants Say McGwire Was Juiced," Michael O'Keefe, T.J. Quinn, and Christian Red (March 13, 2005).

289 *The day the story broke, Reggie called Wenzlaff*: ND, "Jax Upset His Name Was Dragged In," Jim Baumbach (March 14, 2005).

Index